IMAGES
of Rail

EAST TEXAS LOGGING RAILROADS

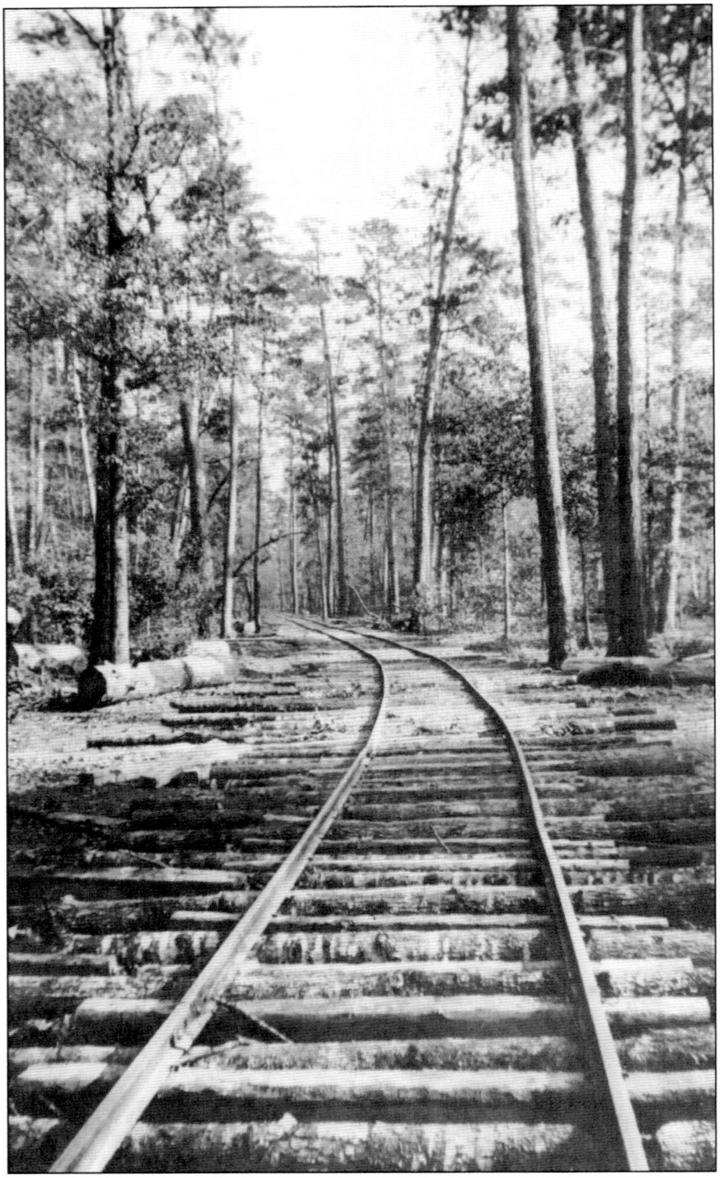

This unknown stretch of tram railroad was photographed by a traveler headed through East Texas in the 1920s. Crossties made out of small tree trunks were cut to widely differing lengths with no attempt to remove the bark. The construction practices displayed were typical of trams all over Texas during the heyday of logging. (Courtesy Texas Transportation Archive.)

On the Cover: Houston County Railroad Locomotive No. 5 pauses mid-trip in 1915 on its way to the 4-C mill at Kennard, Texas. "Houston County Railroad" was a name given to trams that branched off the short-line Eastern Texas Railroad. When the mills closed in 1917, the No. 5 went to Peavy-Byrnes Lumber Company at Kinder, Louisiana, then to Peavy-Moore Lumber Company at Deweyville, Texas, where it operated into the 1940s. (Courtesy Texas Transportation Archive.)

IMAGES
of Rail

EAST TEXAS LOGGING RAILROADS

Murry Hammond

ARCADIA
PUBLISHING

ISBN 978-1-4671-1574-2

Published by Arcadia Publishing
Charleston, South Carolina

Printed in the United States of America

Library of Congress Control Number: 2015948605

For all general information, please contact Arcadia Publishing:
Telephone 843-853-2070
Fax 843-853-0044
E-mail sales@arcadiapublishing.com
For customer service and orders:
Toll-Free 1-888-313-2665

Visit us on the Internet at www.arcadiapublishing.com

For the people of East Texas and all who love its history.

Contents

ACKNOWLEDGMENTS

The people of East Texas are warm and generous by nature, and I have long been the grateful recipient of their willingness to share history. Richard Moody, Bob and Edna King, and Joan Weatherly have all invited me into their homes. They—along with Jack Langston, Mary Kirby, Ruel Young, Bob Bramlett, and so many others over the years—have contributed their stories and precious photographs to these pages. I am deeply grateful to you.

The institutions and libraries that opened up their collections were no less wonderful. Grateful thanks go to Kaitlin Wieseman and Kendall Gay at the Texas Forestry Museum, Tim Ronk at the Houston Metropolitan Research Center, Serena Keech at Stella Hill Memorial Library in Alto, Melissa Booker and Pearl Phillips at the Kirbyville Public Library, Renee Hart Wells at the Hardin County Museum, Kathy Knighton at the Newton County Museum, John Anderson and Halley Grogan at the Texas State Library and Archives, and all the staff at Jasper County Archives and Museum. At Arcadia Publishing, Samantha Langlois got me started, and Sarah Gottlieb took me the rest of the way through my project. Sarah's advice was always so helpful and welcome.

Special thanks go to Jonathan Gerland at the History Center at Diboll for his help, counsel, and friendship. Rail historian Lester Haines is a treasured friend who was beyond generous in the contribution of his own images and those from the Keeling Collection that he lovingly maintains. Finally, thanks to my most significant other and talented editor, Anne Crawford, who more than once has prevented my grammar from standing in the way of a good caption.

INTRODUCTION

The southern forest was once a stand of virgin timber that stretched unbroken from the Atlantic Ocean to its far western edge, the old-growth forests of East Texas. Pines were dominant—especially the longleaf, shortleaf, and loblolly varieties. Cypress grew along rivers, as did hardwoods such as oaks and gums. In all, merchantable timber covered 36,000 square miles across 48 East Texas counties, an area the size of Indiana.

The first industrial-minded lumbermen came mostly from northern states. They taught themselves by trial and error the methods of efficient logging as they worked the great eastern white pine forests of New England and the Great Lakes. As those regions were exhausted of their timber stands in the 1870s, the lumbermen brought their expertise, drive, and capital to the southern forests.

Up until this time, Texas lumbering had taken the form of local operations that harvested timber adjacent to tiny mills. Rivers were utilized where timber could be floated, and larger mills were established along the coast at the mouth of these rivers. For the most part, however, much of the forest was hard to reach, the mill output was small, and the markets remained entirely local. The yield simply could not keep up with the increasing demand for Texas lumber. This was the extent of the Texas lumber industry until railroads penetrated the region, connecting commercial centers with each other and with the world beyond.

The first significant infiltration by rail into the heart of the longleaf belt was by the Houston East & West Texas Railway (HE&WT), which began construction in 1876 and completed a route to Shreveport, Louisiana, in 1886. On the Texas side, the HE&WT (locally nicknamed the "Hell Either Way Taken") traversed some of the densest sections of East Texas forest. Dozens of mill towns emerged along its route, and some, such as Lufkin in Angelina County, would be counted among the most important lumber centers in the South.

Elsewhere in East Texas, a surge of new railroad construction was happening. The Texas & Pacific Railway completed its east-west line through the northern section in 1873 at the same time that the International–Great Northern Railroad was building northward from Houston along the forest's western edge. The Sabine & East Texas Railway completed its route northward from Beaumont through the densely forested border counties, while numerous smaller but significant lines were filling in the railroad map with branches and bridge routes across every county that offered merchantable timber.

By the end of the 1880s, there was no longer a point in East Texas that was not within a tramline's reach of either a rail outlet or a navigable river. Large-scale harvesting of forests was now a possibility waiting to be exploited, and lumbermen from all over the United States answered the call. Some of these early entrepreneurs were able to raise enough capital to purchase huge sections of timber, while others established themselves with only moderate amounts of capital and timberland, and still others manufactured on a small scale, utilizing only lands in their immediate vicinity. All built sawmills, and many built railroads.

To maximize output, mill owners built their own industrial tram railroads, greatly extending a mill's reach into remote forestlands. The first trams were animal-powered: small carts pulled over short distances on wooden rails to feed logs into one of the rivers that connected with the coastal mills at Beaumont and Orange. The first steam locomotive to be used on a Texas tram was brought up the Neches River in 1878 and used on the "Yellow Bluff Tram," a wood-railed line that extended eight miles from a point on the Neches River near modern-day Evadale to a logging camp at Cairo Springs. The Yellow Bluff Tram engine was able to pull a whole string of log cars with exponentially less energy and expense than older methods.

The success of the Yellow Bluff inspired others to adopt its model, and soon steam engines, iron rail, and heavier logging equipment began to arrive along the new railroads and rivers. In the 1870s, there were less than 10 trams of any variety operating in Texas, but by the end of the 1880s, that number increased to more than 70—nearly all of which were built along recently constructed rail lines. Large mill towns like Call and Deweyville in Newton County and Village and Olive in Hardin County were established during this time.

In the most heavily forested counties with rail routes, mills might be found every few miles. For example, in the author's collection is an 1890 timetable for the 66-mile-long Trinity & Sabine Railway, which stretched across Trinity, Polk, and Tyler Counties. The timetable makes note of 22 spurs—amounting to a spur every two to three miles—nearly all of which served one or more sawmills.

Railroad logging became its own industry as manufacturers and inventors sought ways to increase efficiency and production. Technologies only dreamed of in the 1870s became standard by 1900. The "cable skidder," a machine that used long cables to drag logs to a central loading point, much the way a fisherman reels in a catch, came to prominence in the 1890s. Also coming into wide use in the 1890s was the "steam loader," which so greatly decreased the amount of time required to assemble a log train that a crew might be able to double the number of trains sent daily to the mill.

Locomotive manufacturers followed suit, patenting designs specifically with the lumberman in mind, in the form of the Shay, Heisler, and Climax locomotives. As opposed to the traditional side-rod engines that transferred power directly from the steam cylinder to large driving wheels, these new engine designs used a system of gears to transfer power to the wheels, slowing down the locomotive but greatly enhancing its pulling power. And because the power was transferred using universal joints and shafts, the wheels were free to move as irregularly as the often crude track dictated. The Shay locomotive was the most commonly used of all these designs, and many operated in Texas well into the 1940s.

An overview of railroad logging in Texas would not be complete without mention of the many common carrier short-line railroads that began as lumber trams. Short-lines formed when a lumber company determined that its main line could be organized and improved to provide passenger and freight service and, in some cases, even obtain contracts to move the mail. There are dozens of examples, and while most are gone along with the lumber companies that built them, two survivors are worth mentioning here. At Lufkin, the Angelina County Lumber Company built the Angelina & Neches River Railroad out of the company tram in the 1890s, and at Camden in Polk County, the W.T. Carter & Brother Lumber Company formed the Moscow, Camden & San Augustine Railroad out of the main tram artery the company built in 1898. Both railroads are still regularly moving freight as of 2015.

As the bonanza era entered the 20th century, many companies hastened their own demise by good markets and the sheer efficiency of their operations. This was especially true of larger mills, which had the facilities and workforce for two and even three shifts, depending on market demand. A mill that in 1900 was considered good for 20 years' worth of cutting might be considered exhausted by its 15th year, and so on. The 1900s and early 1910s especially saw a fever pitch of activity, when Texas was third only to Louisiana and Washington in lumber production. By 1915, however, the boom was essentially over. Timberlands declared inexhaustible by the first generation of lumbermen in the 1870s were completely cut over by 1920. Unable to replenish their supply of timber, smaller companies sold their machinery and lands to larger companies. If tram railroad equipment could not be resold to another firm, as was increasingly the case in the 1920s, then the equipment was sold to a scrap dealer to be salvaged for metal.

To some extent, established lumber giants—such as W.T. Carter & Brother, Kirby, Angelina County, Southern Pine, and Temple Lumber Companies—were able to continue logging by railroad but with increasingly diminishing returns. Highway trucks were inexpensive and powerful, and their entry into the industry in the 1920s spelled the end for railroad logging in the piney woods of Texas. A few old tram routes remained into the 1950s, moving logs to the large mills at Lufkin, Temple, Diboll, Camden, Silsbee, Voth, and Jasper. By the early 1960s, however, what railroad facilities remained at the lumber mills were reduced to plant facilities, for the purpose of switching cars around the mill.

The last regular steam-powered log train in Texas was sent out by the Southern Pine Lumber Company at Diboll in the spring of 1963. The engine was Southern Pine Lumber's No. 13, today on display in fine condition at the History Center at Diboll, Texas. After the No. 13 was taken out of service, a pair of small diesels leased from the Cotton Belt were tried, but the logging department decided to retire the railroad program altogether and let highway trucks do the work.

The great era of Texas railroad logging was over, in the end to be noted by only a few individuals who wished to be there—perhaps with camera in hand—to witness the conclusion of a story that would not be repeated. The goals of this book are to let the photographic record convey the arc of that story and explain why it remains significant among the families and communities who still pass around its anecdotes, tall tales, history, and old photographs.

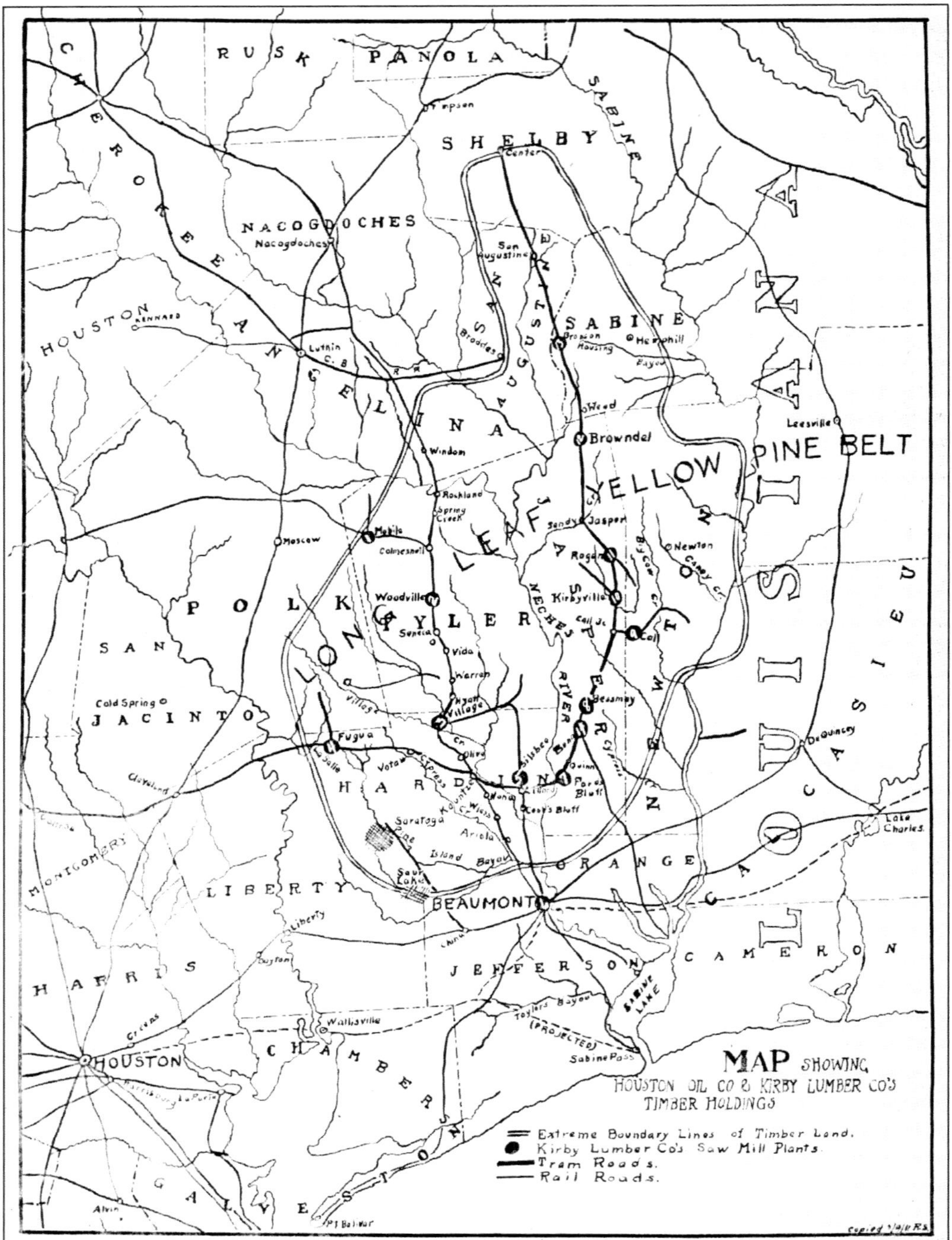

Kirby Lumber Company's 1911 map of its mill properties reveals an empire of sawmills inhabiting every section of the "Long Leaf Yellow Pine Belt." While the number of mills dwindled over the decades, Kirby remained among the most significant enterprises in the history of the Texas lumber industry. The last Kirby mill at Silsbee closed in 1987. (Courtesy Kirby Lumber Company Records, Houston Metropolitan Research Center.)

One

Early Railroad Logging in Texas

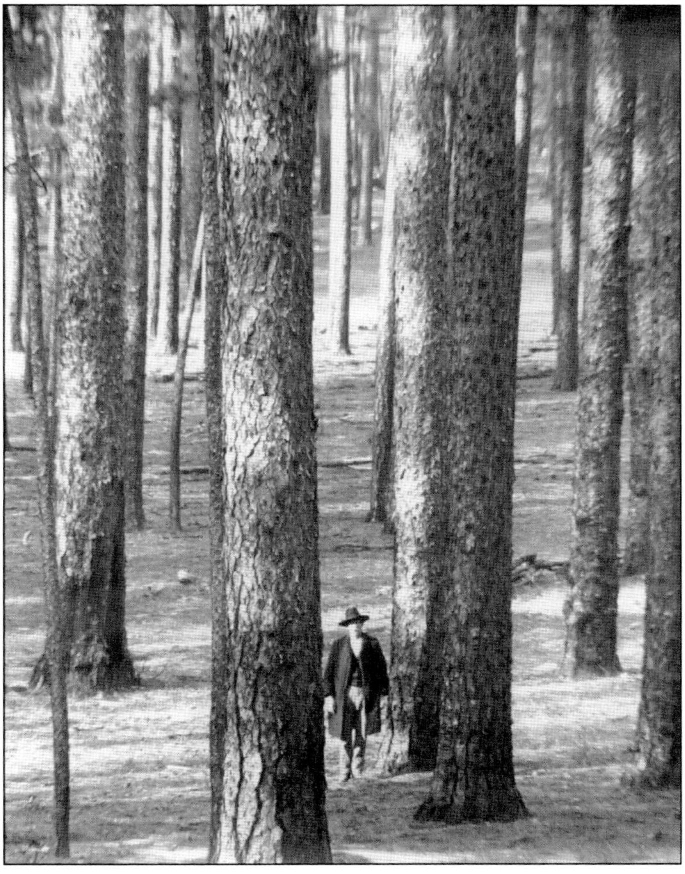

The photographic record vividly reveals the park-like floor of the old-growth East Texas forests. One old-time logger recalled, "When I was a boy, I could ride a horse a hundred miles cross-country through virgin timber. . . . you could see a deer a half-mile across the piney woods. I sawed trees [so large] I had to walk around them to saw them. . . and when they hit the ground, you'd hear 'em three, four mile." The identity of the man in this early view has been lost to time, but one certainty is that, for the next several decades, there would be many such men and women entering East Texas forests to claim their portion of its promised wealth. (Courtesy East Texas Research Center, Stephen F. Austin State University.)

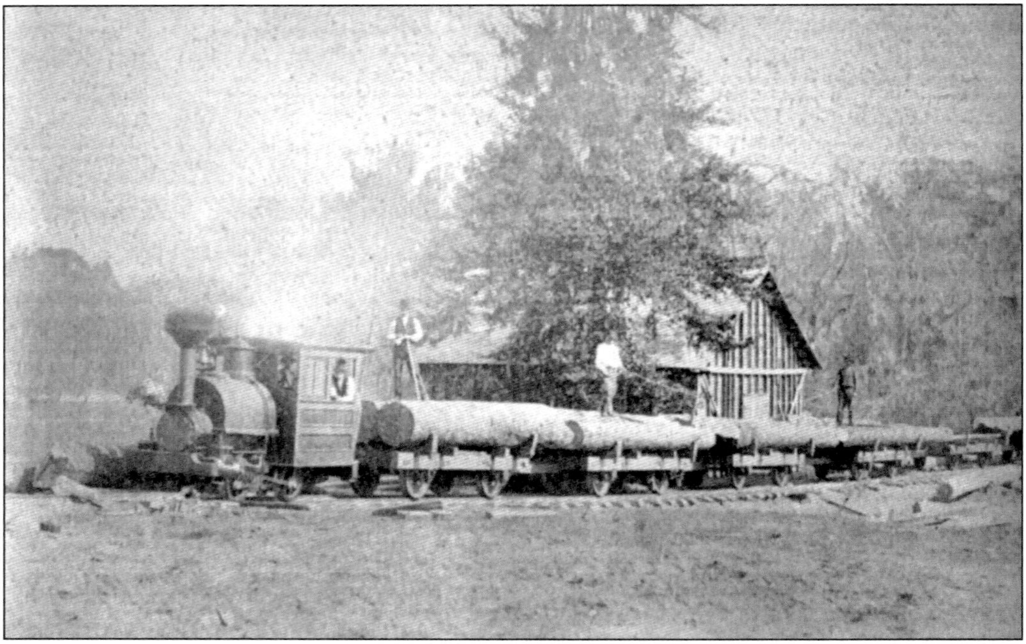

Engine No. 1 of Long & Company was first brought up the Neches River in 1876 aboard the steam vessel *Laura*. The tram's eight-mile line moved logs out of the Cairo Springs area of Jasper County to the banks of the Neches, where they were floated 116 miles to Beaumont. This 1878 image is the oldest known view of railroad logging in Texas. (Courtesy Marjorie Carroll Collection, History Center at Diboll.)

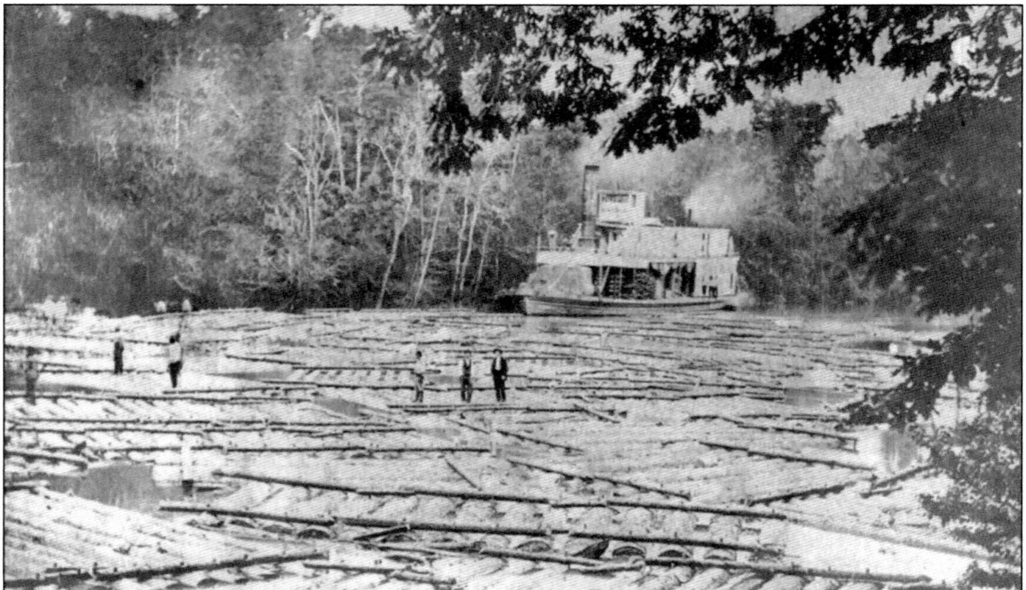

The *Laura* helps to clear a tangle of lumber rafts on the Neches in 1879. These rafts were placed in the river by Long & Company logging crews. Once they were untangled, they moved downriver to the company's mill at Beaumont. The *Laura* is the same vessel that transported the first East Texas logging locomotive into the forests. (Courtesy Jasper County Museum.)

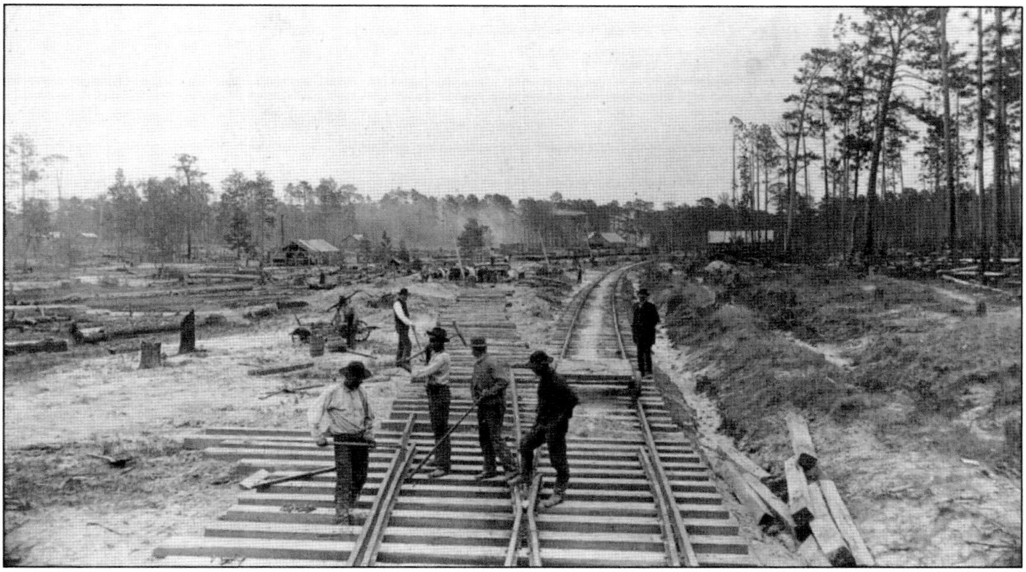

Large-scale harvesting of East Texas forests began in earnest as mainline railroads made possible the high-volume movement of cut timber. At this unknown station, the International–Great Northern was hardly ballasted before crews installed the trackage necessary to service a small sawmill that had just been situated along its line. (Courtesy DeGolyer Library.)

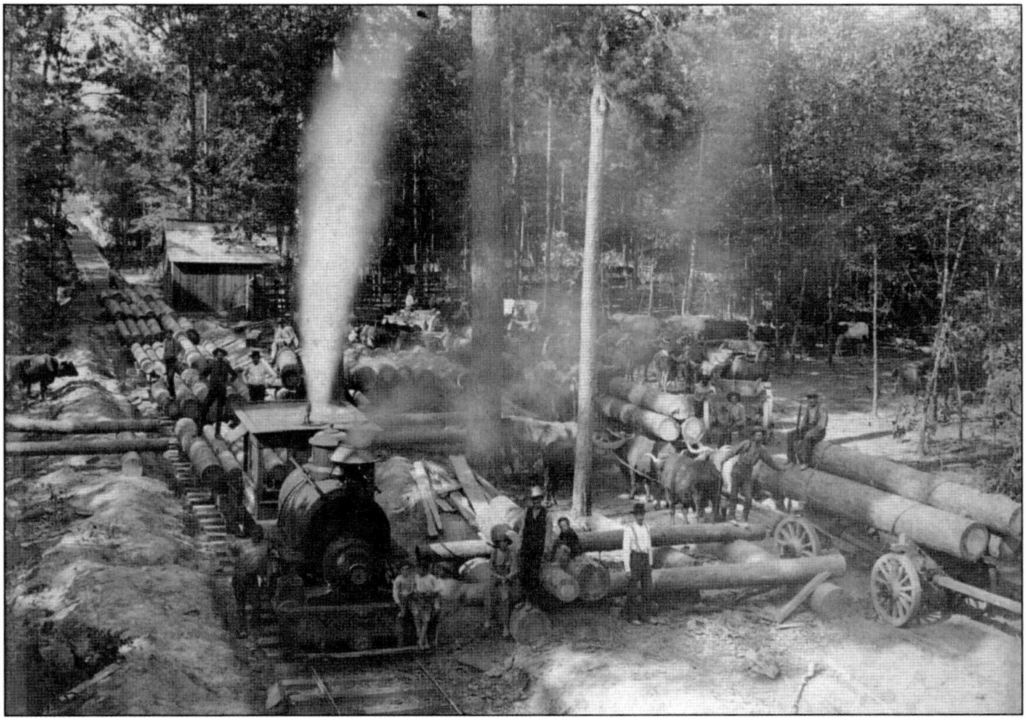

Loading areas or "fronts" began to appear in every forested county that enjoyed a navigable river or railroad connection. East Texans learned quickly the methods of efficiently moving timber from the woods to the mill. This small but busy operation used skids that were placed level with the tiny log rail cars to ease the transferring of heavy timber from wagons onto log cars. (Courtesy DeGolyer Library.)

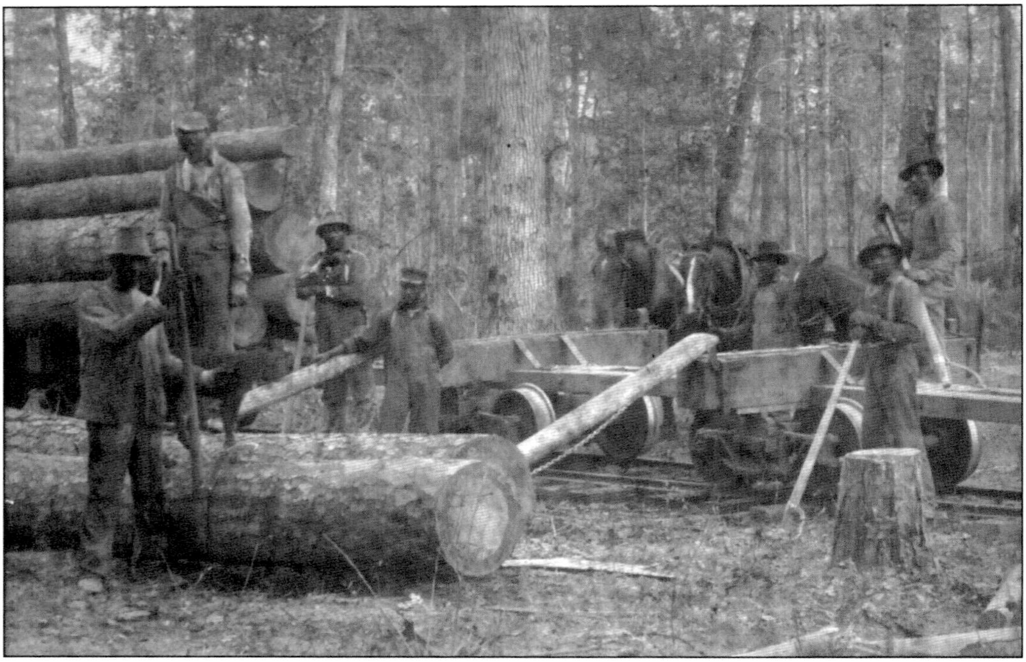

Before mechanical log loaders became common, early loading crews used skids set at an incline to roll logs onto railroad cars, as seen in this early Jasper County view. This could be dangerous work, generating injuries especially to the fingers and hands. Even fatalities could be caused by the unpredictable movement of the logs. The below photograph is of an early loader used by the Kirby Lumber Company at the commencement of its operations. This simplified the loading process and substantially decreased the time it took to assemble a log train. (Above, courtesy Jasper County Museum; below, courtesy Richard W. Keeling Collection.)

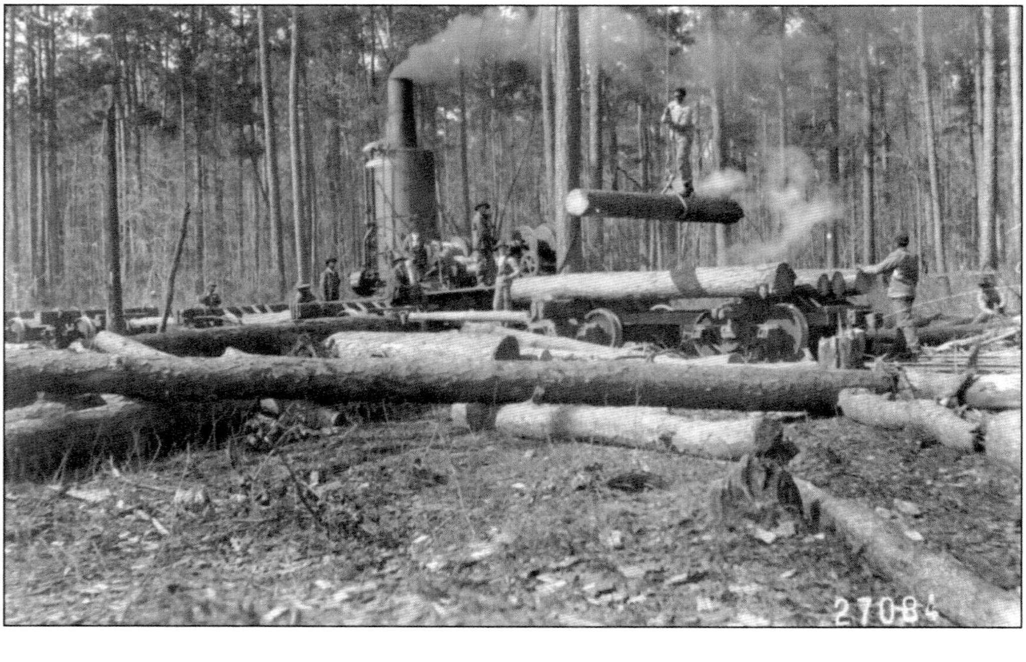

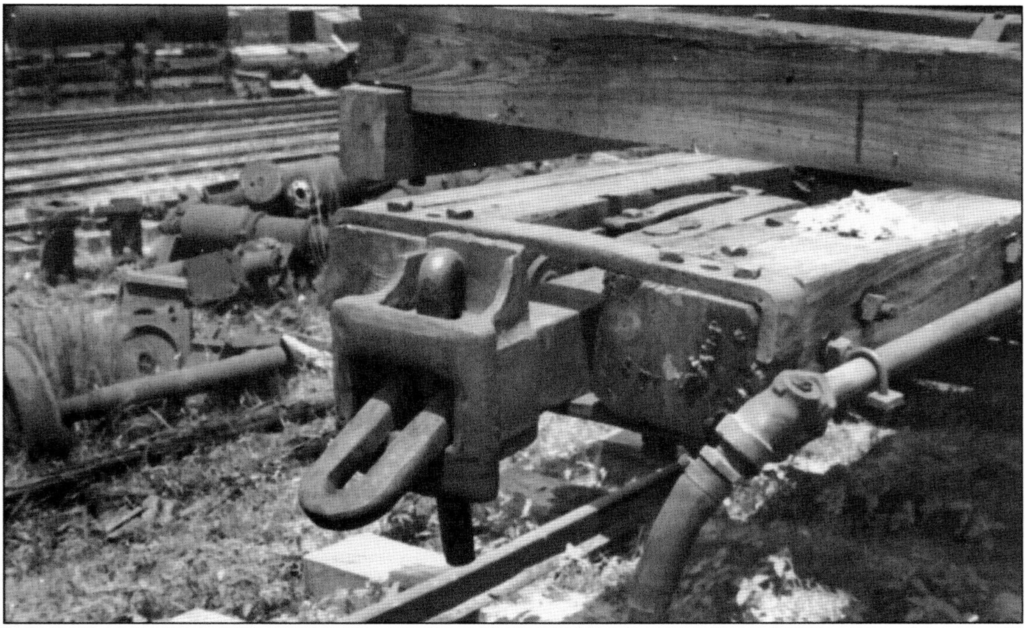

The link-and-pin coupler was a primitive but universal method of coupling cars on early logging roads. The coupler worked when the brakeman held a long metal "link" in place as cars were moved together. The brakeman removed his hand out of harm's way just as the cars bumped, and then the "pins" were placed through the top of each drawbar and through the link to form the connection. The practice was notorious for mashing or taking off fingers or even hands, and was outlawed by the 1950s. (Both, courtesy Richard W. Keeling Collection.)

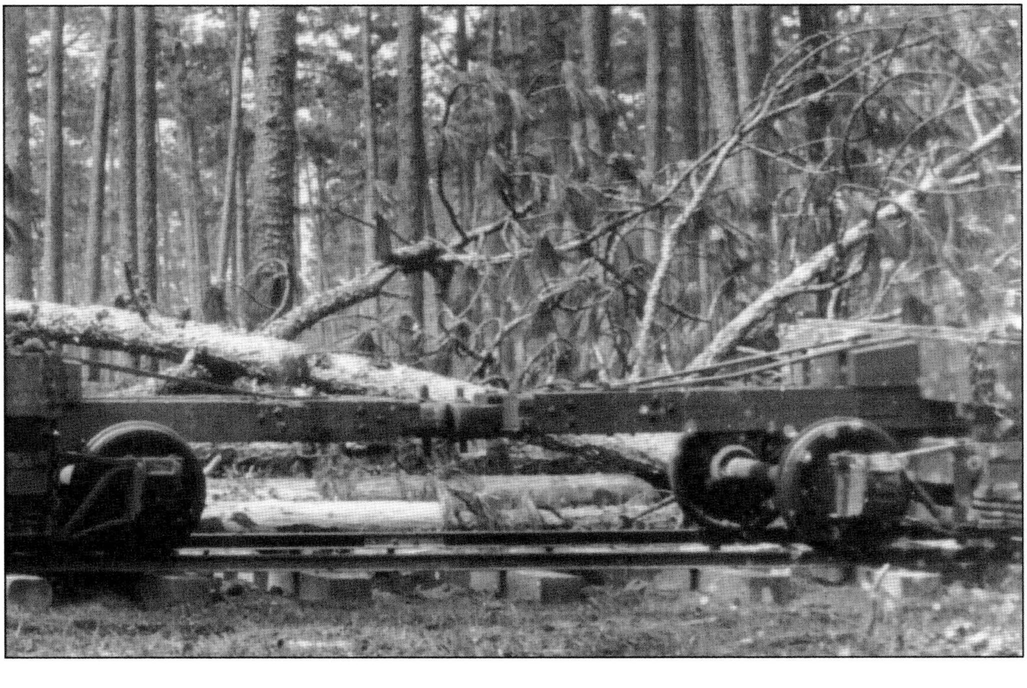

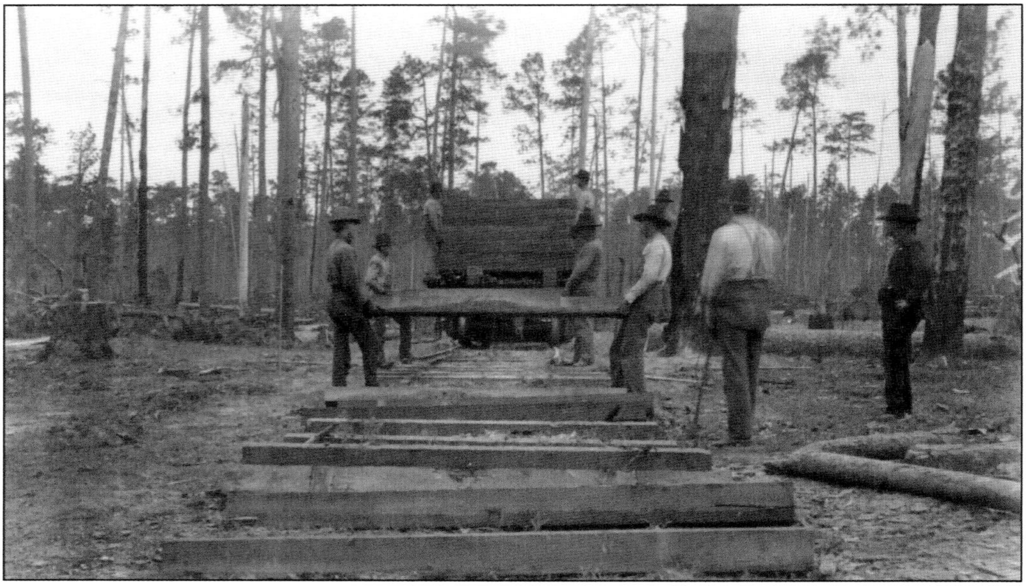

Depending on the amount of timber to be cut, ease of rail access, and efficiency of the logging crews, a tram might be active for years or only a few months. In this early view, the timber has been cut on a tract of Kirby Lumber land, and the tram crew has returned to reclaim any good rail and ties for use on future spurs. (Courtesy Richard W. Keeling Collection.)

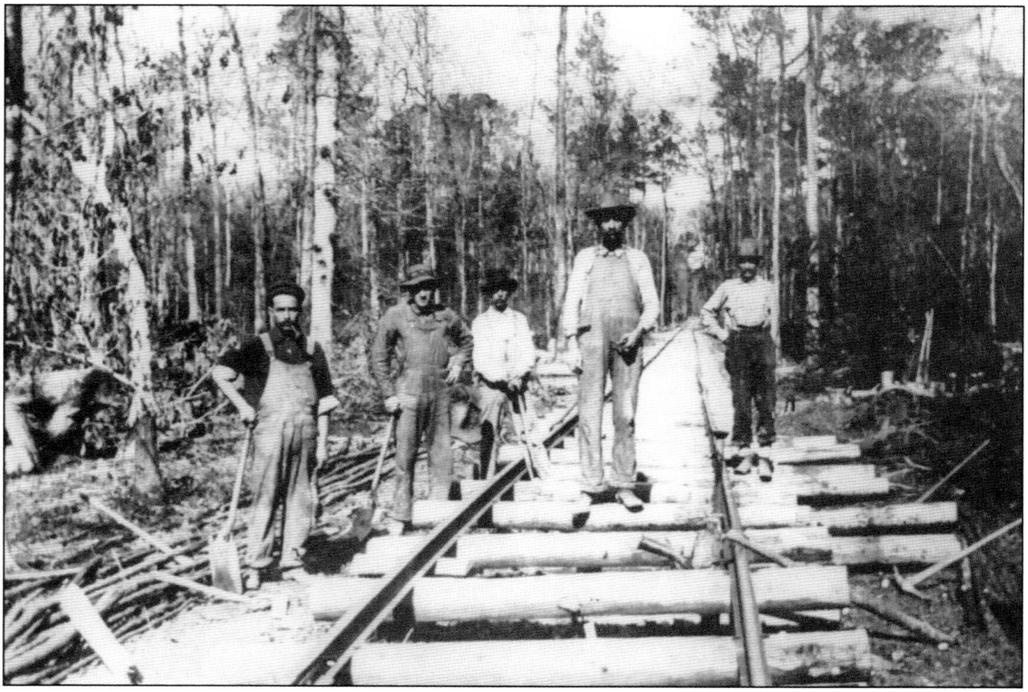

Trams were as varied as the terrain and available materials dictated. Here, a Jasper County crew inspects a tram constructed with iron rails laid directly onto raw poles of widely varying lengths. As crude as this tram appears, the crudest practices belonged to the pole and stringer roads, which used wood in place of iron rails. (Courtesy Jasper County Museum.)

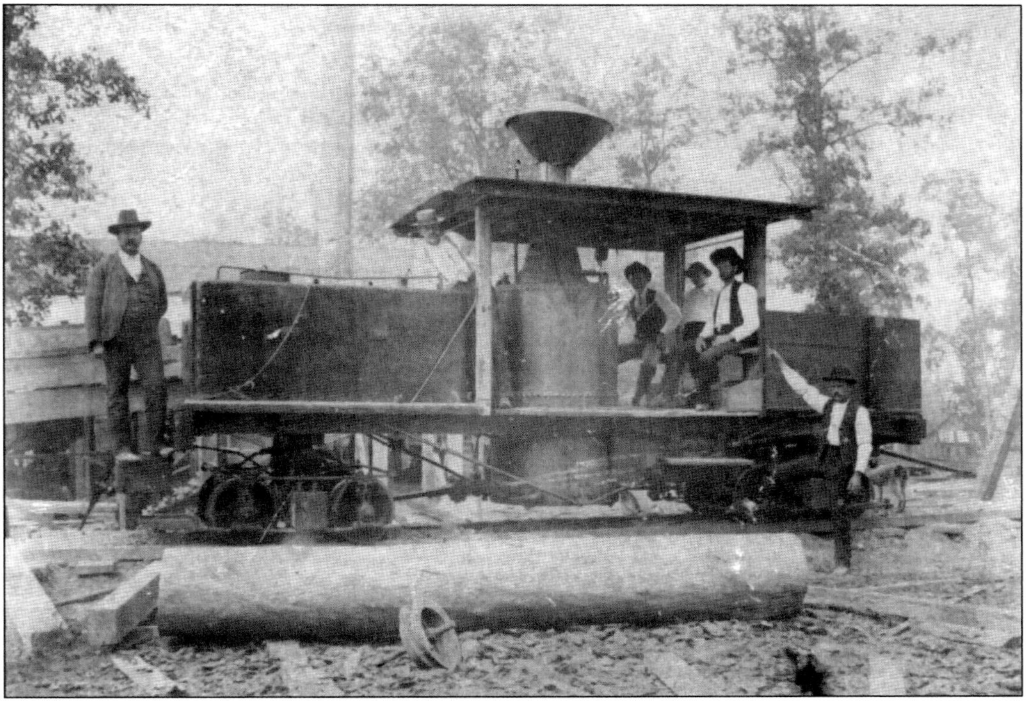

Along the Houston East & West Texas Railway in Polk County, the Lamont Lumber Company employed a light vertical-boiler Shay locomotive operating over wooden rails (above). Such trams were inexpensive to construct but fared poorly under the stresses of even the lightest equipment. Elsewhere in Polk County, a similar machine (below) was used by Thomas Hackney. The *T.L. Hackney* operated over a stringer road at Lone Star and Valda. The Shay's tiny boiler was fueled with pine knots and wood waste, while its tank was filled with water drawn directly from nearby Menard Creek. (Above, courtesy Polk County Museum; below, courtesy Richard W. Keeling Collection.)

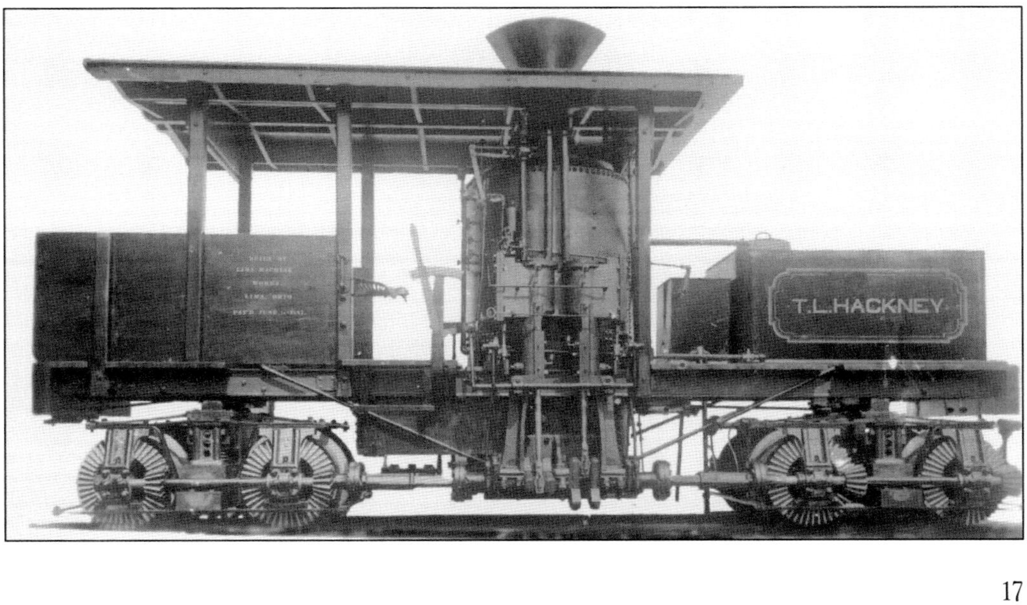

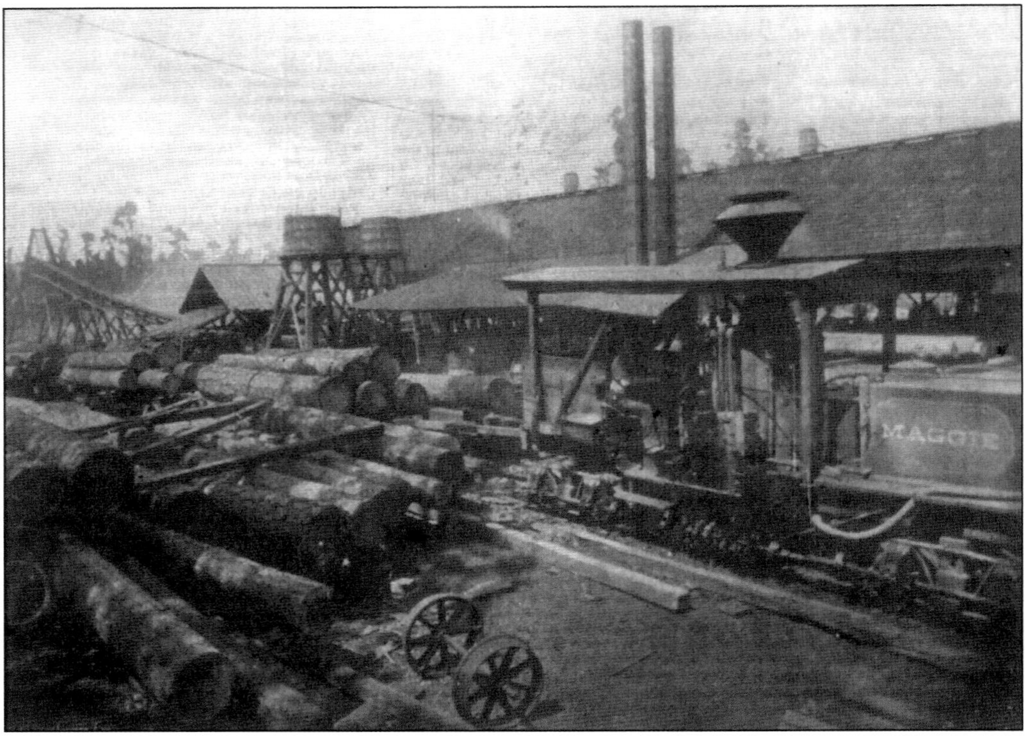

Beginning in 1882, brothers Frank and Peter Josserand began milling three miles east of Groveton at Josserand Station on the Trinity & Sabine Railway, which was powered by this vertical-boiler Shay locomotive affectionately named *Maggie*. (Courtesy Texas Transportation Archive.)

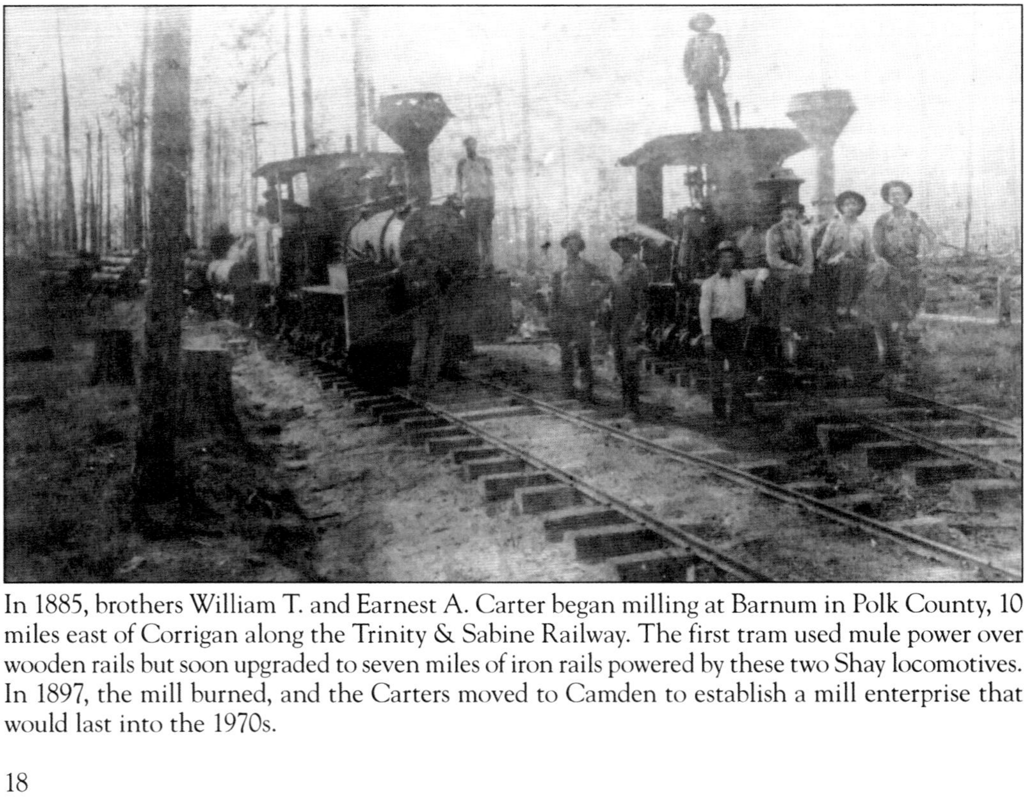

In 1885, brothers William T. and Earnest A. Carter began milling at Barnum in Polk County, 10 miles east of Corrigan along the Trinity & Sabine Railway. The first tram used mule power over wooden rails but soon upgraded to seven miles of iron rails powered by these two Shay locomotives. In 1897, the mill burned, and the Carters moved to Camden to establish a mill enterprise that would last into the 1970s.

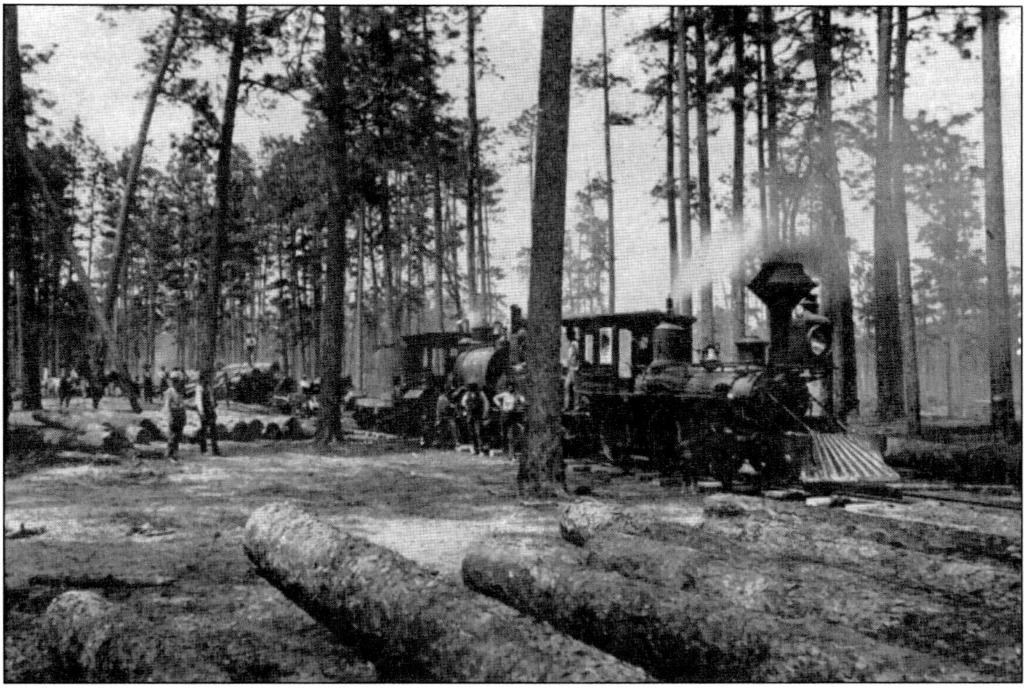

In 1886, the Village Mills Company established its mill at Village, a new station in northern Hardin County on the Houston East & West Texas Railway. A narrow-gauge tram was laid from Village to the Neches River in southeastern Tyler County. This view shows the company's two locomotives at the log front around 1890. (Courtesy Texas Transportation Archive.)

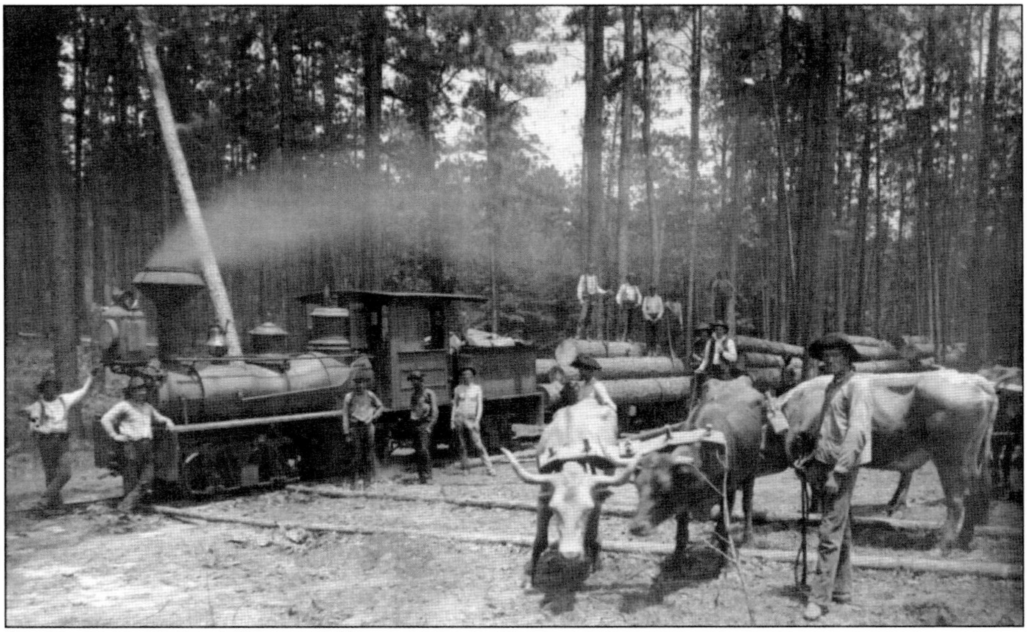

Angle Lumber Company built its mill in 1883 at Stryker, about five miles east of Corrigan in Polk County. Depending on the needs of the mill, the tram varied in length from three to six miles. Shay No. 2 was built for the company in 1888 and was affectionately known among the crews as "Mala." (Courtesy Polk County Museum.)

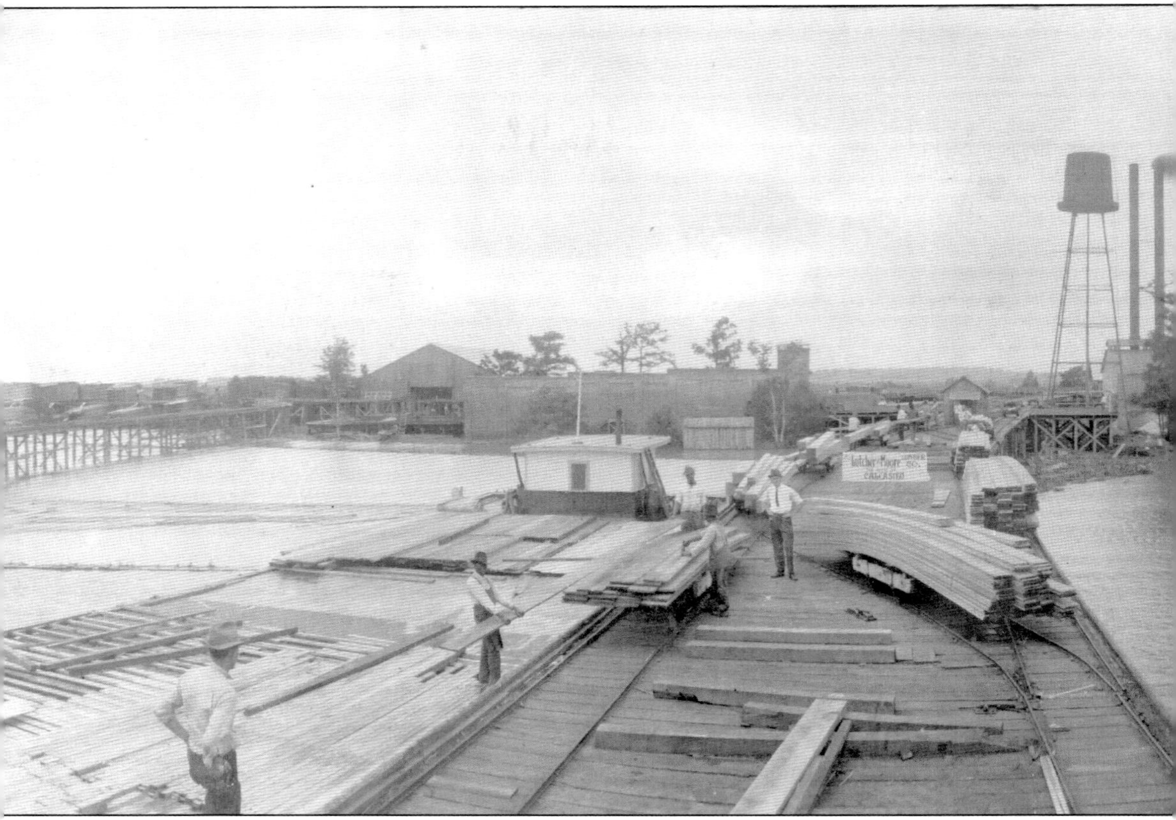

In 1877, Pennsylvanians Henry Jacob Lutcher and Gregory Bedell Moore purchased more than a half-million acres of Louisiana land and established at the port city of Orange their Star & Crescent Mill, which lumber historians regard as the first big mill in Texas. This panorama from around

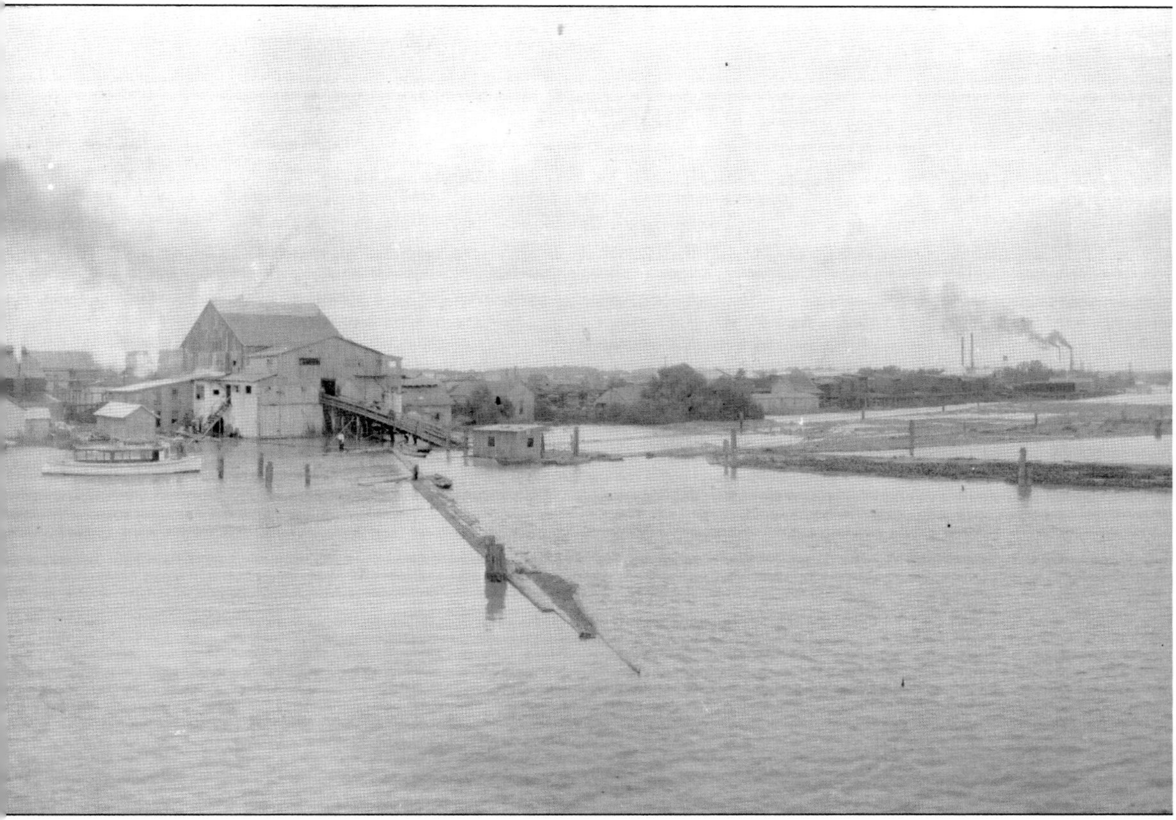

1890 shows the mill complex spread along a horseshoe bend on the Sabine River. To supply the mill's initial capacity of 150,000 board feet, timber was cut on both the Texas and Louisiana sides of the Sabine and transported by both rail and water. (Courtesy Texas Transportation Archive.)

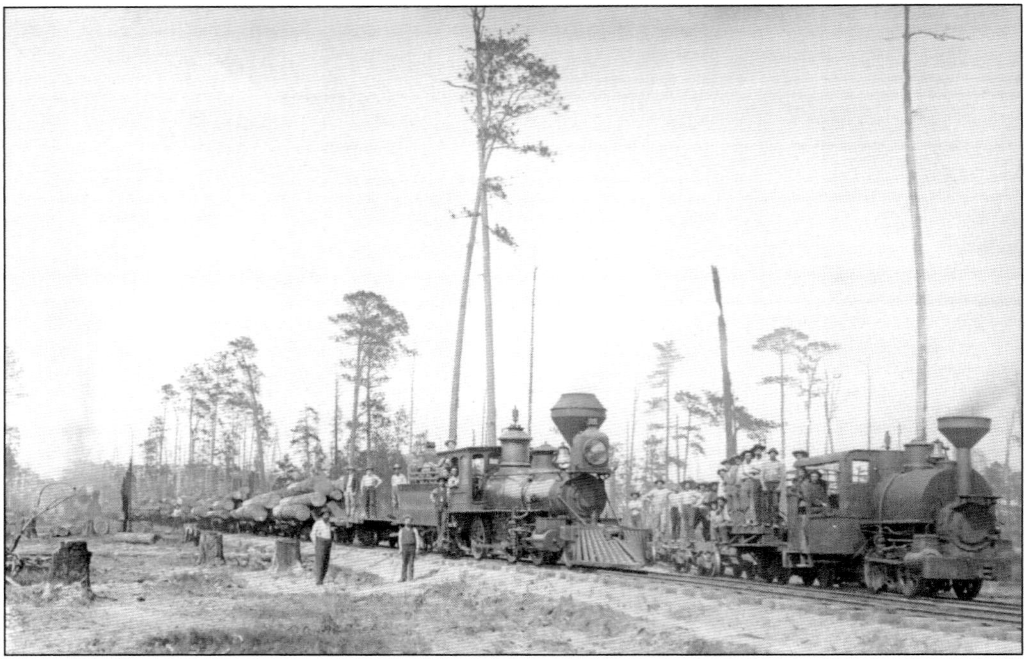

To move timber to the banks of the Sabine on the Louisiana side, a 100-mile tram was constructed and dubbed the Gulf, Sabine & Red River Railroad. Pictured is Engine No. 1 with a train of logs destined for the landing at Niblett's Bluff, while a small tram engine readies to transport two cars of woodworkers. (Courtesy Texas Transportation Archive.)

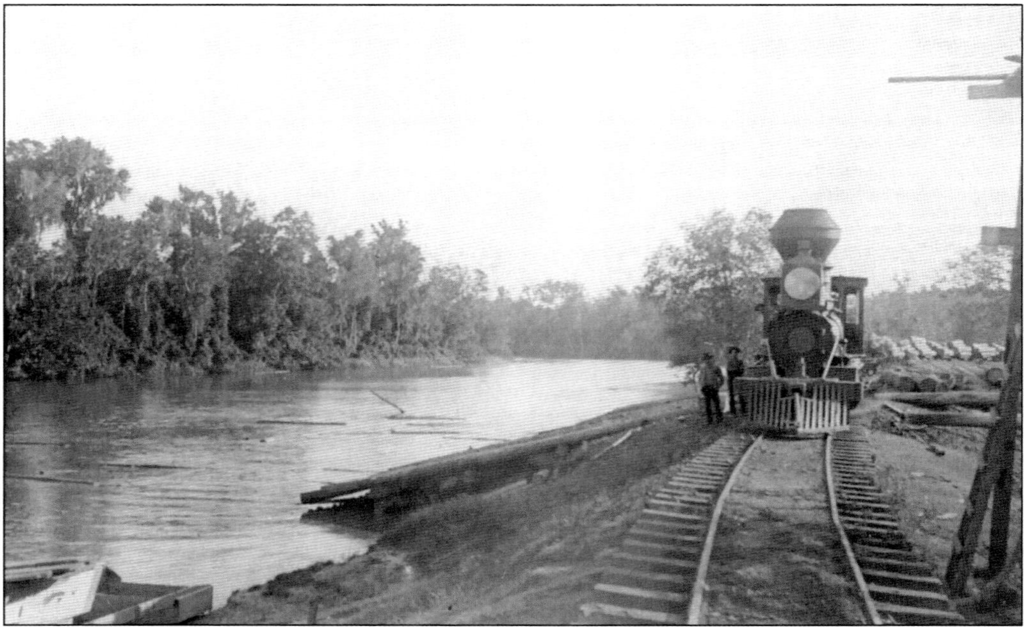

Lutcher-Moore's tram, the Gulf, Sabine & Red River Railroad, was said to have been constructed with standards and equipment worthy of a mainline road. In this 1890s view, Engine No. 1 waits at the Niblett's Bluff landing for the crew to unload the logs into the Sabine River, where they will be assembled into rafts and floated 16 miles to the Orange mill. The No. 1 will then return to the camps to prepare for the next day's load. (Courtesy Texas Transportation Archive.)

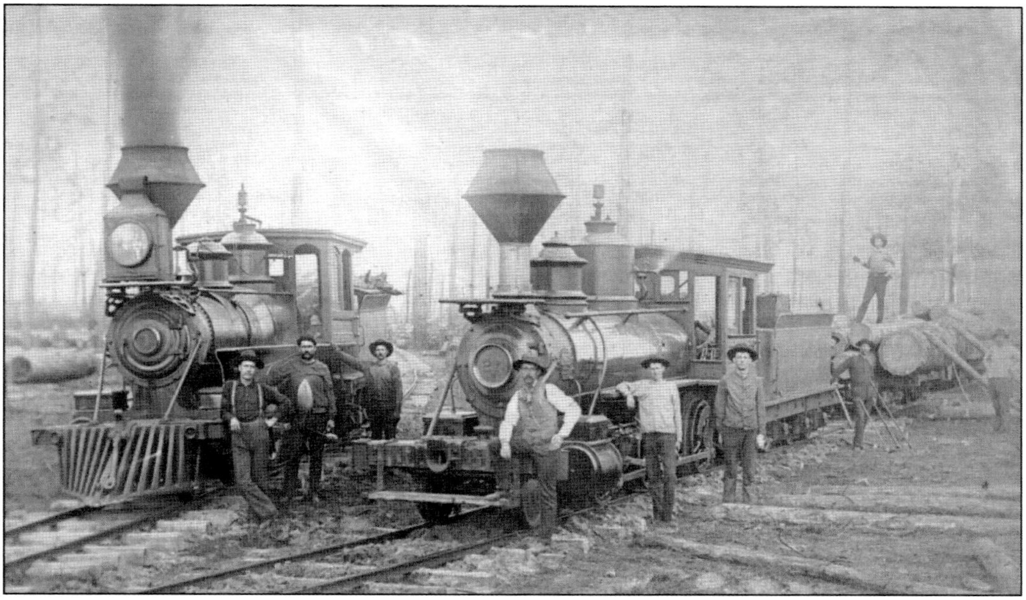

Sabine Tram operated the Laurel logging camp in Newton County from 1889 until 1904, when the company moved its woods operations into Louisiana. In this 1891 view, Engines Nos. 1 and 27 meet in the woods. The No. 27 (right) previously pulled trains through the Rocky Mountains for the Denver & Rio Grande Railroad before coming to East Texas. (Courtesy Dolph Briscoe Center for American History.)

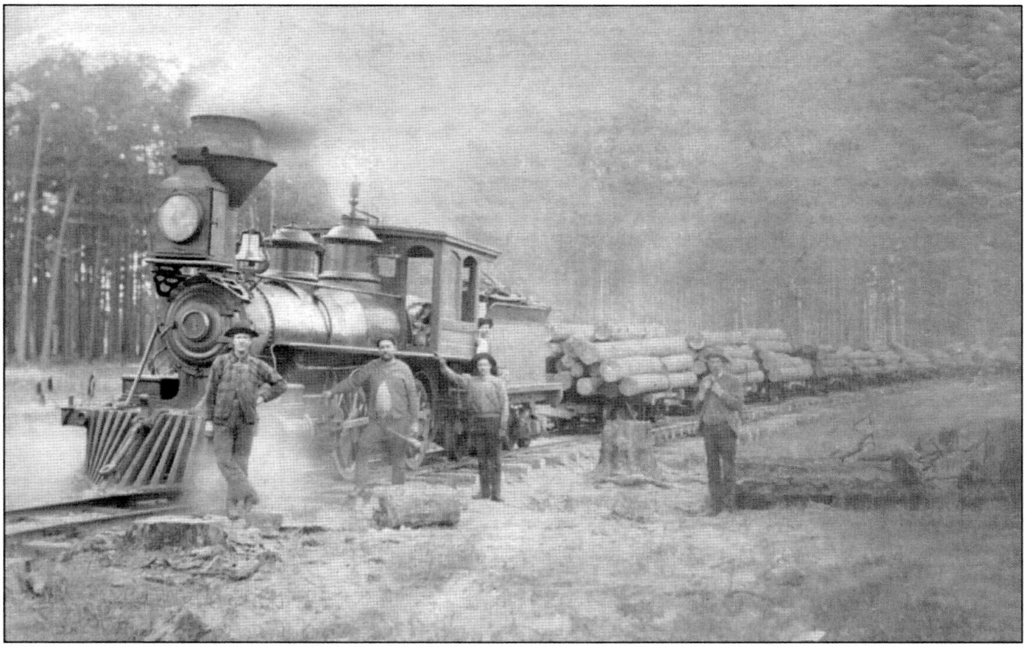

Sabine Tram No. 1 is pictured with its crew and the day's log train. The fully loaded train will dump its contents into the Sabine River at a point called Sudduth's Bluff, from which the logs will float to the mill at Deweyville in the southern part of Newton County. (Courtesy Dolph Briscoe Center for American History.)

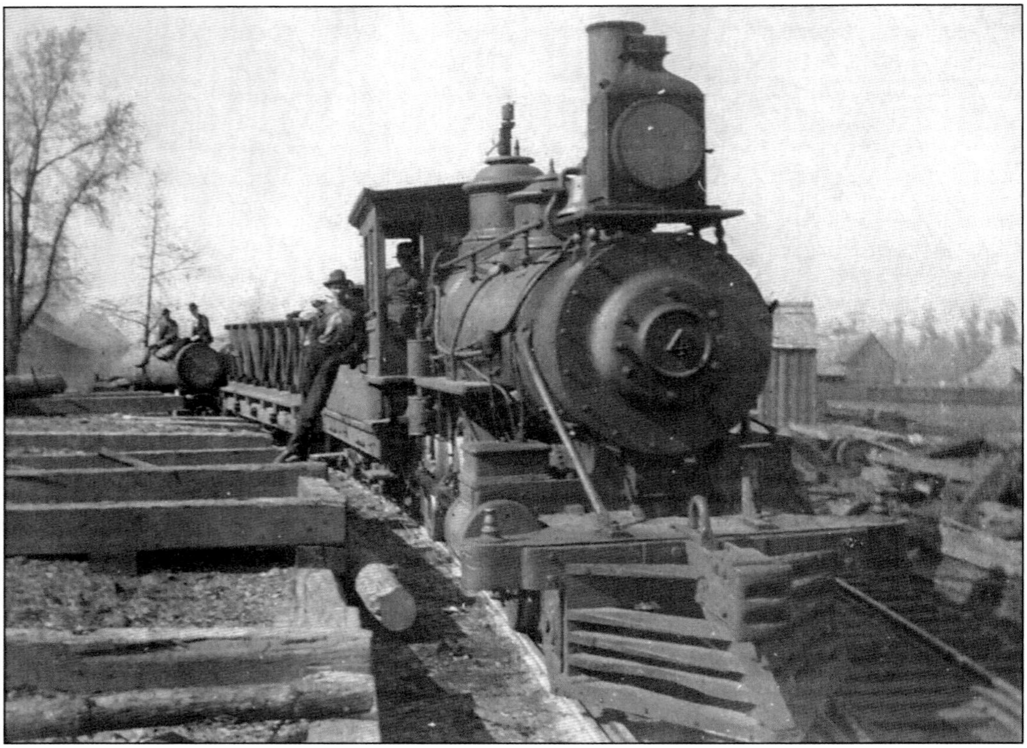

In 1881, Sidney Olive and John Sternenberg established their Sunset Mill at Olive in Hardin County. The narrow-gauge Olive & Sternenberg Timber Railroad was laid five miles northwest from Olive and began with just one locomotive and five flatcars. In the above 1890s view, Engine No. 4 switches the Olive mill. Below is the original 1881 mill as it looked in the 1890s. Its capacity of 40,000 board feet made it one of the largest in Texas at the time. Olive-Sternenberg operated until 1912, when the timber was finally depleted. Olive became a ghost town overnight, and by 1920 was no longer included on state maps. (Both, courtesy Hardin County Museum.)

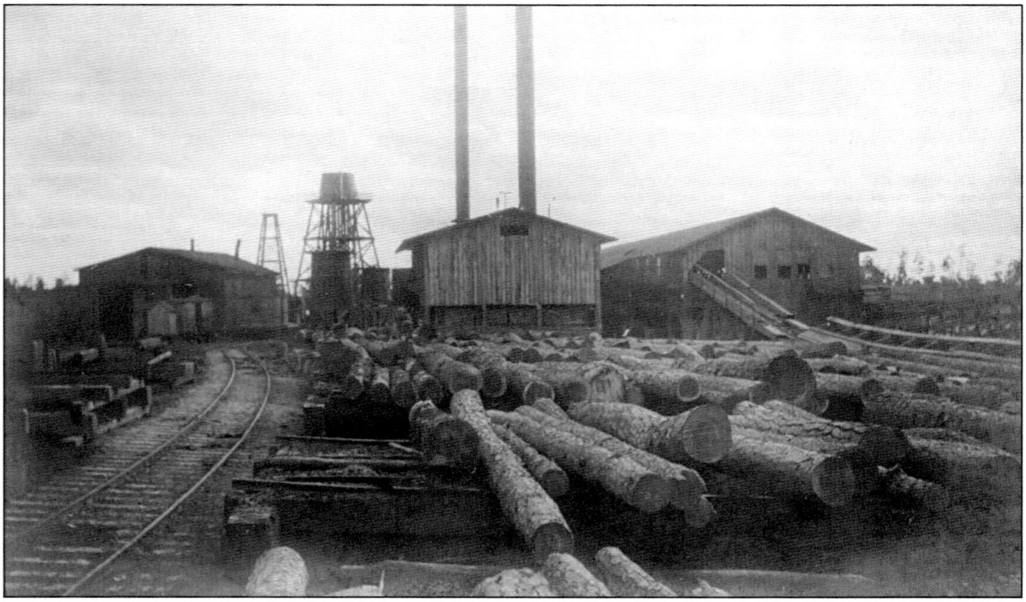

Two

Logging in the North East Counties

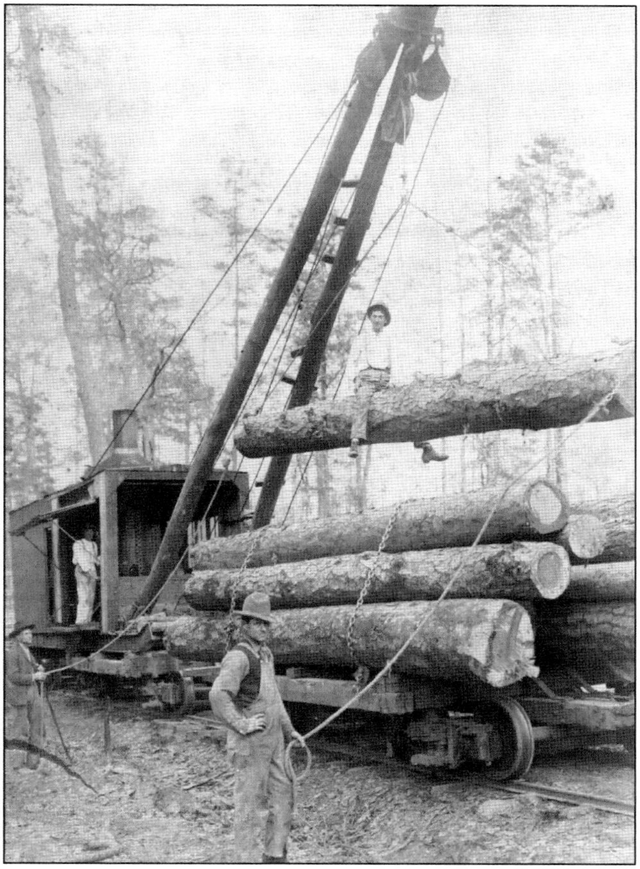

The entry of interstate railroads into northeast Texas starting in the 1870s opened up vast sections of forest to commercial exploitation. Lumber mills appeared in every timbered county, much as their counterparts farther south. Here, a moment of levity is captured at the Clark & Boice Lumber Company camp west of Linden in Cass County around 1900. On the log is Prue Freeman, who would serve as fireman, engineer, and master mechanic for both the lumber company and its railroad counterpart, the Jefferson & Northwestern Railway. Prue was on the job when the railroad was incorporated in 1899 and was on hand to "shut off the lights" when the company closed operations in 1941. (Courtesy Robert S. Bramlett.)

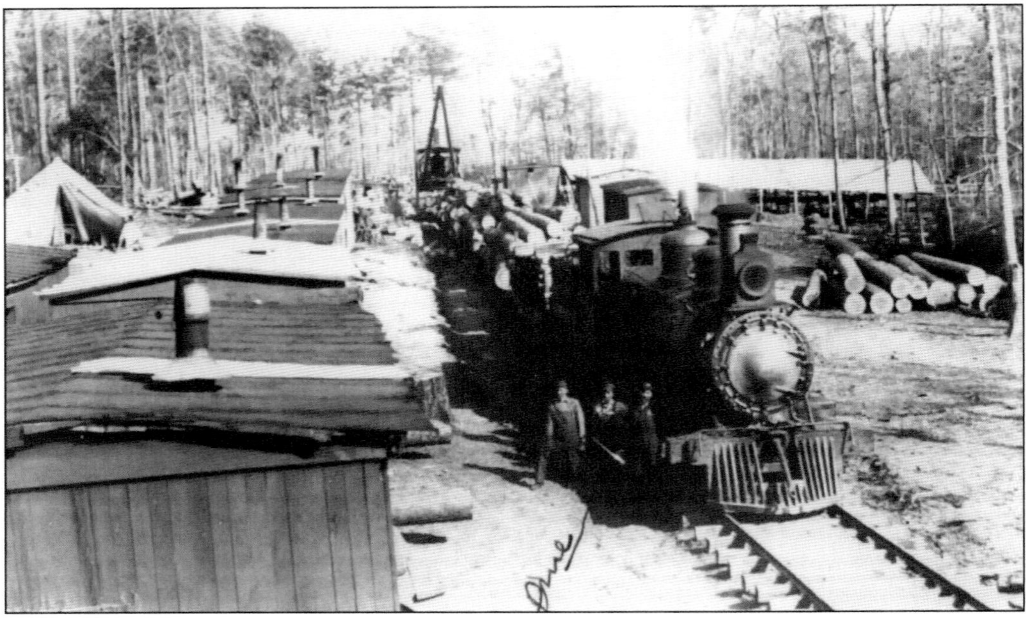

Around 1900, the Clark & Boice Lumber Company established a camp four miles southwest of the Cass County seat of Linden. The line of cars to the left served as housing for loggers and their families. Trains were moved from here to the mill at Jefferson. The railroad was incorporated separately as Jefferson & Northwestern and would outlive the lumber company that built it. (Courtesy Texas Transportation Archive.)

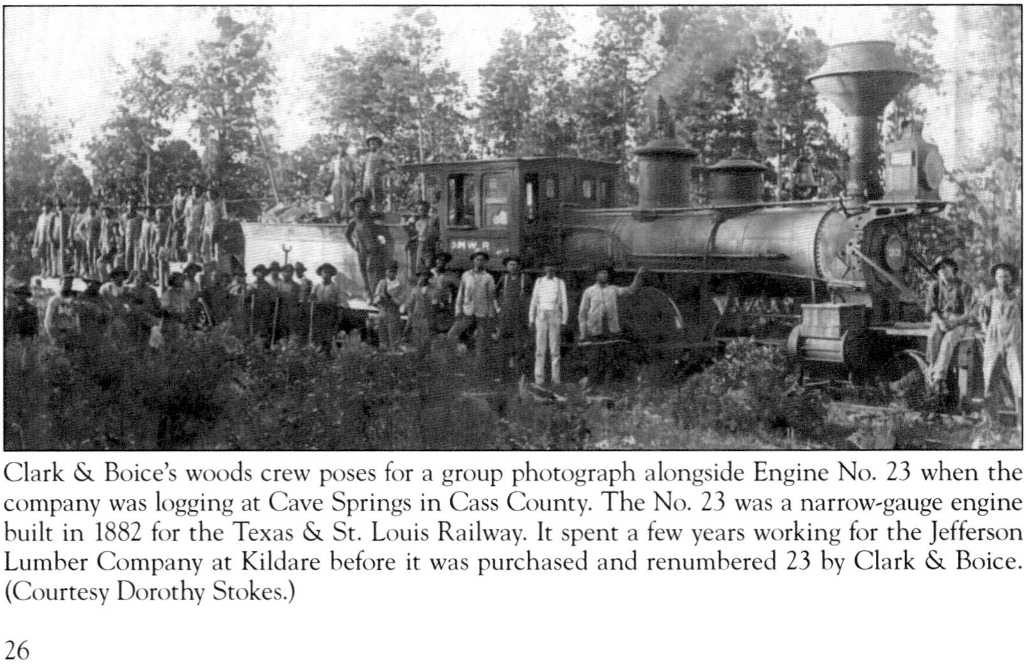

Clark & Boice's woods crew poses for a group photograph alongside Engine No. 23 when the company was logging at Cave Springs in Cass County. The No. 23 was a narrow-gauge engine built in 1882 for the Texas & St. Louis Railway. It spent a few years working for the Jefferson Lumber Company at Kildare before it was purchased and renumbered 23 by Clark & Boice. (Courtesy Dorothy Stokes.)

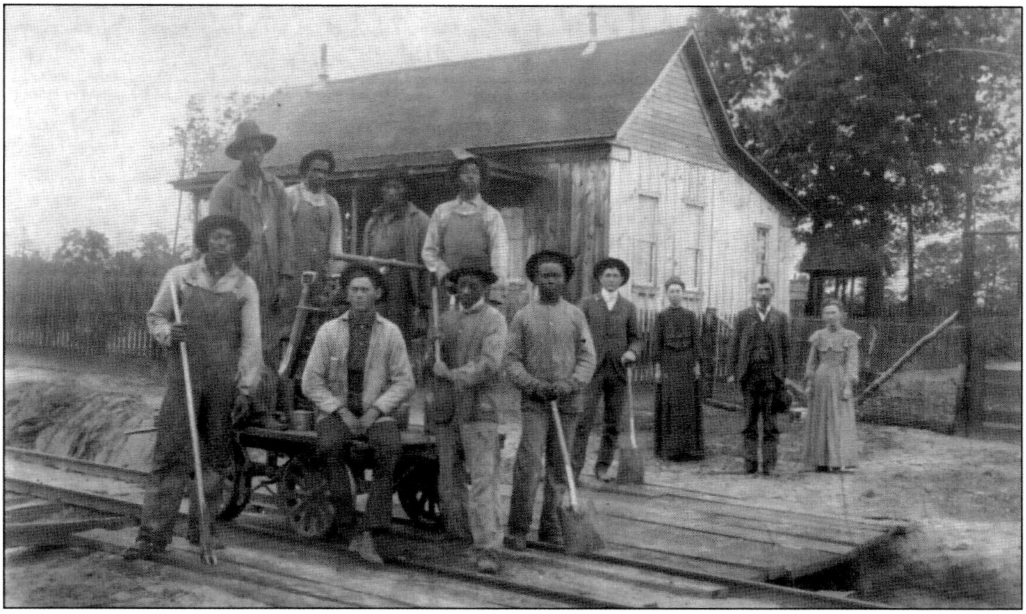

At Lanier, a section gang under the charge of roadmaster Luster Hughes (seated in front) maintained both Clark & Boice lumber spurs and the Jefferson & Northwestern line between Jefferson in Marion County and Linden in Cass County. (Courtesy Mrs. Luster Hughes.)

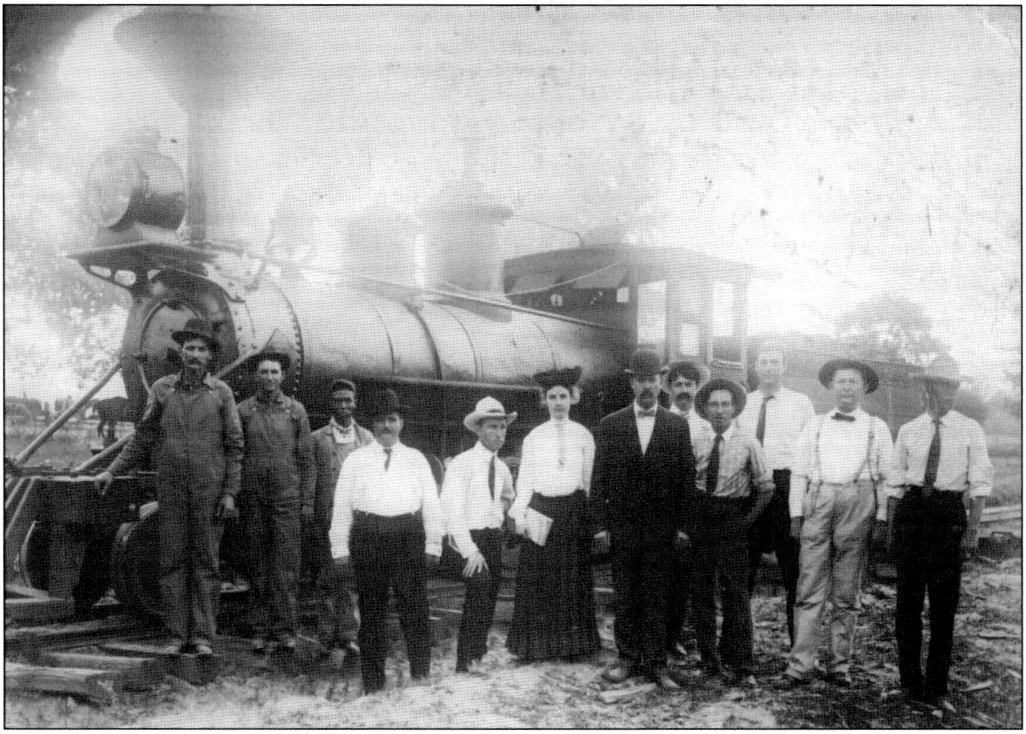

A group of managers and their families ride out on the Clark & Boice tram for an afternoon picnic at Lanier. Shortly after this photograph was taken, the company changed the road's gauge from narrow to standard, completed its line into the Cass County seat of Linden, and sold or scrapped the old narrow-gauge engines. (Courtesy Kyle Fant.)

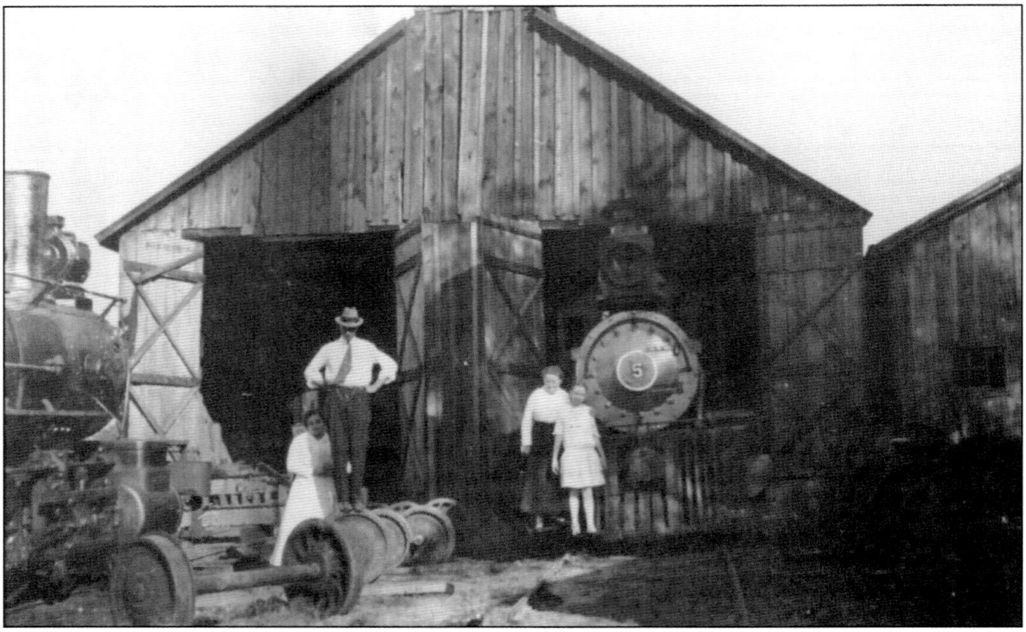

Clark & Boice used this rough-hewn board-and-batten building to house and maintain its fleet of logging locomotives and those of the Jefferson & Northwestern Railway. On this day, Engine No. 5 received a visit from master mechanic and occasional engineer Prue Freeman and family. (Courtesy Ruel Young Sr.)

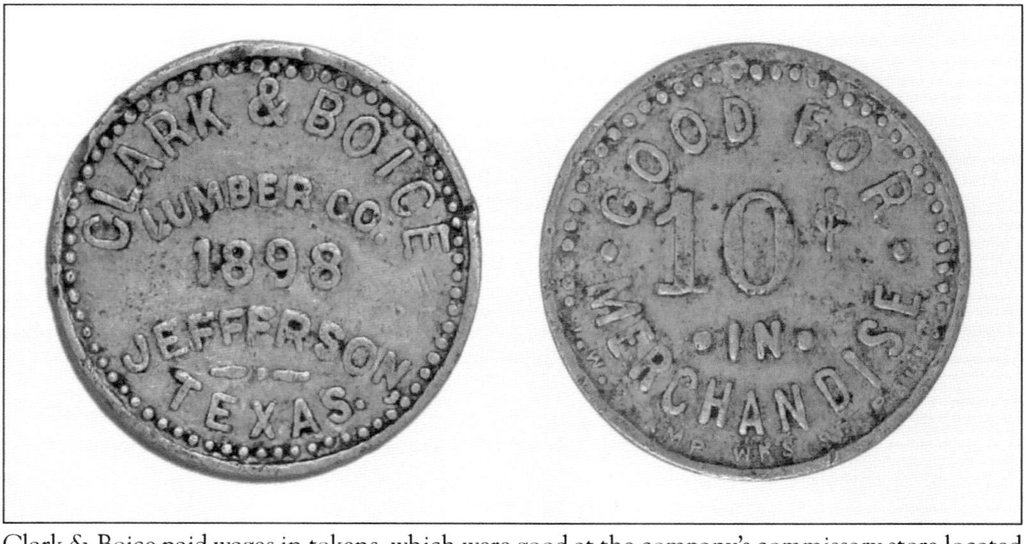

Clark & Boice paid wages in tokens, which were good at the company's commissary store located at the mill. This system was nearly universal among the larger lumber mills across the South. This token was issued in 1898 and was good for 10¢ worth of goods at the store. (Courtesy Robert S. Bramlett.)

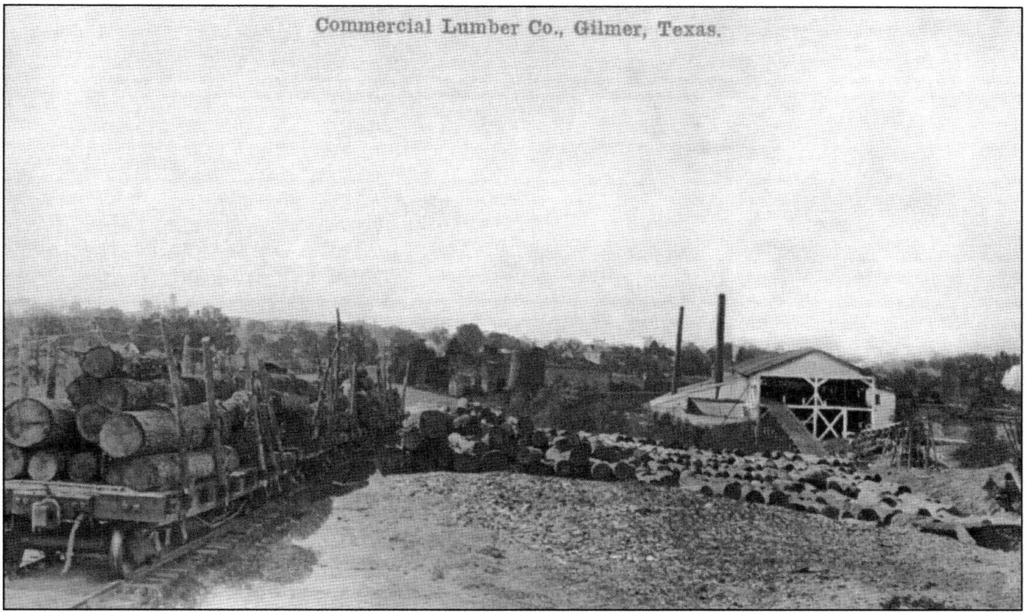

The Commercial Lumber Company, also known as Clark's Mill, was built on the northern end of Gilmer in Upshur County around 1892. A tram was laid out 16 miles from Gilmer to Ashland and operated until 1897, when it was purchased for inclusion in a new railroad venture, the Texas Southern Railway. Only three miles ended up in the final Texas Southern route; the rest of the tram was deemed too steep and the curves too tight. Commercial Lumber continued milling until a devastating fire in 1907 ended operations. Below, Commercial Lumber No. 2 has been "wooded up" with mill waste and pine knots and is pictured with its crew in the early 1890s. The engine seems to have recently arrived on property, as evidenced by the pristine and glossy condition of its boiler and tender. (Above, courtesy Texas Transportation Archive; below, courtesy Mary Laschinger Kirby.)

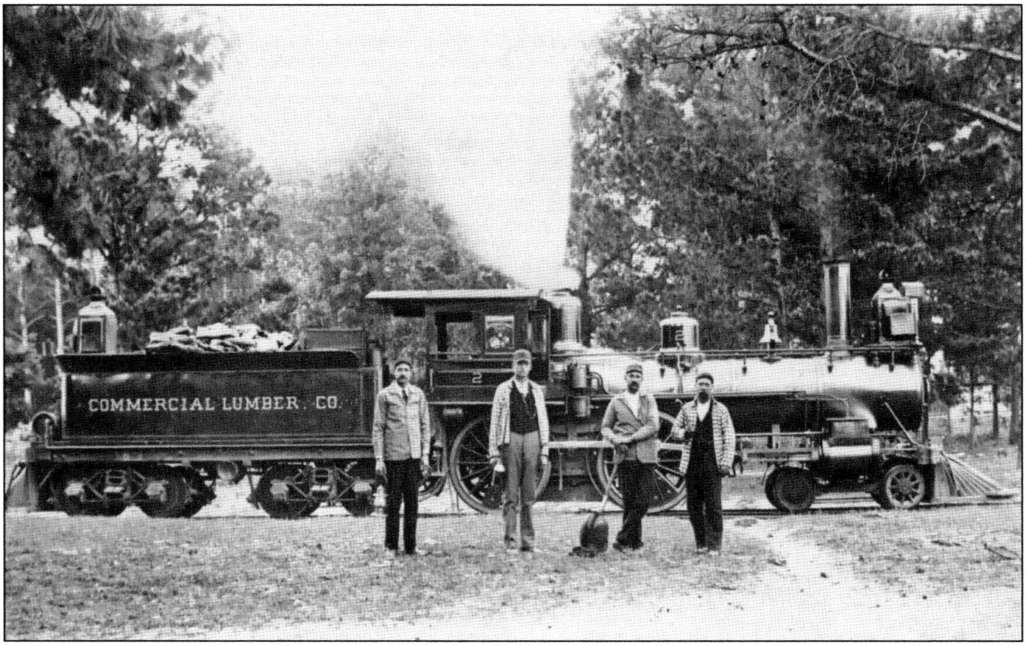

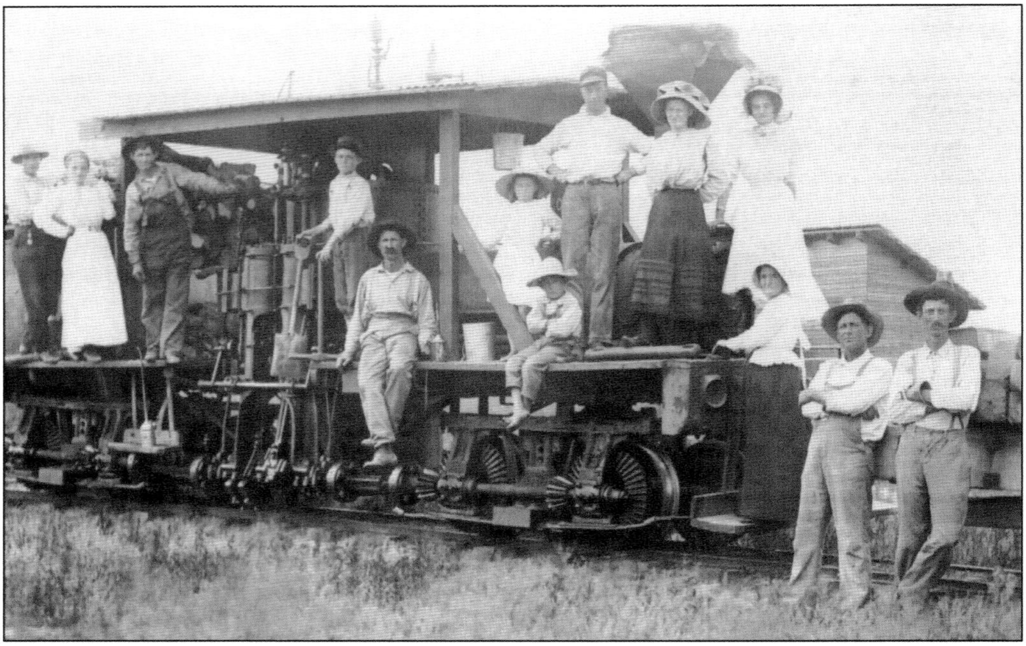

In 1905, a tram was laid northward from Saltillo to tap the oak forests that lined Fish Branch and Stouts Creek in Hopkins and Franklin Counties. The hardwood lumber was used for making staves and barrels at Mount Pleasant and for treated railroad ties at the National Creosote Company at Texarkana. The tram was initially operated by the King family, until the elder Seth King was killed trying to board a moving train in 1910. The firm of Markham & Brosius continued operations for another two years until the supply of oak was deemed exhausted and the lands sold to local farmers for cultivation. (Both, courtesy Bob King.)

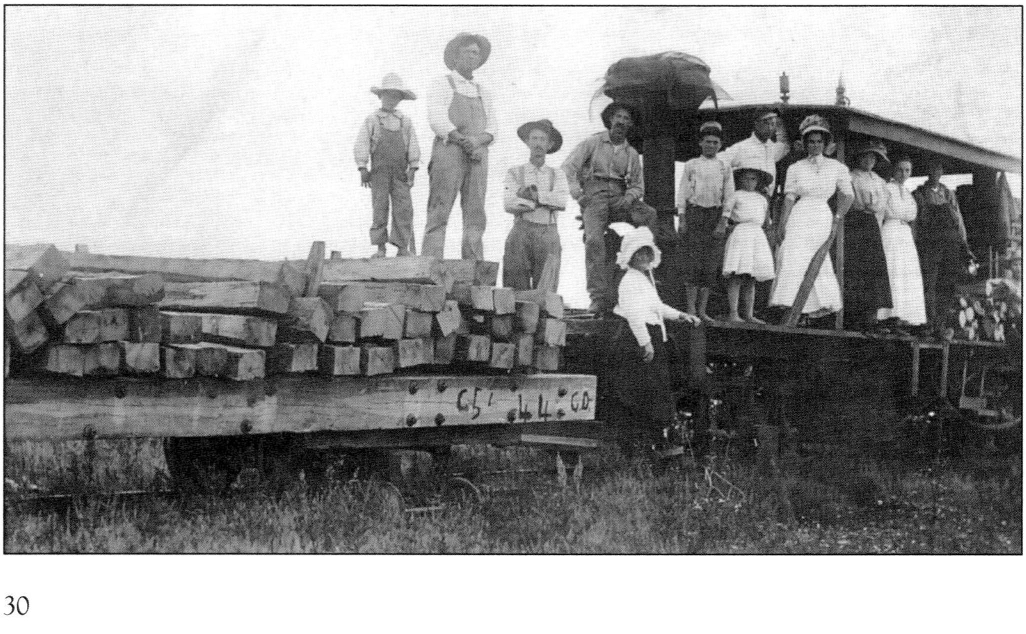

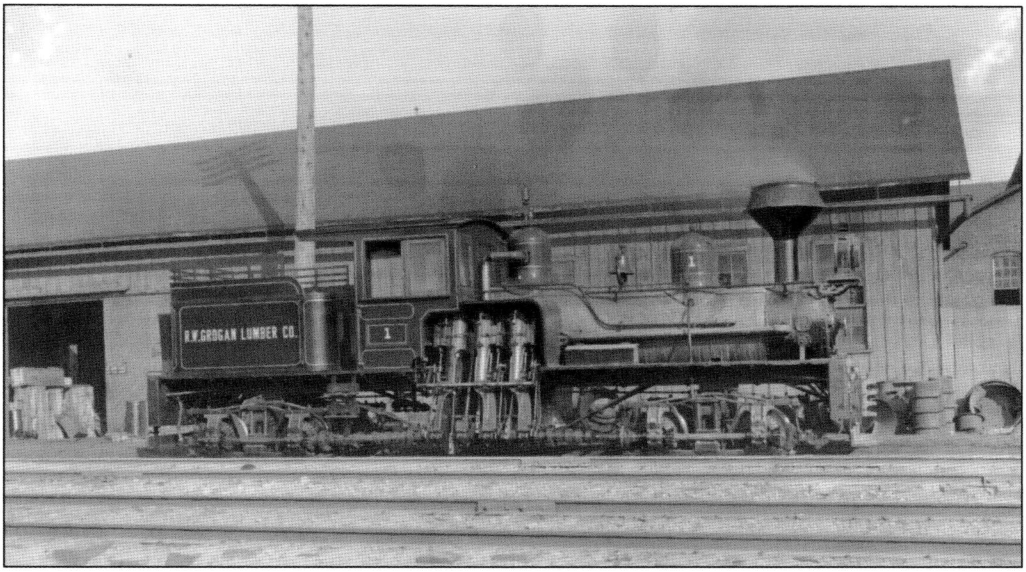

At Harleton in Harrison County, the R.W. Grogan Lumber Company took delivery of this 29-ton standard-gauge Shay locomotive in 1902. After a few years at Grogan, the No. 1 worked the forests for several companies in Harrison, Upshur, and Cass Counties, until 1922, when it went to Arkansas for a few more years of use before it was finally scrapped in 1926. (Courtesy Texas Transportation Archive.)

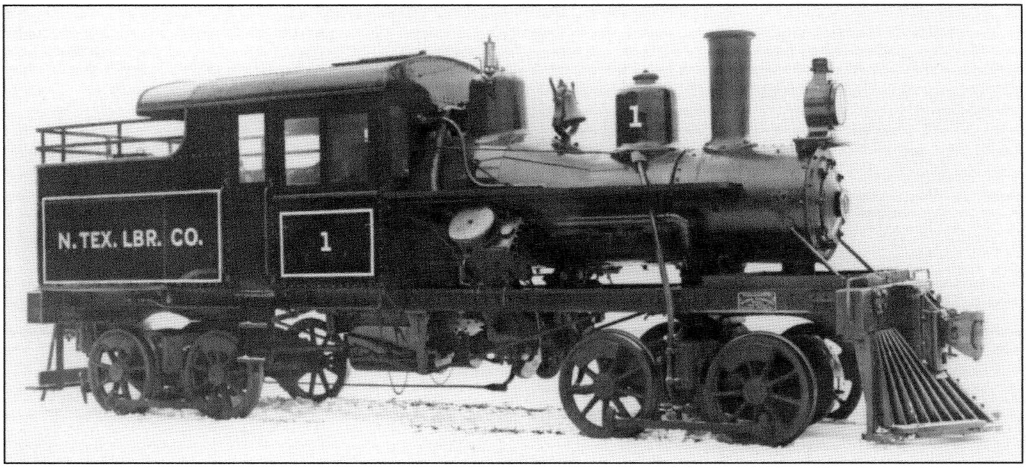

North Texas Lumber Company at Kildare used Heisler locomotives to log its timberlands near Linden in central Cass County. The North Texas tram operated until at least 1917 and extended 15 miles at its peak. This builder's portrait was taken when the No. 1 was delivered new in December 1909. No. 1 later worked for Clark & Boice at Jefferson before being scrapped in the 1930s. (Courtesy Texas Transportation Archive.)

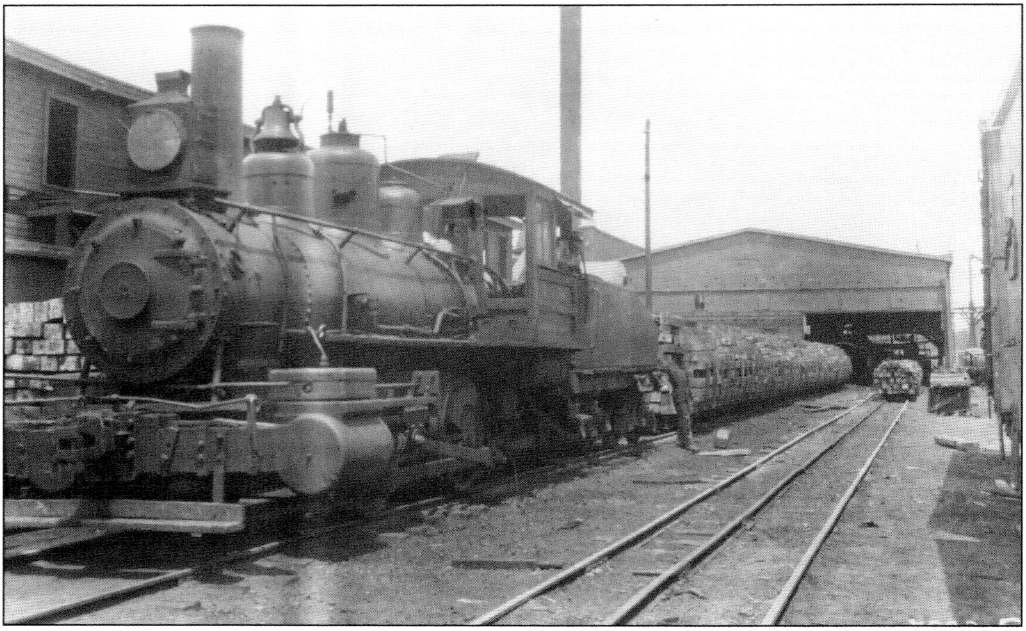

The Texas railroad construction boom began in the 1870s and continued into the 1910s. A contract for supplying crossties meant even a small lumber mill could be busy for weeks or even months. At Texarkana, thousands of raw ties passed through the pressurized creosote cylinders of the International Creosote and Construction (ICC) Company on their way to new railroad construction. In the above 1922 view, ICC's Engine No. 2 is busy shuttling loaded tramcars around the plant. Below, a sea of crossties surrounds the company's many plant spurs, all awaiting shipment to new construction across the state and beyond. (Both, courtesy Texas Transportation Archive.)

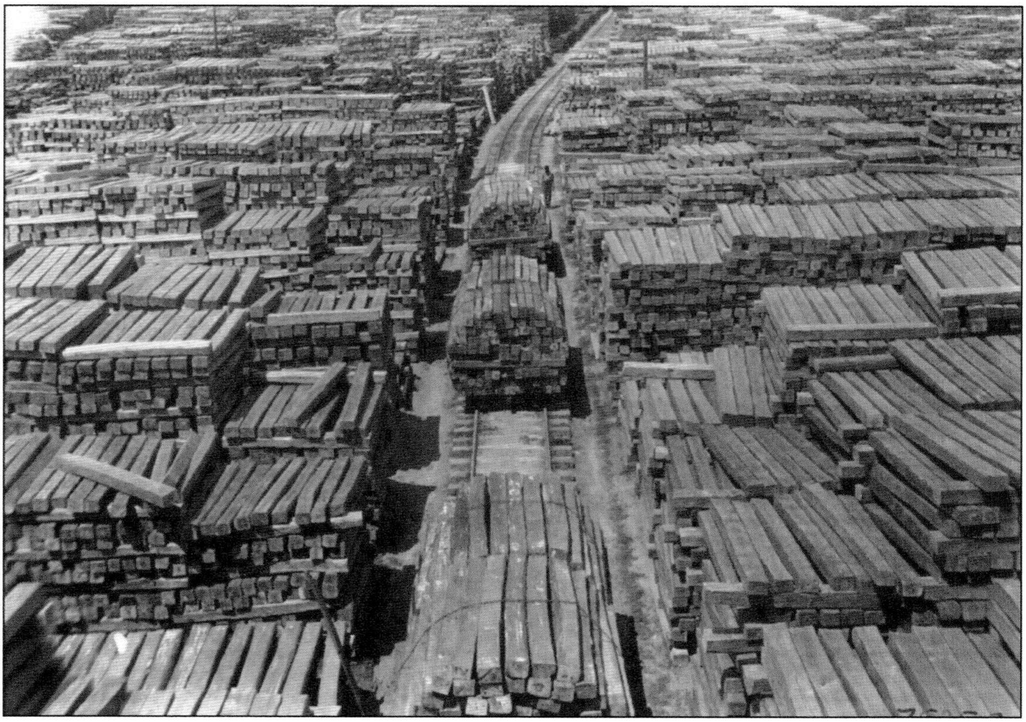

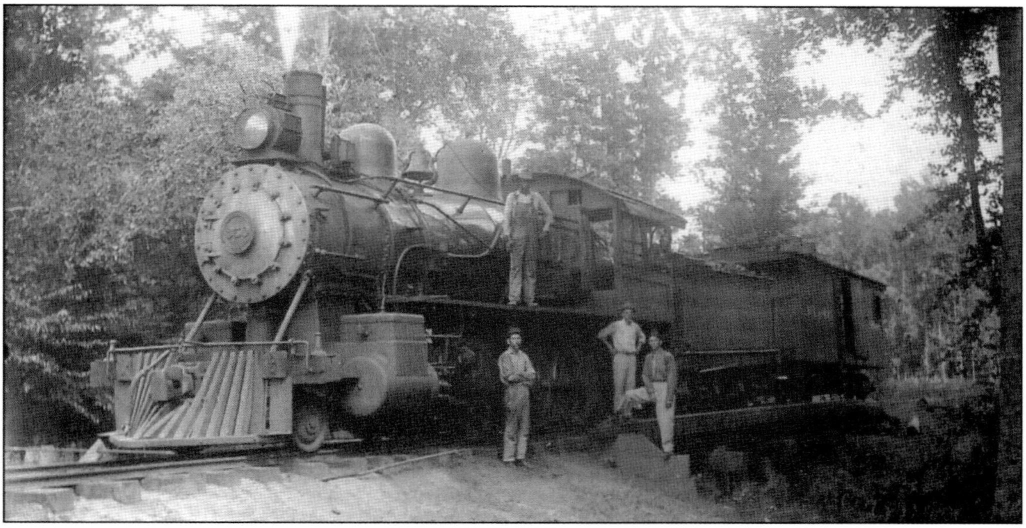

Waterman Lumber & Supply Company operated mills in the Shelby County towns of Waterman and Timpson, about 15 miles apart. In the above photograph taken in the 1910s, Waterman Engine No. 350 is pulling a single crew car used in the transportation of loggers from the Waterman mill to the company's timberlands east of town. Below, Engine No. 3 is pictured with engineer Samuel Tilton Smith in the mid-1910s. (Above, courtesy Terry Passmore; below, courtesy John Minton.)

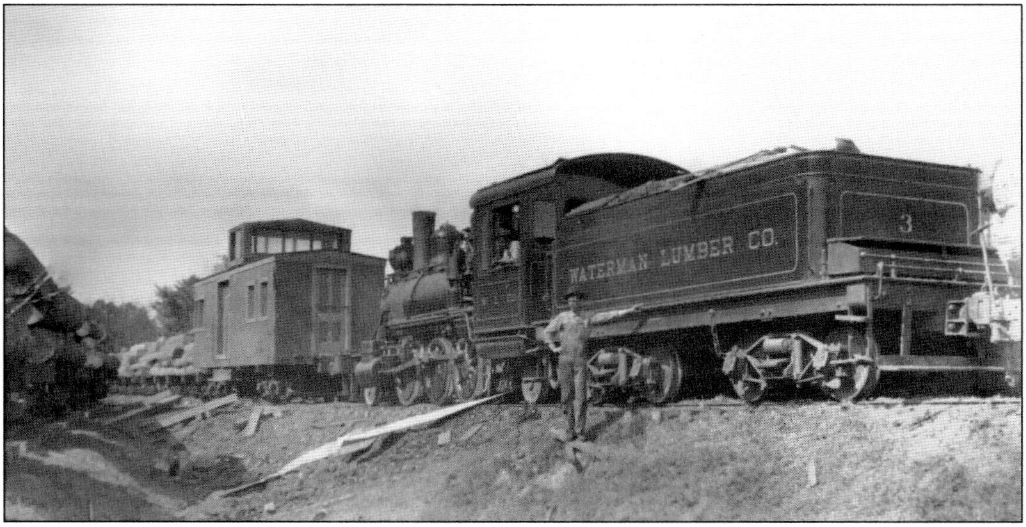

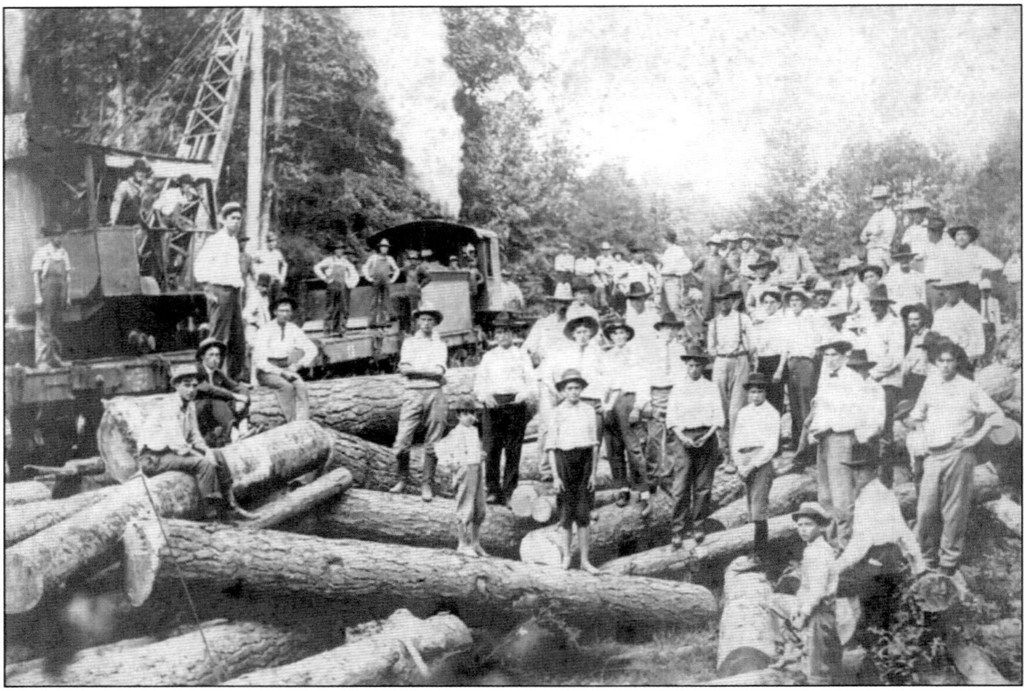

The violence of a major log train accident is on display in the above photograph, which was taken the day after a Waterman train derailed on September 1, 1911. The contents of the heavily loaded train were spilled, and three crew men who were riding atop the cars were killed. The event inspired the folk song "The Waterman Train Wreck," which was passed around East Texas locals for decades afterward. The locomotive involved in the Waterman wreck was the No. 200, pictured below with crew in the Shelby County woods. The engine was a total loss in the accident. (Both, courtesy Texas Transportation Archive.)

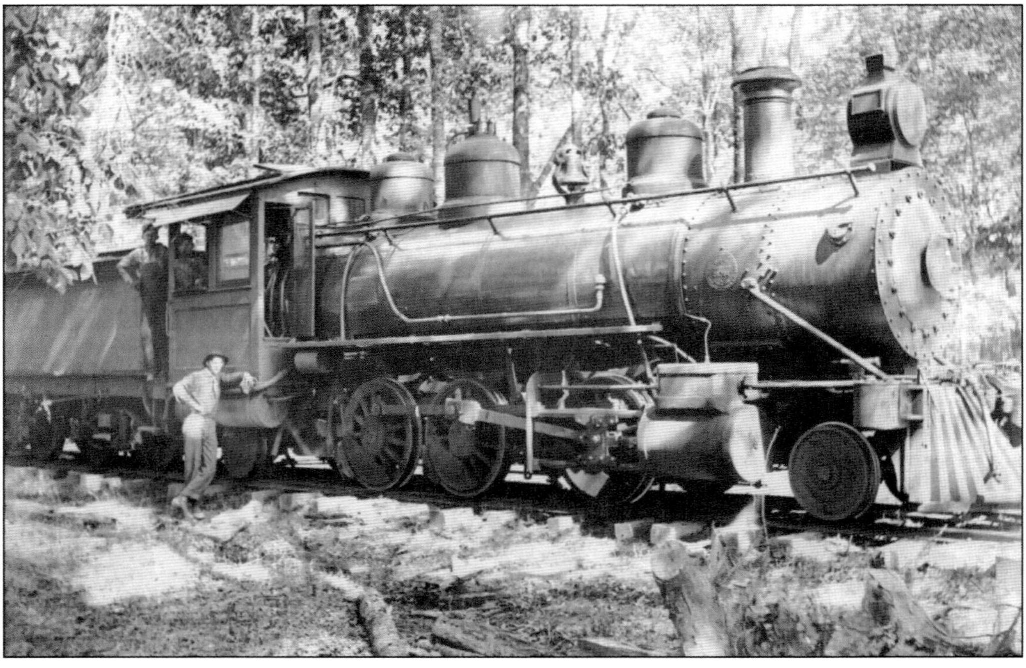

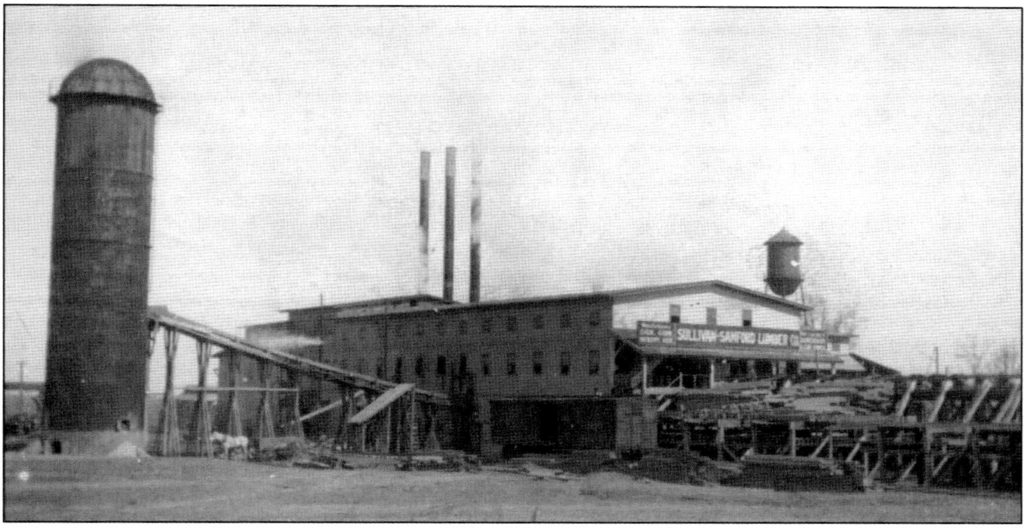

In 1906, at Naples in Morris County, the Sullivan-Sanford Lumber Company erected the above mill to process hardwoods harvested along the bottoms of White Oak Creek and the Sulphur River northwest of town. Timber was moved to the mill via a 16-mile narrow-gauge tram that extended in a northwesterly direction from the mill. The Sullivan-Sanford tram, below, was known locally as the Naples & Sulphur River Railroad, and while no photographs have surfaced of its equipment, this view captures the former Sullivan-Sanford Engine No. 2 in storage at the Dayton Lumber Company in Liberty County in the 1930s. (Both, courtesy Texas Transportation Archive.)

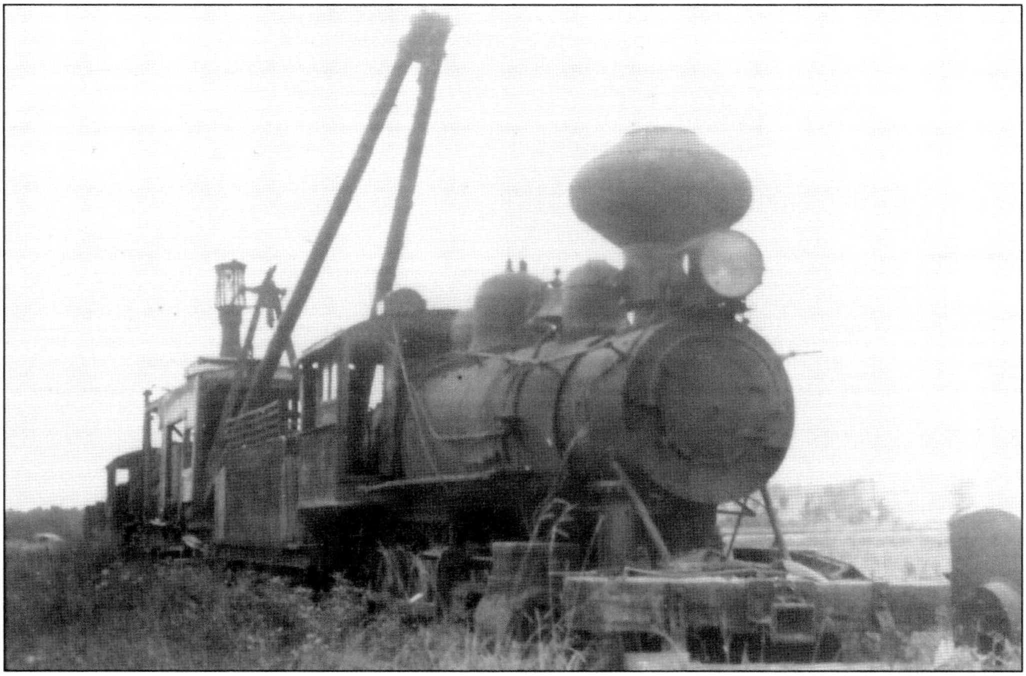

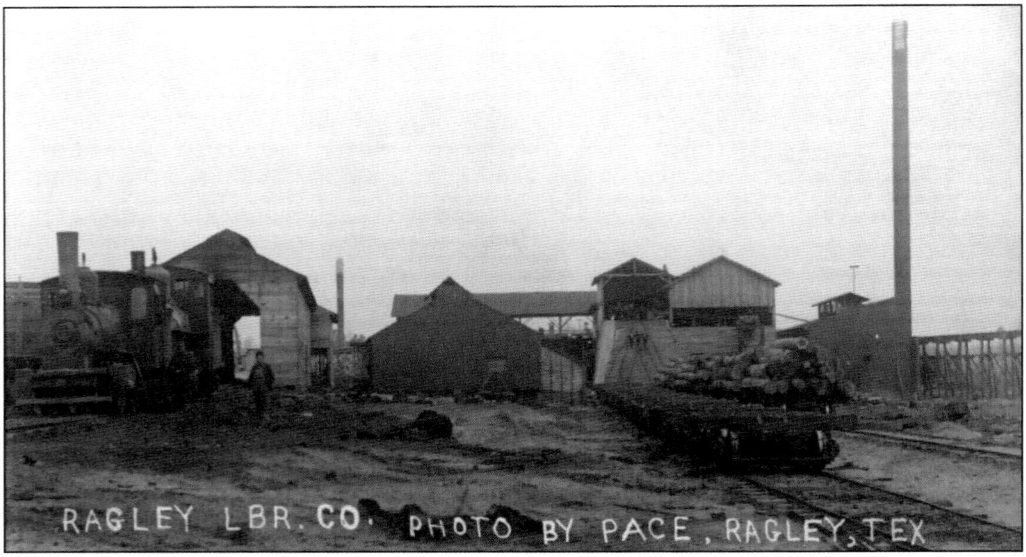

As Wolfgang Ragley wound down operations at Winnsboro in Wood County, he purchased several thousand acres of timber in Panola and Shelby Counties and built a mill and the new town of Ragley. In 1901, an eight-mile connection was laid between Ragley and Timpson, while a tram was built 12 miles to Pinehill. This 1909 view shows the Ragley machine shop and main mill building. (Courtesy Texas Transportation Archive.)

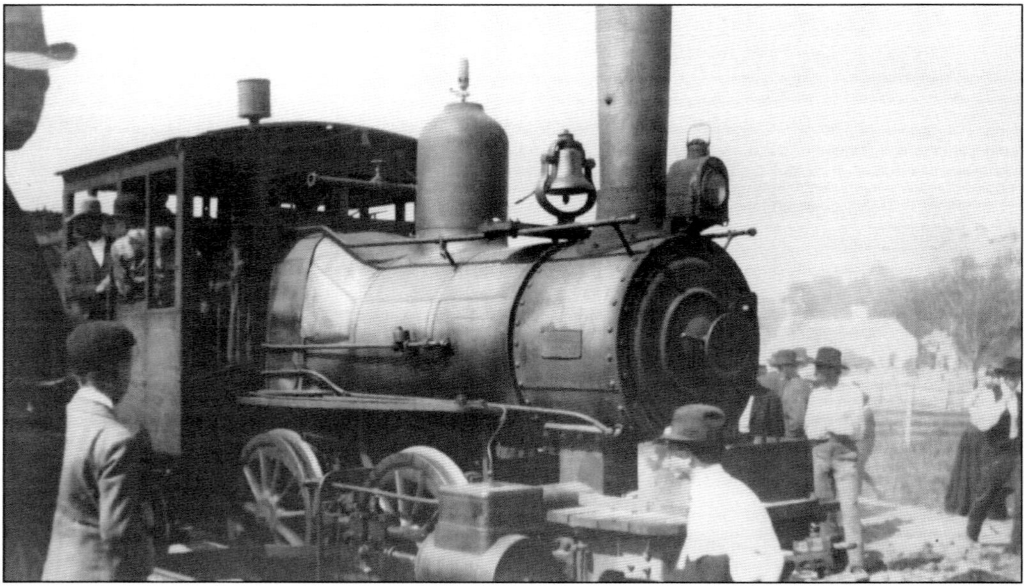

Ragley's No. 2 was an 1887 engine purchased in 1903 from New York City's Manhattan Railway, where it worked in commuter rail service. In this photograph taken on November 20, 1909, No. 2 is in Henderson to take part in ceremonies celebrating the completion of the Timpson & Henderson Railway. The Timpson & Henderson was a common carrier promoted by Ragley to link the two towns, utilizing former Ragley Lumber right-of-way. (Courtesy Texas Transportation Archive.)

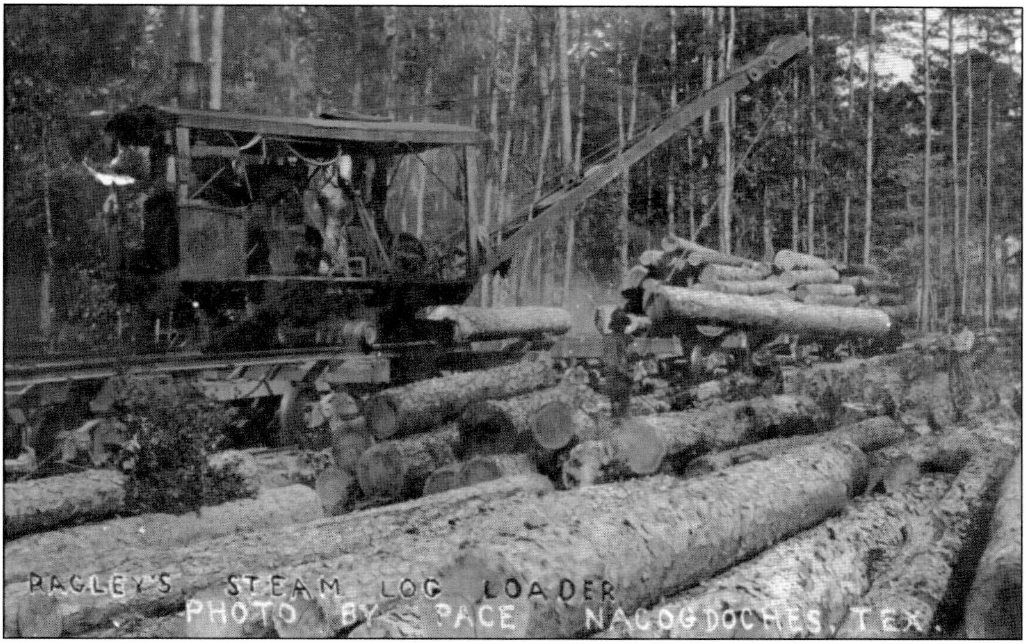

The Ragley Lumber loader clears out a congestion of logs that are waiting to be moved to the mill. It is unclear where this front was located, but records indicate that Ragley cut along Murvaul Creek and near the towns of Pinehill and Long Branch. (Courtesy Texas Transportation Archive.)

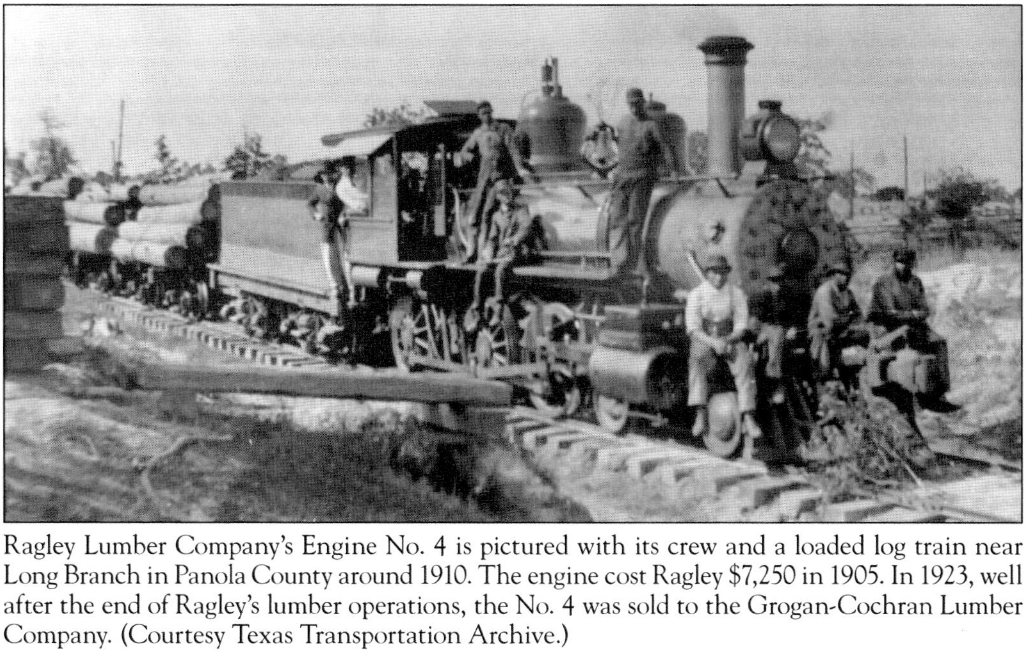

Ragley Lumber Company's Engine No. 4 is pictured with its crew and a loaded log train near Long Branch in Panola County around 1910. The engine cost Ragley $7,250 in 1905. In 1923, well after the end of Ragley's lumber operations, the No. 4 was sold to the Grogan-Cochran Lumber Company. (Courtesy Texas Transportation Archive.)

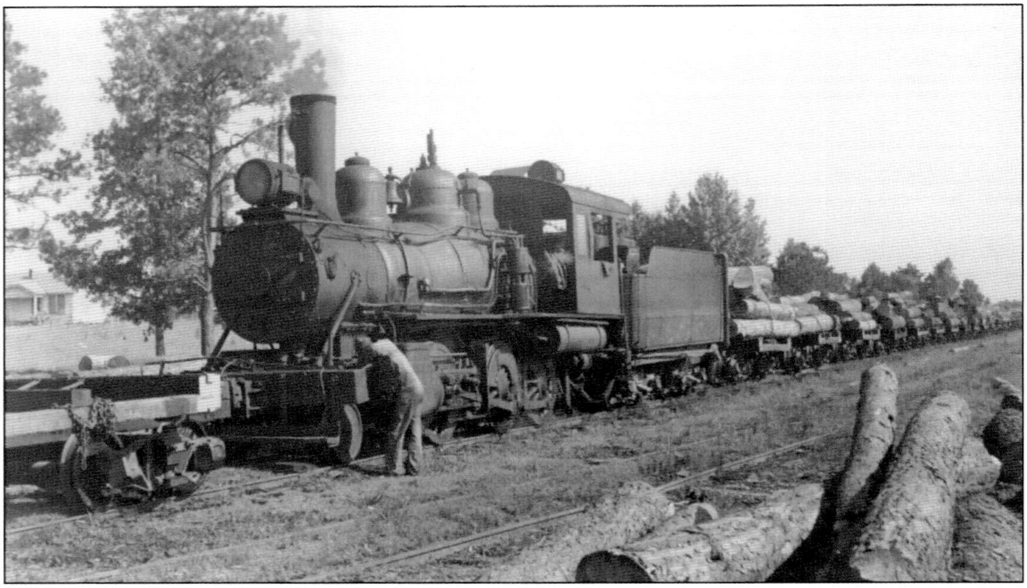

In this late 1940s view, Frost Lumber Industry's Engine No. 8 pulls its loaded train into Waskom on the far eastern edge of Harrison County. Frost purchased the Waskom mill and its 20-mile tram in 1928 from the Waterman Lumber Company, which built the mill in 1919. (Courtesy Richard W. Keeling Collection; photograph by C.W. Witbeck.)

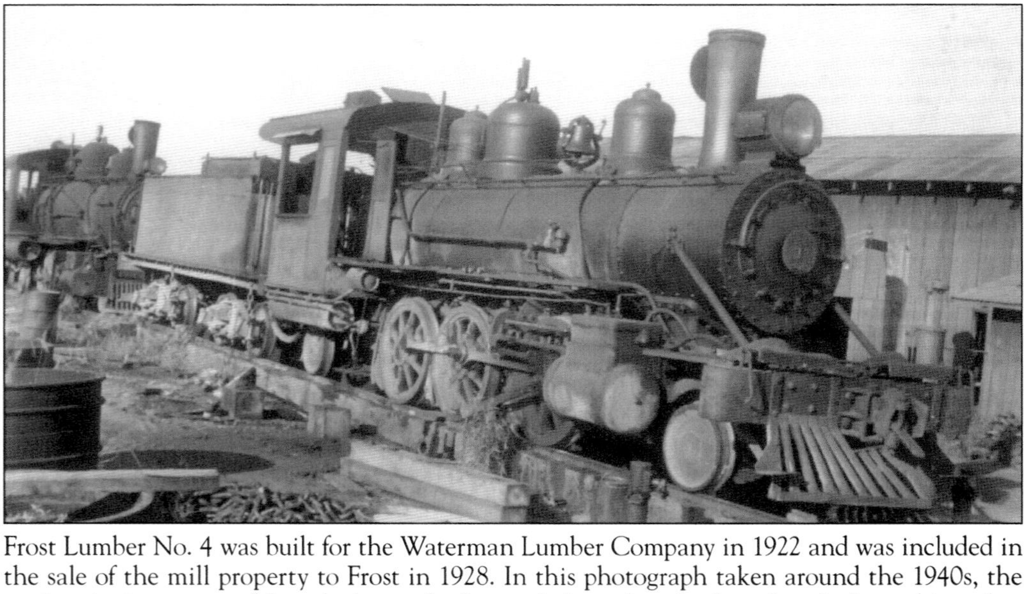

Frost Lumber No. 4 was built for the Waterman Lumber Company in 1922 and was included in the sale of the mill property to Frost in 1928. In this photograph taken around the 1940s, the engine sits in storage, although the mud splattered along the wheels and underframe hints that the engine has recently been steamed up. (Courtesy Texas Transportation Archive.)

Three

Logging in the Central East Counties

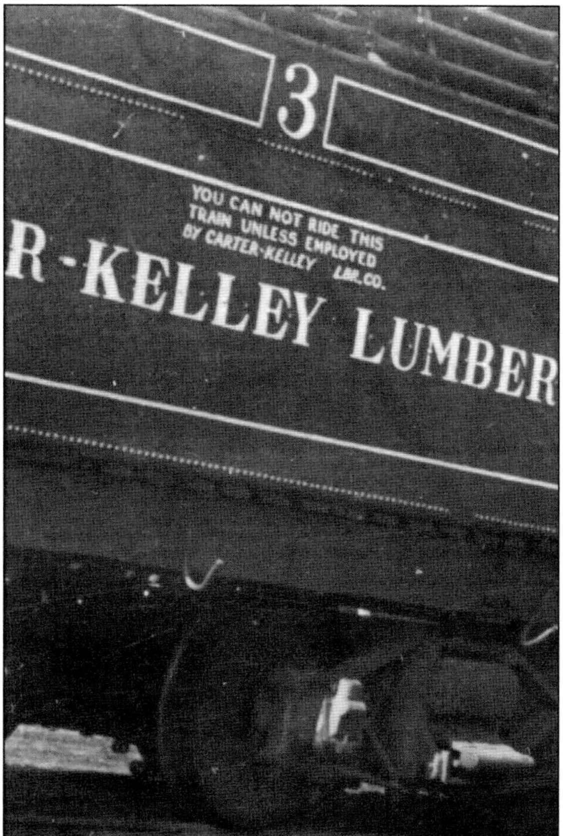

Carter-Kelley's busy mill town of Manning in Angelina County was one of many such communities that dotted the densely-forested middle-heart of East Texas. Many of Texas's most storied lumber centers were located here, with names like Lufkin, Diboll, Nacogdoches, Trinity, and many others. As seen here, Carter-Kelley's management sought to discourage joy riders on its logging engines by posting this notice on all its locomotive tenders. (Courtesy Richard W. Keeling Collection.)

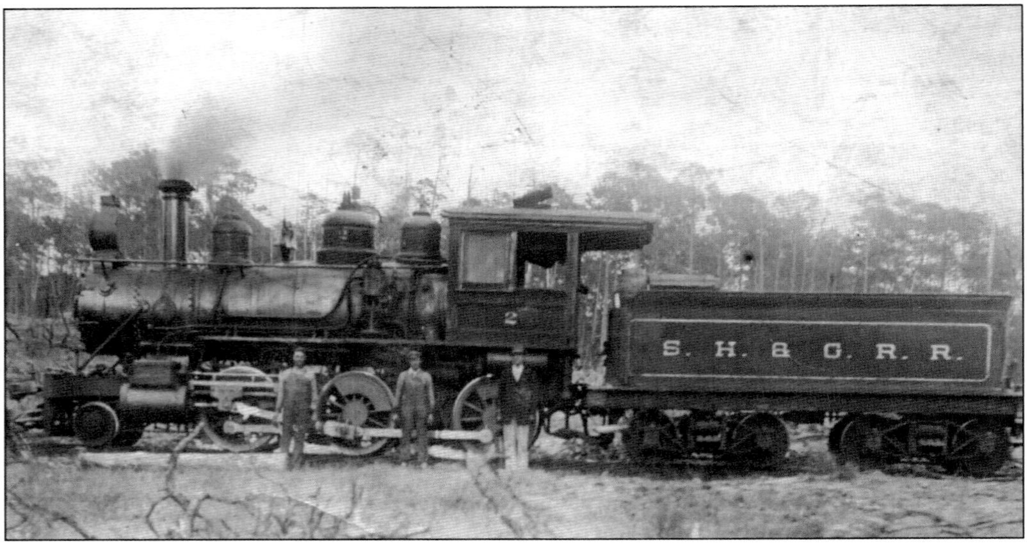

In 1906, the Carter-Kelley Lumber Company established its mill at Manning in the southeastern part of Angelina County. The company tram extended nine miles from the mill to the joint Cotton Belt and Texas & New Orleans Railways station at Prestridge. The tram was incorporated as the Shreveport, Houston & Gulf Railway, playfully referred to as the "Shove Hard & Grunt." Locomotive No. 2 is seen above at Manning around 1910. After the Manning mill closed, all Carter-Kelley engines were transferred to Carter's Polk County operation, the W.T. Carter & Brother Lumber Company at Camden. The engines were used primarily on the company's Camp Ruby tram, which extended into southern Polk County. The below photograph shows the No. 4 shortly after it arrived at Camden. The engines retained their Carter-Kelley paint scheme into the 1950s. (Both, courtesy Richard W. Keeling Collection.)

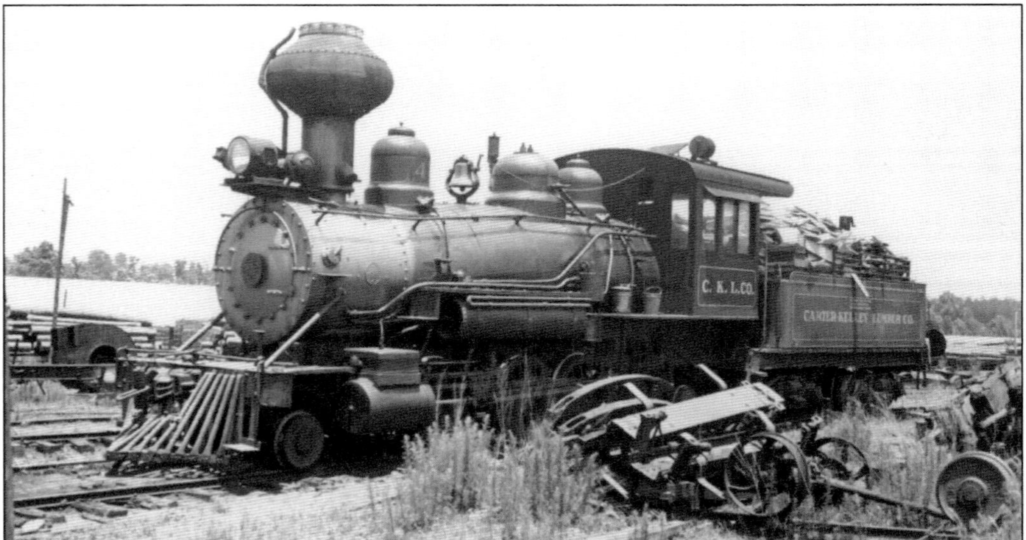

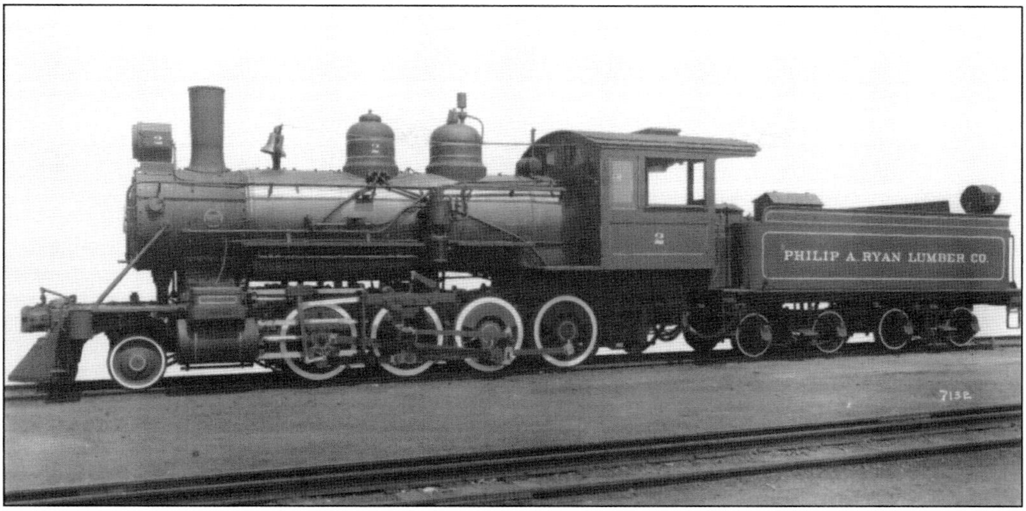

At Lufkin, Philip A. Ryan established a mill and a 10-mile tram in 1919 that used at least two locomotives. The No. 2, pictured, was built new for the company in July 1919. Ryan made a deal with Carter-Kelley to use Manning loggers to harvest hardwoods for shipment to the Lufkin mill. (Courtesy Texas Transportation Archive.)

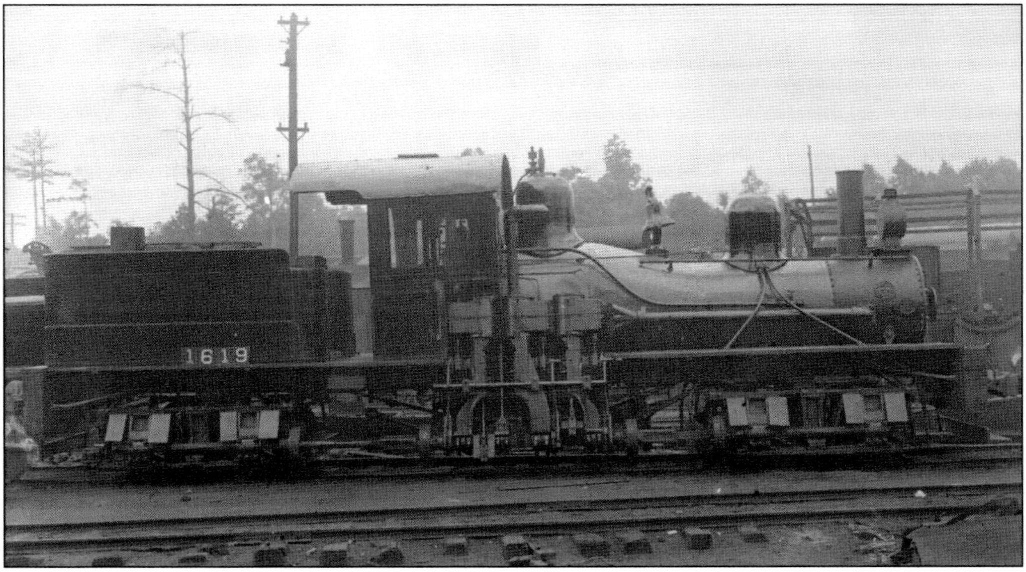

In 1894, the Emporia Lumber Company was built at Emporia, 12 miles south of Lufkin on the Houston East & West Texas Railway. The tram was incorporated as the Emporia & Gulf Railroad and extended 15 miles to a log camp called Crooker. Operations ceased when the mill burned in 1906. This is Shay No. 5 awaiting a buyer in 1919 at reseller Southern Iron & Equipment in Atlanta, Georgia. (Courtesy Texas Transportation Archive.)

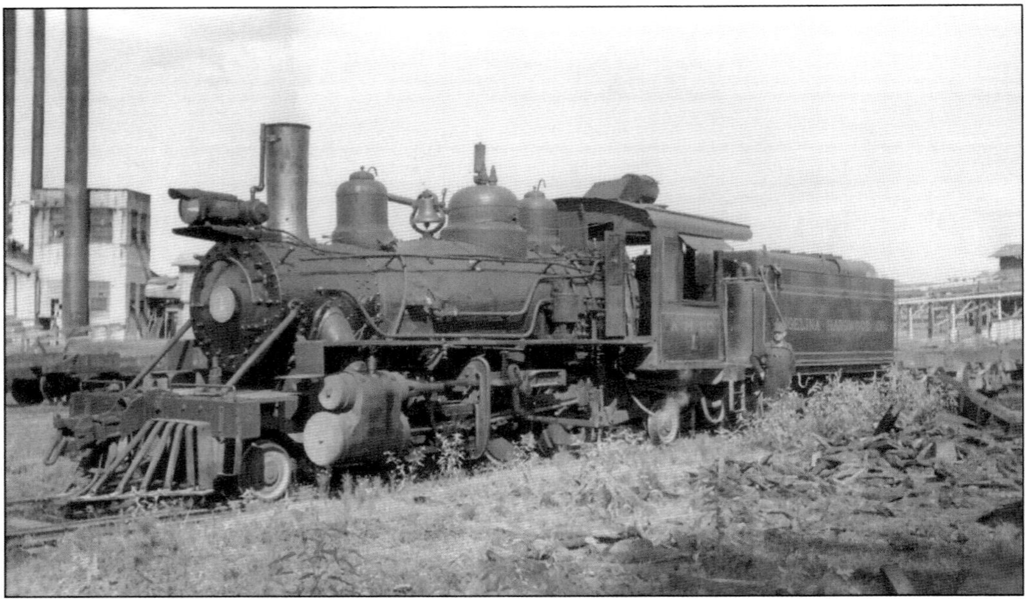

Angelina Hardwood Company's No. 1 was the main workhorse at the company's mill at Ewing in northeastern Angelina County. Before coming to Ewing, No. 1 had worked along the Panama Canal. After operations ended in 1944, the engine went to the Waco, Beaumont, Trinity & Sabine Railway, where it operated until 1959. Today, the No. 1 is preserved at the Galveston Railroad Museum at Galveston, Texas. (Courtesy Texas Transportation Archive.)

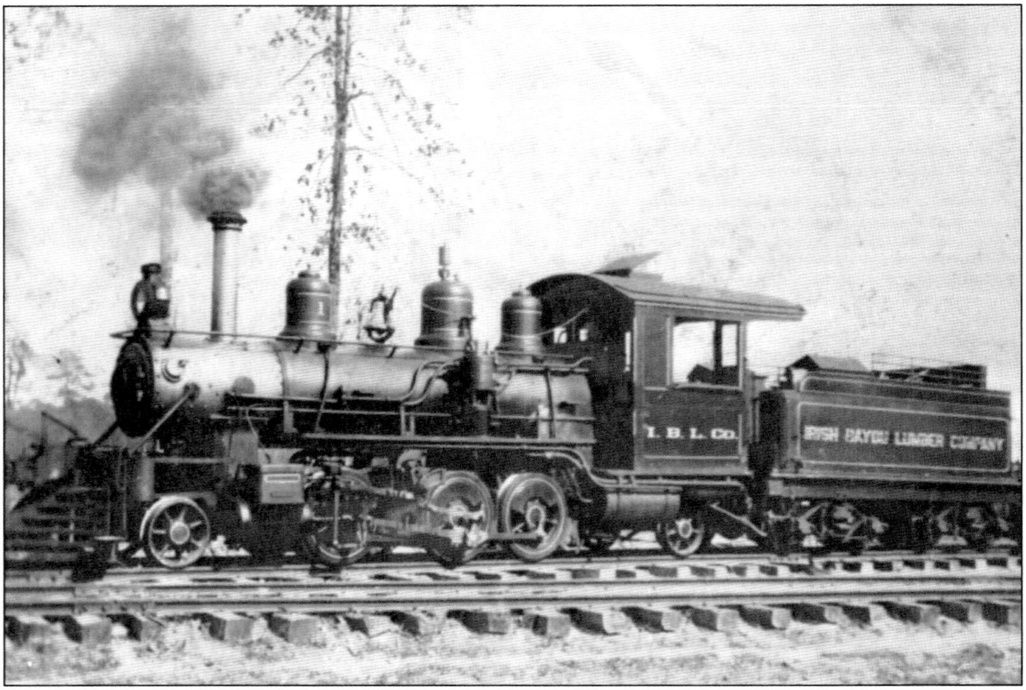

Irish Bayou Lumber Company, a variation of the local misnomer "Ayish Bayou," began logging at Sturgis, near White City in San Augustine County, in the early 1910s. Irish Bayou purchased its No. 1 new from Baldwin Locomotive Works in August 1913. (Courtesy Texas Transportation Archive.)

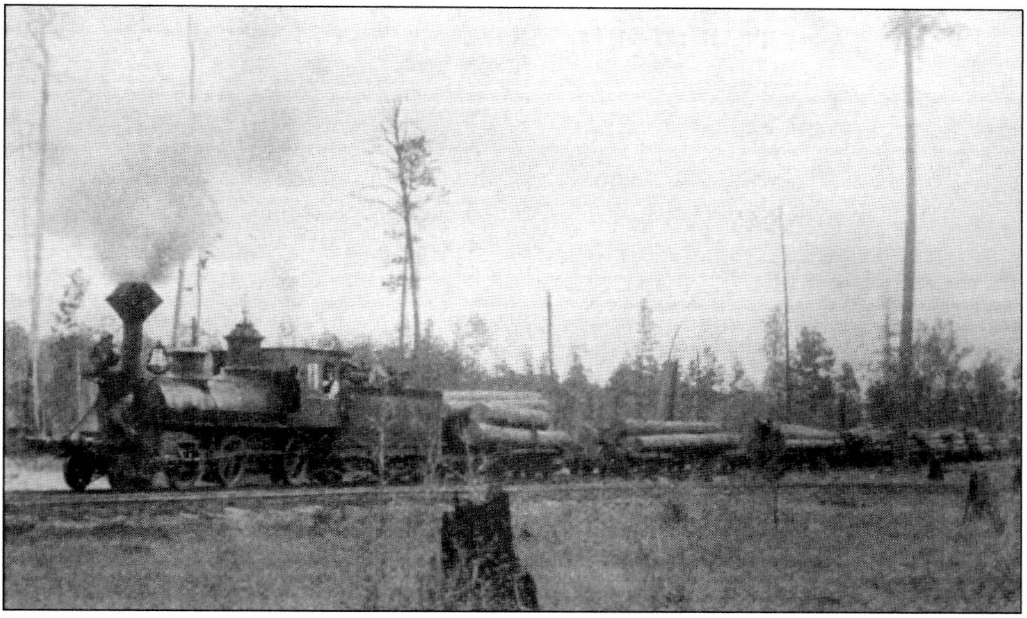

Above, the William Cameron Company log train is pictured under steam near Rockland in Tyler County. Few particulars are known about tram operations, and images are equally scarce. Records indicate that the Cameron trams were gone by 1920. In 1893, the William Cameron Company purchased the sawmill of the Tyler Car and Lumber Company at Michelli, Texas, in Angelina County, due north of Lufkin along the Angelina-Nacogdoches county line. The photograph below shows the woods camp that put logs on the company's 13-mile tram. (Both, courtesy Texas Transportation Archive.)

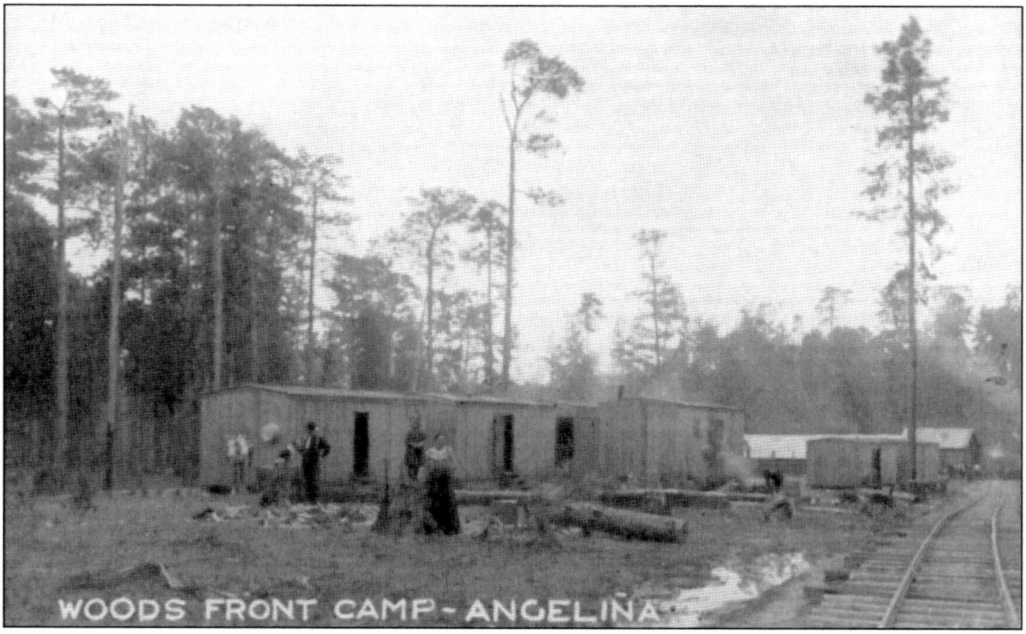

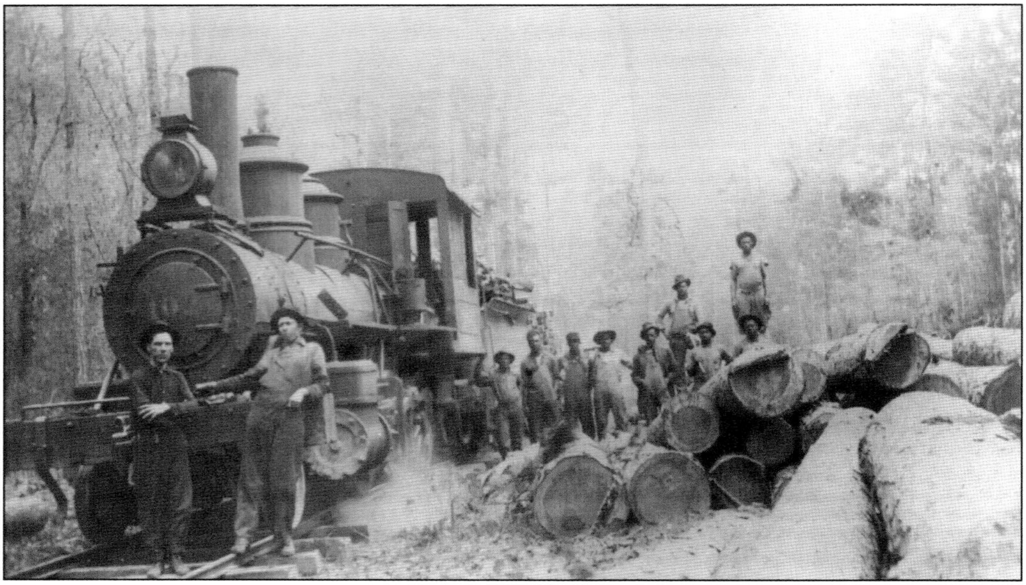

At Chireno in San Augustine County, there was much activity in 1910, as evidenced by this view. Engine No. 102, lettered and working for the Angelina Lumber Company, is pictured at the log front east of town. (Courtesy Richard W. Keeling Collection.)

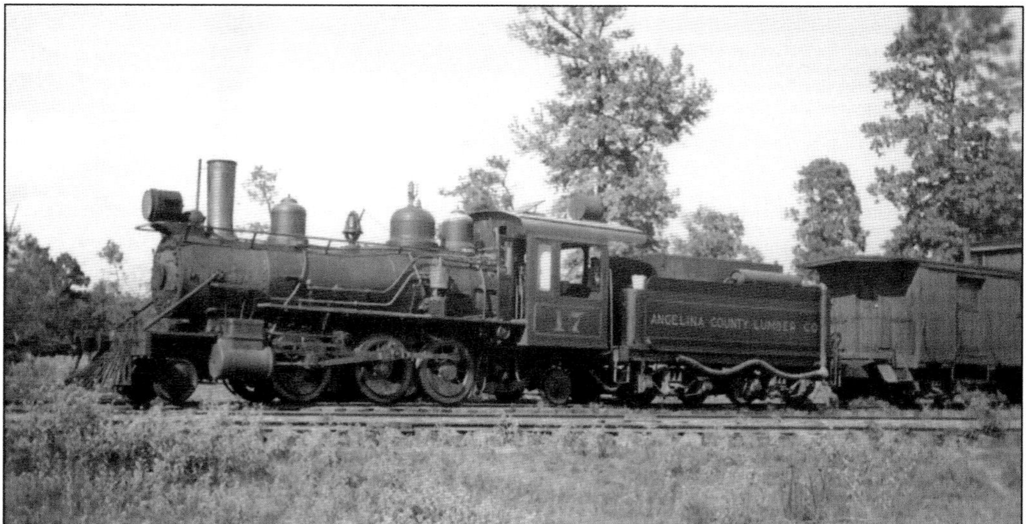

No. 17 was a regular sight at the Angelina County Lumber Company in the 1940s and 1950s. In this 1950s view, No. 17 and its caboose wait as the day's log train is made up. (Courtesy Texas Transportation Archive.)

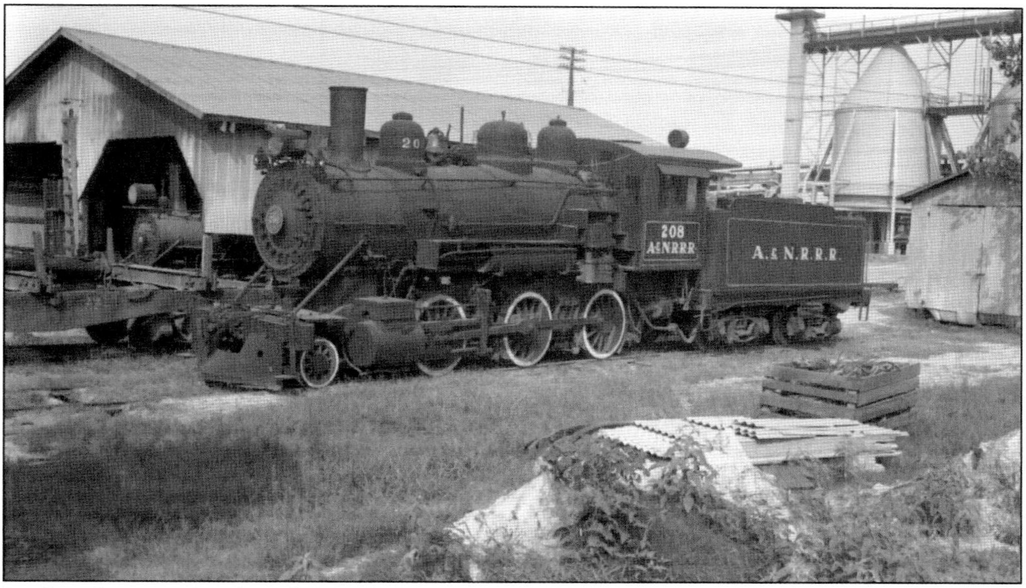

In this photograph taken during the summer of 1955, Angelina & Neches River Railroad No. 208 rests outside the engine shed, while Angelina County Lumber Company No. 17 can be seen stored inside. The No. 208 remained in service until 1962 and was then stored at Keltys. A railfan group purchased the engine to preserve it, and as of 2015, the No. 208 is on lease at the Indiana Railway Museum. (Courtesy Richard W. Keeling Collection.)

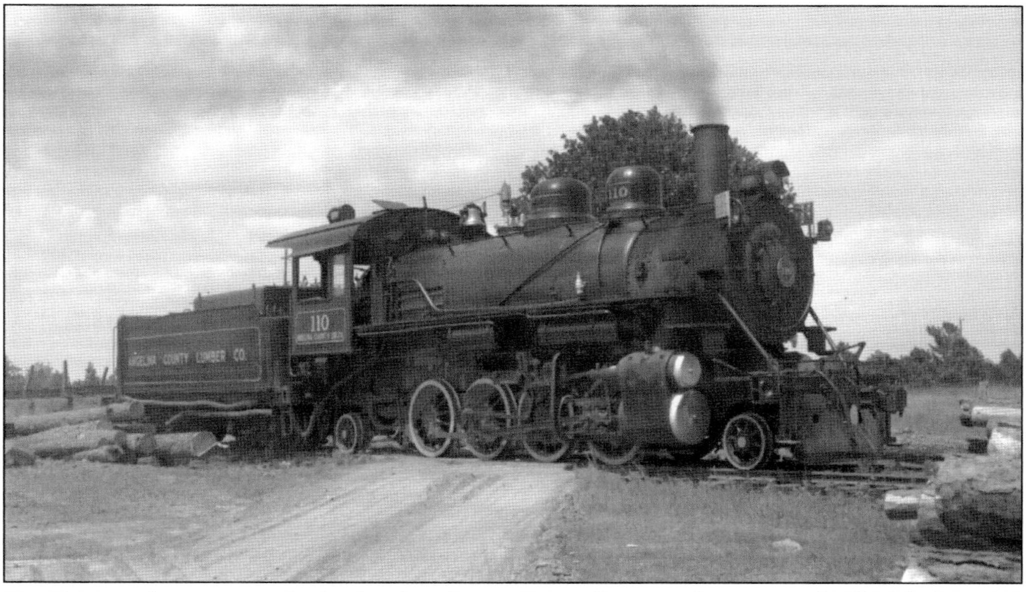

No. 110 is under steam at the log-loading front of New Camp in the spring of 1957. The No. 110 was built new for Angelina County Lumber in 1924 and became the most common sight on tram operations in the late 1950s. (Courtesy Richard W. Keeling Collection.)

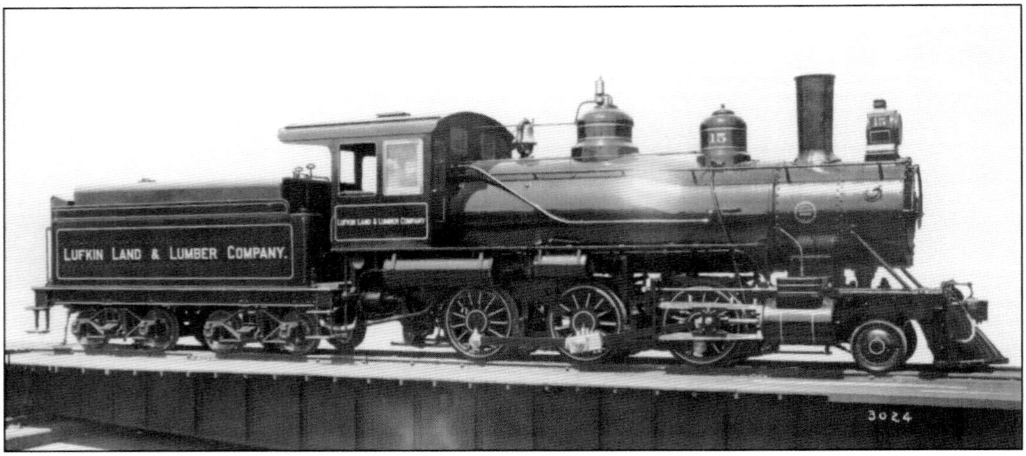

The Lufkin Land & Lumber (LL&L) Company was organized in 1899 as a joint venture of prominent lumbermen E.A. Frost, G.A. Kelley, and T.L.L. Temple. Between 1900 and 1904, the LL&L built the Texas & Louisiana Railroad 38 miles from Lufkin to Broaddus and constructed unincorporated trams beyond that into the White City area. After 1905, Long-Bell Lumber Company of Kansas City, Missouri, operated all properties under both the LL&L and Long-Bell names. The above photograph shows Engine No. 15, built new for the LL&L in 1909. Below, an LL&L engine is pictured in derelict condition at Huntington, Texas, after logging operations ceased in 1930. (Both, courtesy Texas Transportation Archive.)

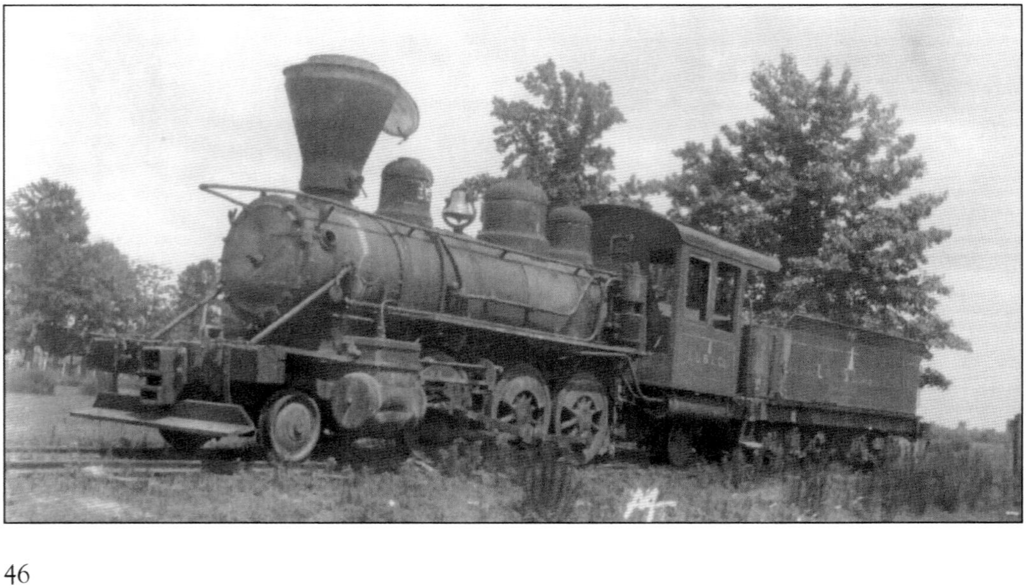

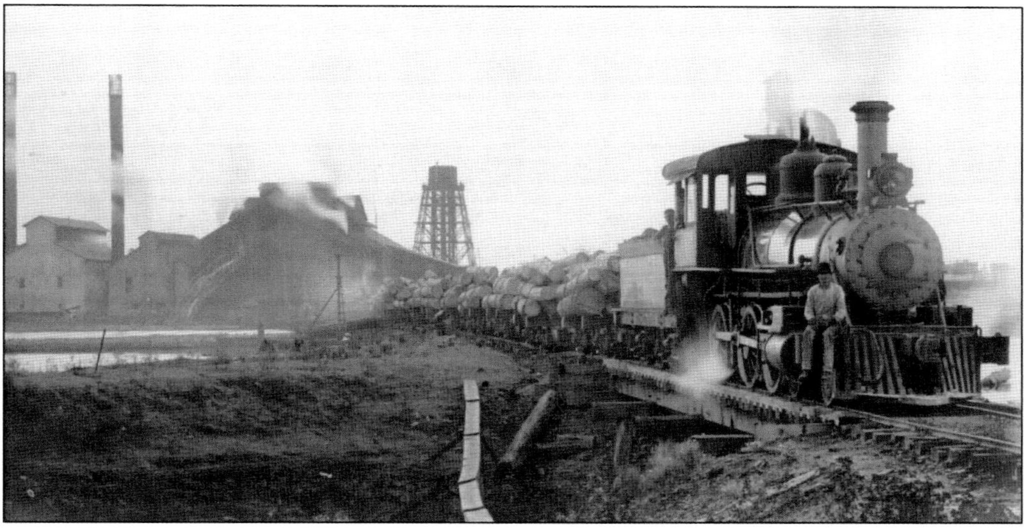

The big mill of the Southern Pine Lumber Company at Diboll in Angelina County had its beginnings in 1894, when Thomas Louis Latane Temple established a mill south of Burke to harvest 7,000 acres of timber he purchased along the Houston East & West Texas Railway. In the above 1907 view, Engine No. 7 pulls alongside the millpond with a full load of logs. Below, from left to right, Texas South-Eastern Railroad's Engines Nos. 1, 2, and 3 are wooded up and have gathered at the junction of a tram spur for an *American Lumberman* magazine photographer in the spring of 1904. (Both, courtesy History Center at Diboll.)

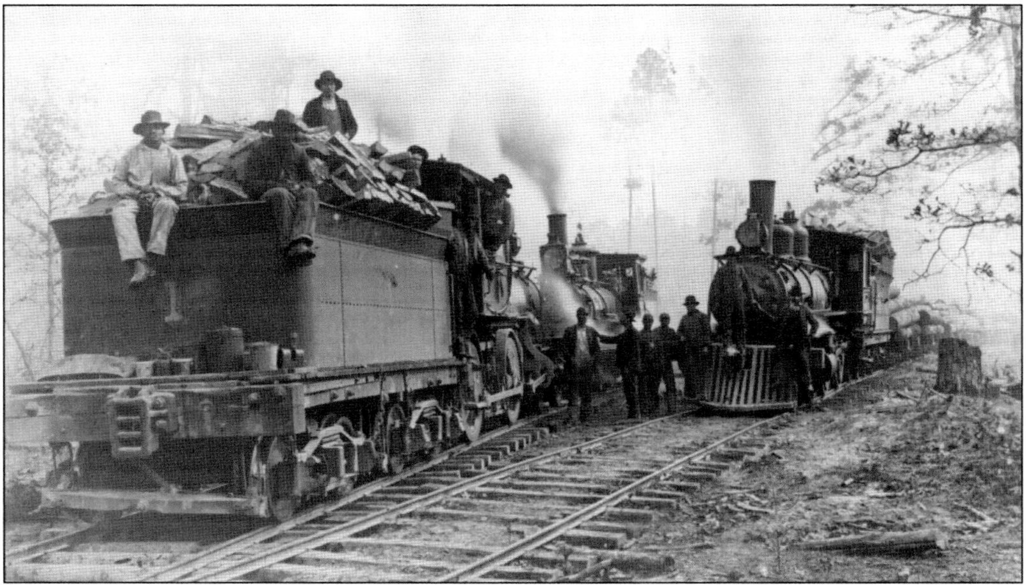

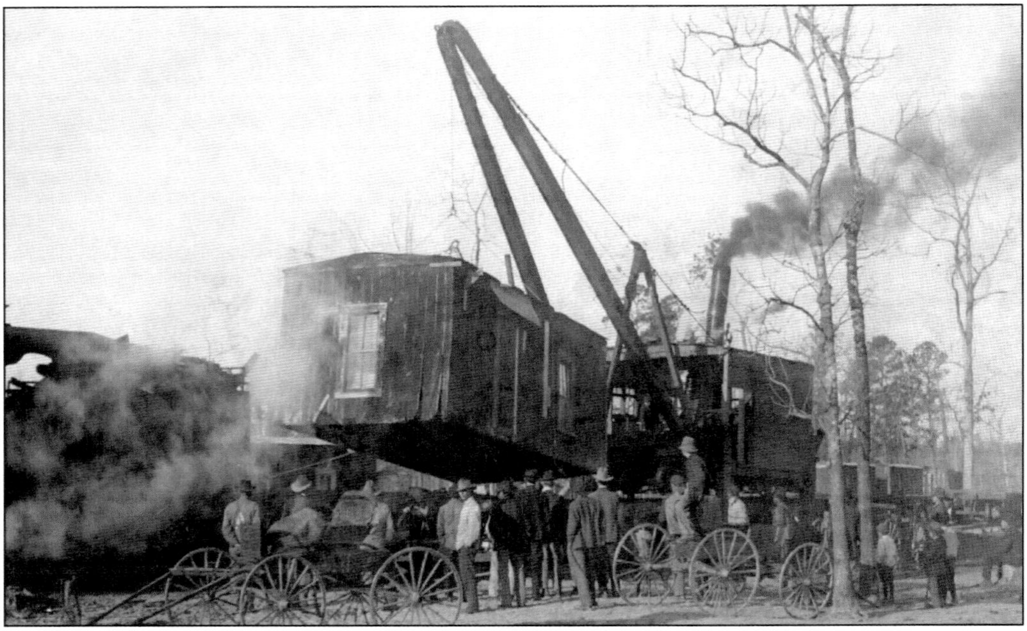

In the above photograph, it is clearly moving day at the Southern Pine Lumber's woods operation known as Camp 1. This camp was established in 1906 at a point on the company tram northwest of Diboll and across the Neches River in Trinity County. These boxcar residences provided the basic shelter necessities for Southern Pine woods employees and their families. Camp 1 operated until 1912, when its residents were moved to a new camp in Houston County. Terms such as serenity and community come to mind when pondering the below photograph of life at Camp 1 taken in 1907. Free-range pigs and a young boy with his wagon hitched to a goat can be seen. (Both, courtesy History Center at Diboll.)

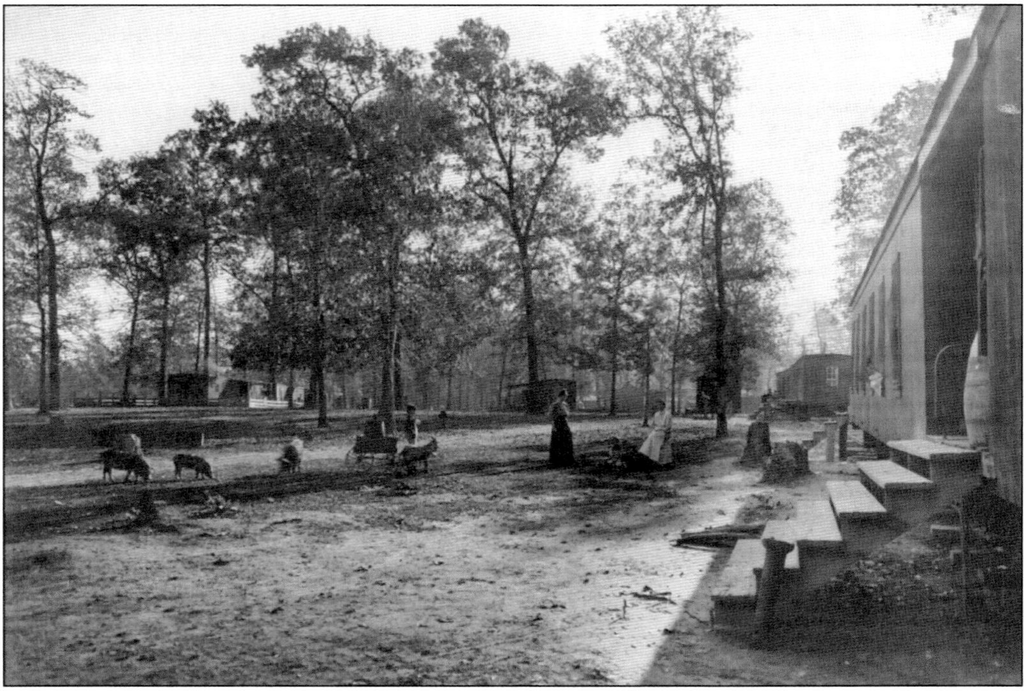

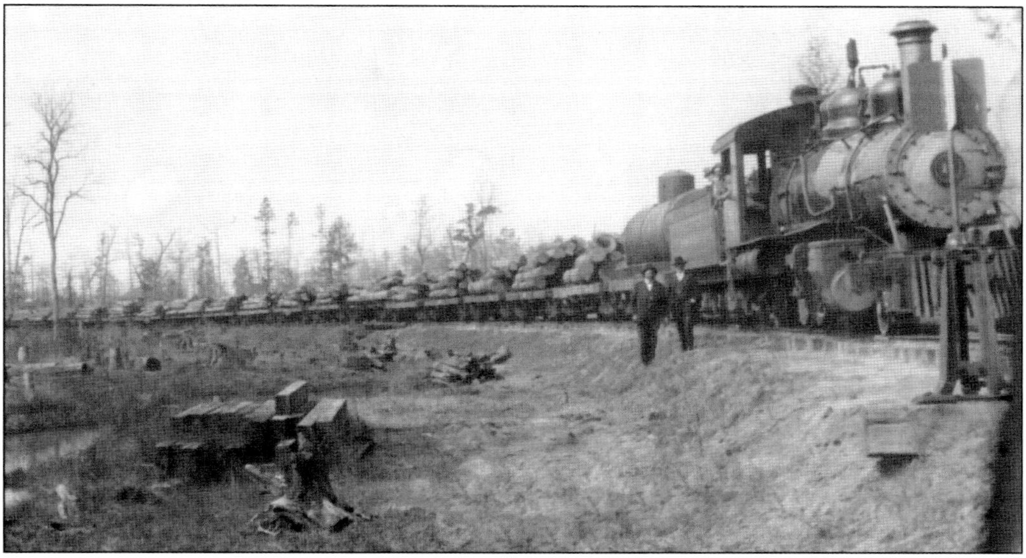

Southern Pine Lumber established a large camp at Fastrill in Cherokee County in 1922, after logging was concluded in San Augustine County. In this 1930 view, Engine No. 11 pulls more than 30 cars on the Fastrill tram. (Courtesy History Center at Diboll.)

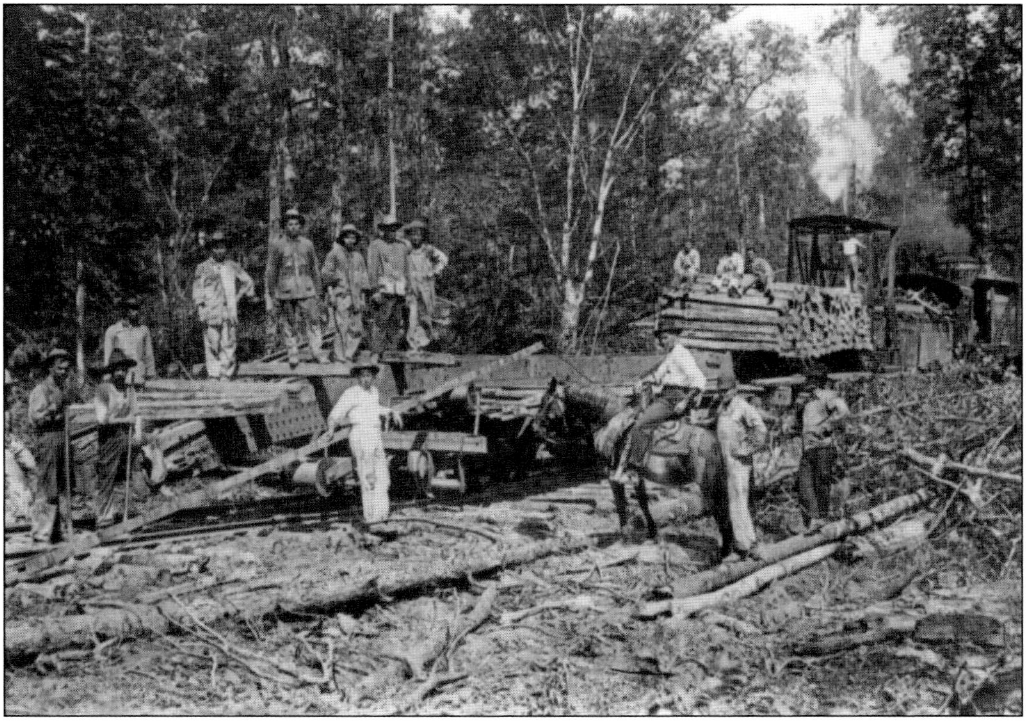

In this undated view, the tram crew is laying in a new spur near Fastrill. By 1941, Fastrill was largely cut out, and most residents were relocated by the company to Diboll, effectively ending community life at the camp. (Courtesy Newton County Museum.)

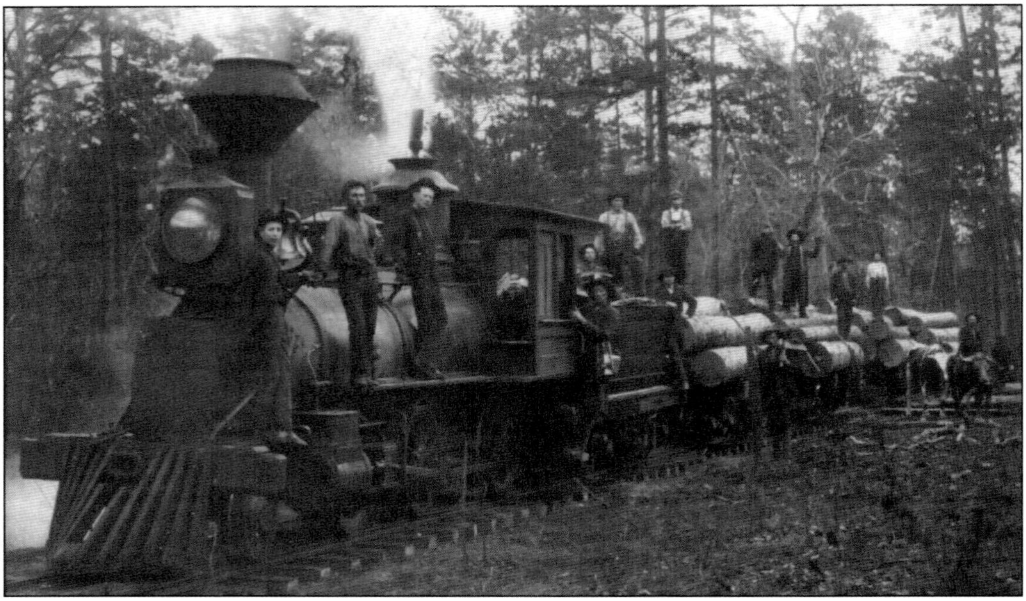

Chronister Lumber Company began sawmilling in 1899 at Wildhurst, one mile north of Forest on the St. Louis–Southwestern Railway in Cherokee County. Chronister's tram was known as the Durham Transportation Company; at its peak, it extended 25 miles across the Angelina River into Nacogdoches County. The above view captures an early Chronister train inbound to Wildhurst on May 6, 1900. At the Chronister logging camp, below, housing was provided by portable camp cars that could be moved around on the tram. Other images of this camp reveal that canvas tents were also used for living quarters. (Both, courtesy Stella Hill Memorial Library.)

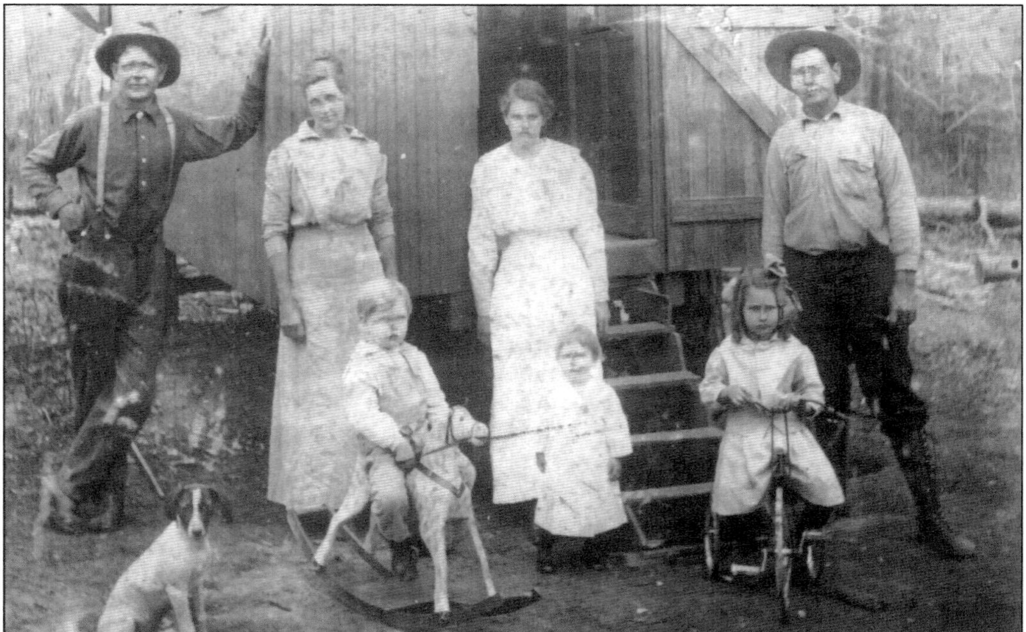

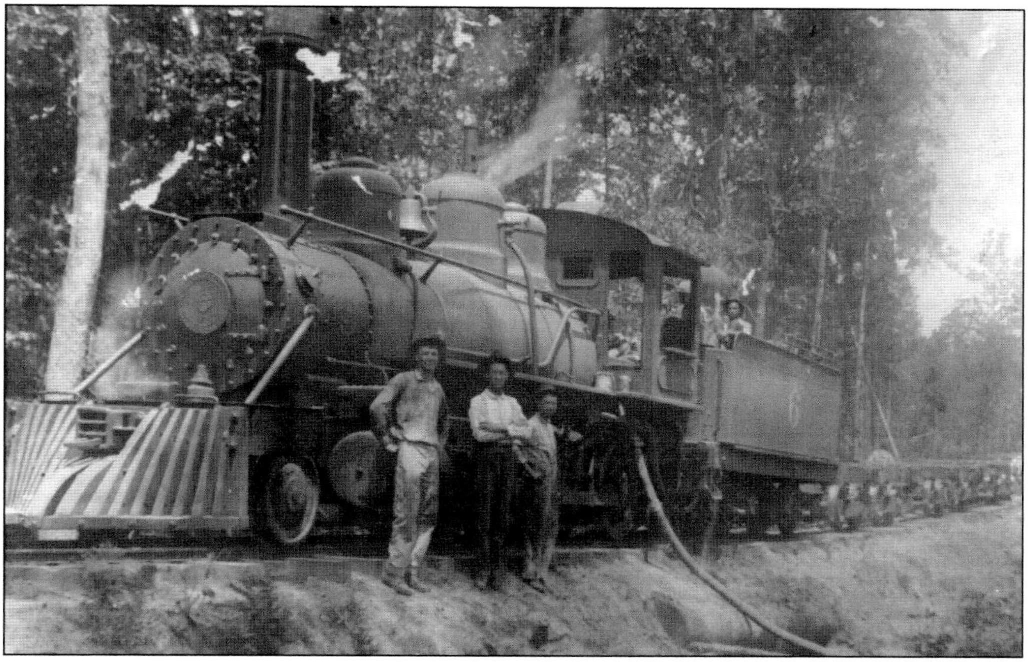

In this photograph taken around 1920, the crewmembers of No. 6 pause to pump water from a nearby creek into the engine's tank using a steam siphon. From left to right are Ramsey Starling, Harris Anderson, and engineer Tom Creekmore. (Courtesy Stella Hill Memorial Library.)

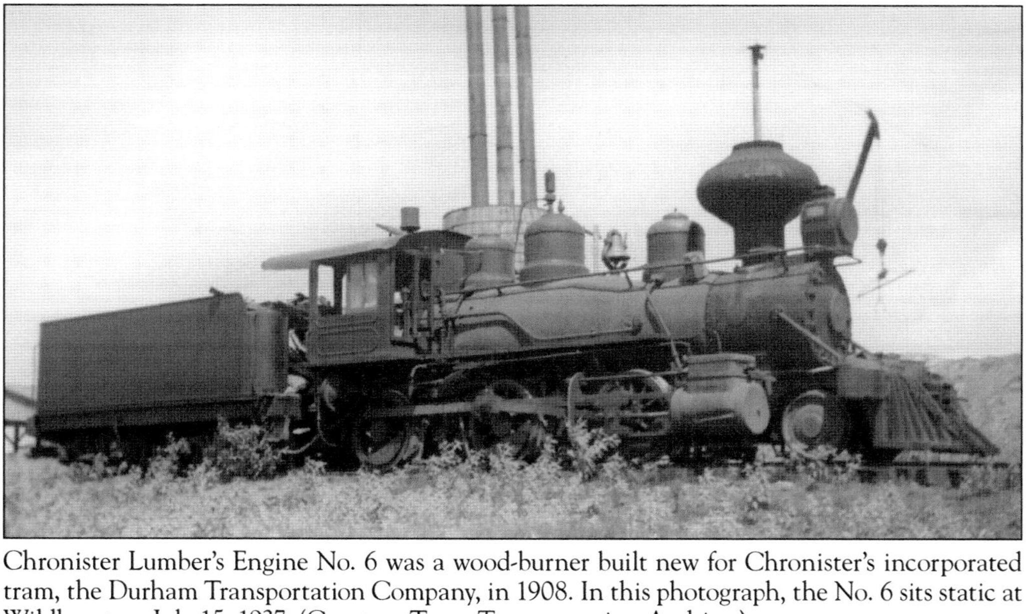

Chronister Lumber's Engine No. 6 was a wood-burner built new for Chronister's incorporated tram, the Durham Transportation Company, in 1908. In this photograph, the No. 6 sits static at Wildhurst on July 15, 1937. (Courtesy Texas Transportation Archive.)

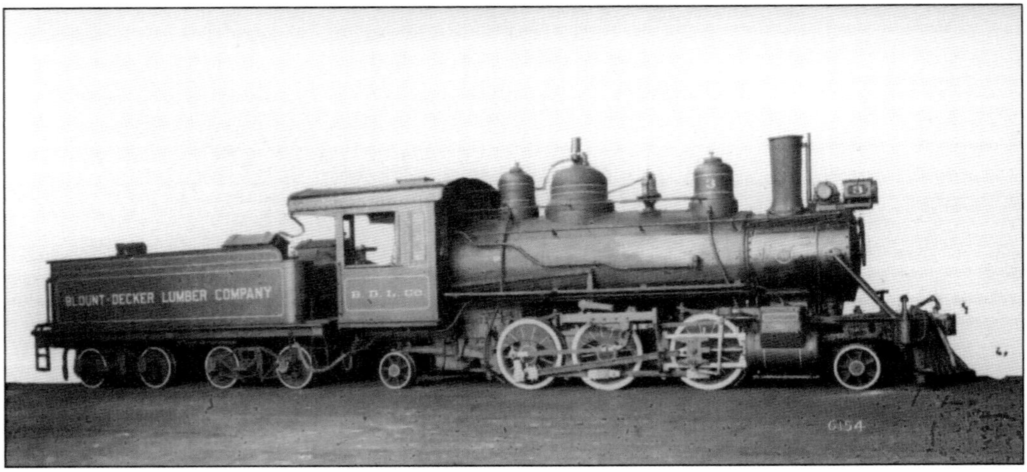

Blount-Decker Lumber Company established a sizeable mill at Alto in Cherokee County in 1909. An eight-mile tram was put in, which at its peak extended to 25 miles of mainline and spurs, operating until at least 1922. Locomotive No. 3, pictured here in its official Baldwin Locomotive Works builder's portrait, was manufactured new for the company in December 1916. (Courtesy Texas Transportation Archive.)

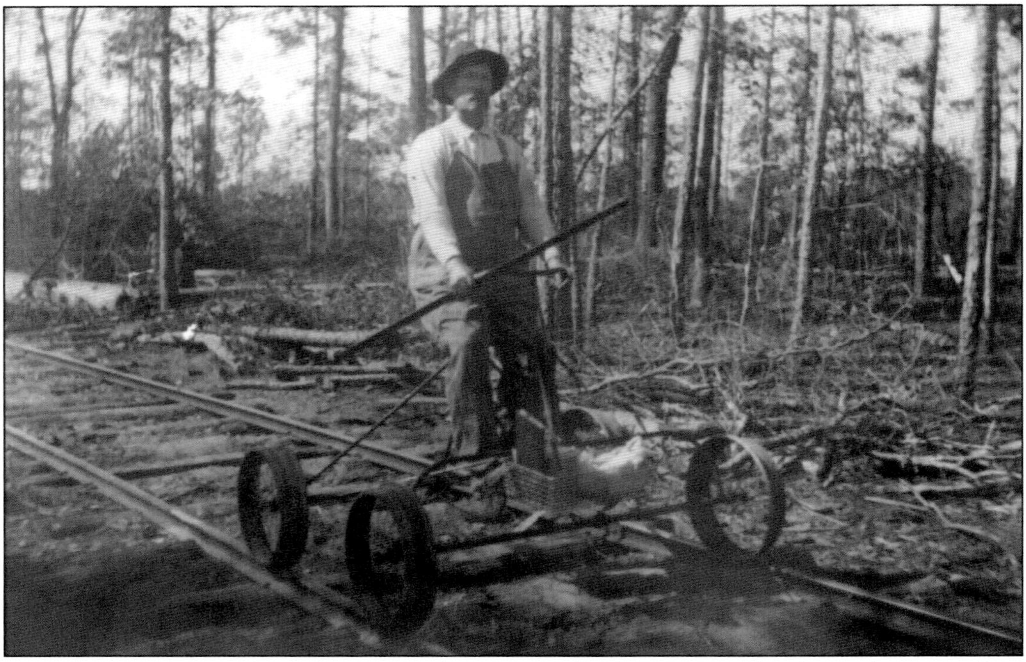

In his duties as log scaler, John H. Singletary used this hand-pumped velocipede to travel up and down the Blount-Decker tram conducting timber estimates. The tram and the mill would operate until 1922, when Blount left the partnership and the firm moved all mill operations to Farmerville, Louisiana, as the Whiteman-Decker Lumber Company. (Courtesy Stella Hill Memorial Library.)

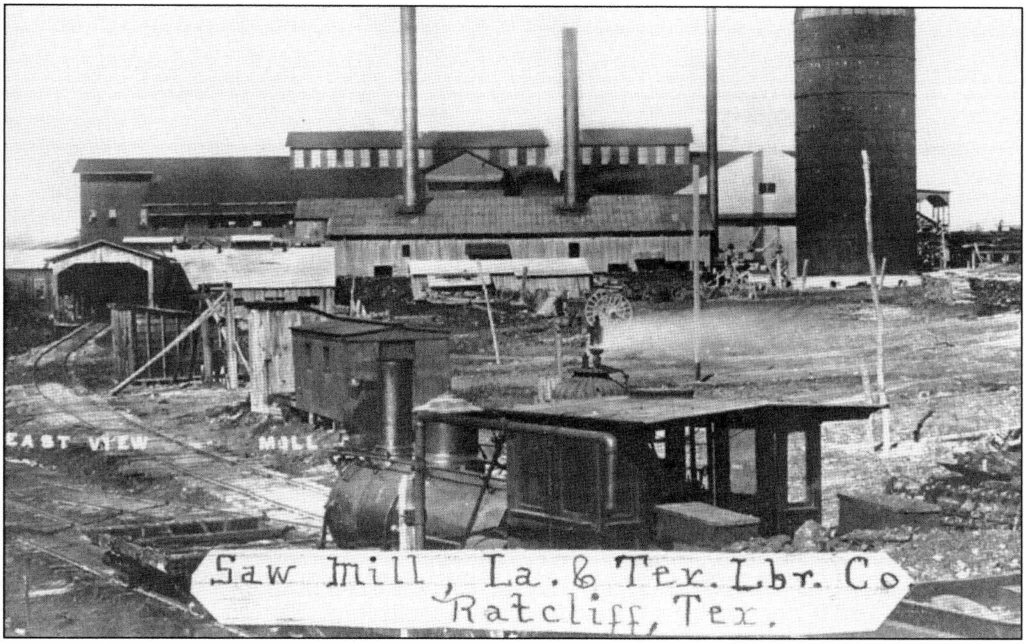

In 1902, the Louisiana & Texas Lumber Company built a very large mill at Ratcliff in Houston County. The Louisiana & Texas was a subsidiary of the Central Coal and Coke Company, and the mill was referred to as the 4-C mill. Capacity was 350,000 board feet per day, fed by a woods operation that spanned Houston and Trinity Counties and sent up to two log trains simultaneously to the 4-C's massive 160-acre log pond. Tram mileage stayed over 30 miles for most of the mill's 16-year existence. The above view gives a glimpse of both the mill and some of the railroad facilities. Below, the Eastern Texas Railroad No. 2 arrives with another load of logs for the millpond in 1902. (Both, courtesy Texas Transportation Archive.)

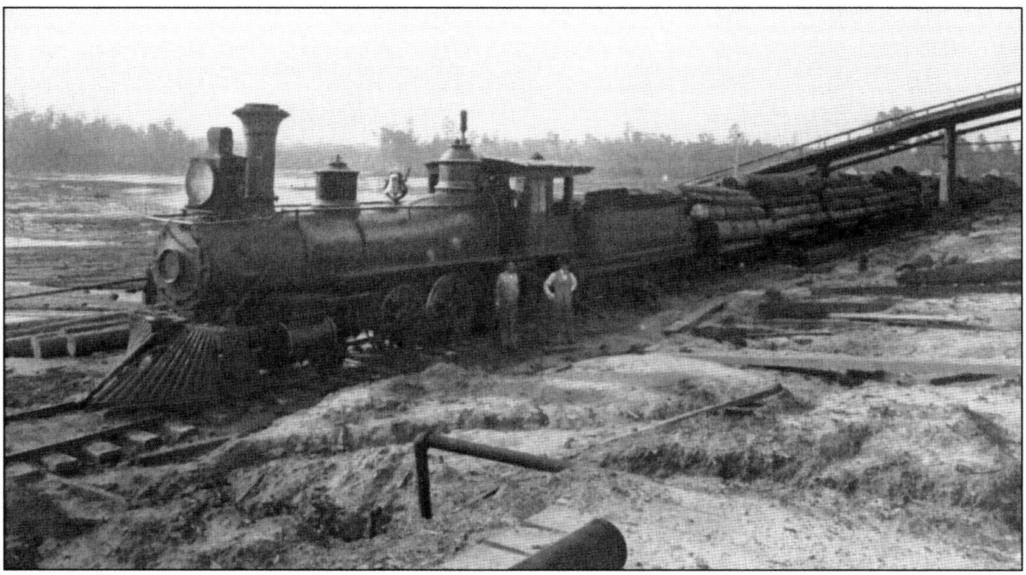

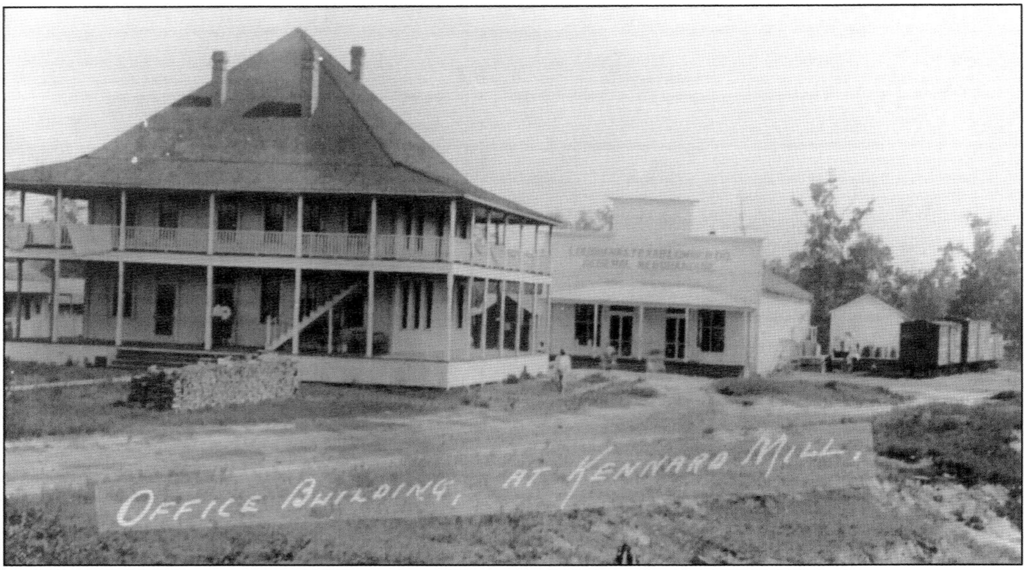

Among Kennard's many buildings, which included 500 company houses for its workers, was a two-story office building (left) and a large commissary store (right). In this photograph taken around 1910, several boxcars of merchandise wait to be unloaded by commissary warehouse workers. (Courtesy Texas Transportation Archive.)

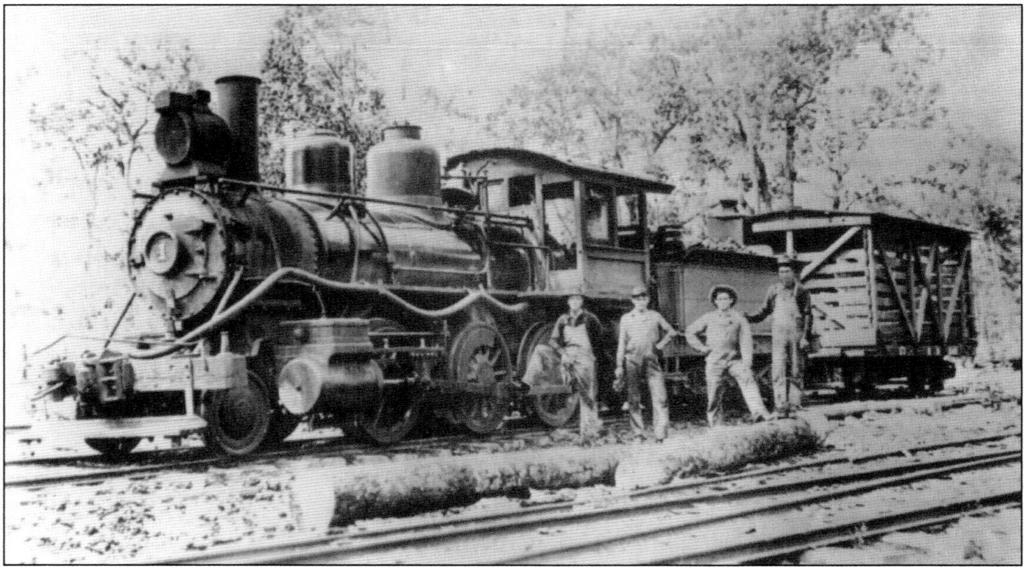

Louisiana & Texas Lumber Company built the Eastern Texas Railroad to connect Kennard with rail outlets at Lufkin, 20 miles away. Prior to 1906, all mileage was recorded as operated by the Eastern Texas Railroad, whether log trains on the forest trams or passenger trains and postal delivery on the Lufkin mainline. In this early view, Eastern Texas Railroad No. 1 pulls one of the lumber company's homemade livestock cars. These cars were used to transport mules and oxen between the company's several loading fronts. (Courtesy Texas Transportation Archive.)

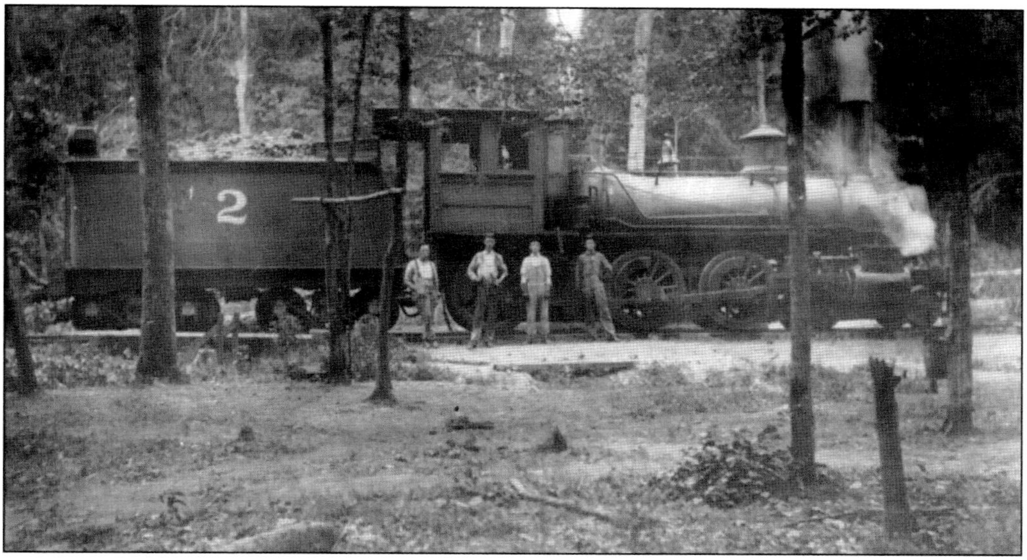

In 1906, the Eastern Texas Railroad came under the control of the St. Louis–Southwestern Railway, also known as the "Cotton Belt." The new parent company organized all woods trains under the new name of Houston County Railroad, while common carrier train service to Lufkin was operated by Cotton Belt crews using Cotton Belt equipment. Above, Houston County No. 2 poses with its crew in the Houston County woods; below, Houston County No. 5 nears the Ratcliff mill with a heavy-loaded log train. As a purely industrial facility, the Houston County Railroad, along with the Ratcliff mill, ceased operations in 1918. With its primary customer gone, the Eastern Texas Railroad ran its last train in 1921 and completed the removal of its rails in 1924. (Both, courtesy Texas Transportation Archive.)

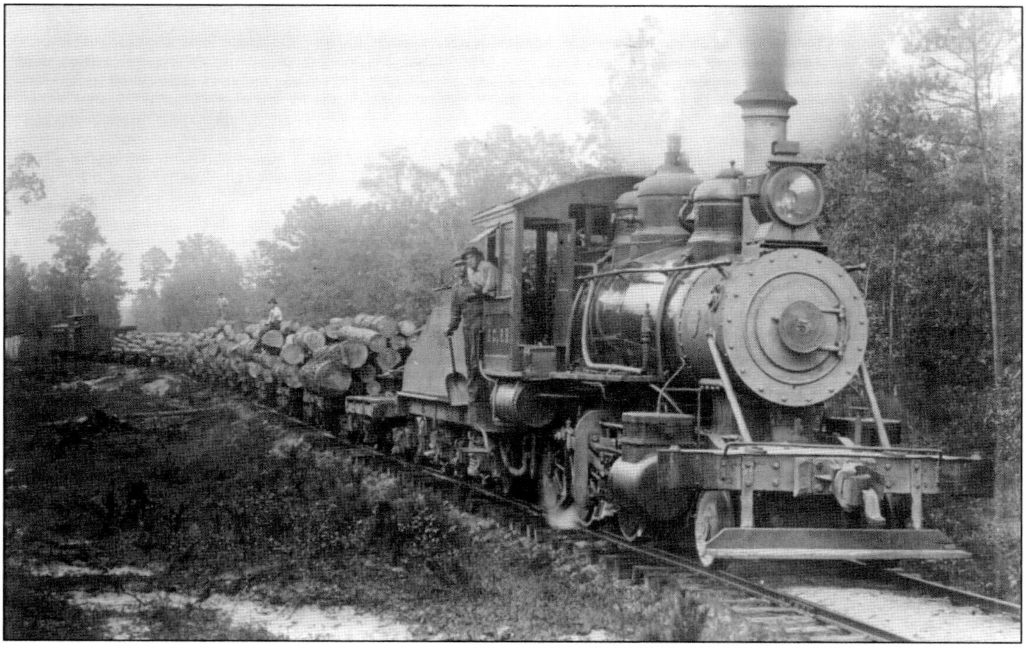

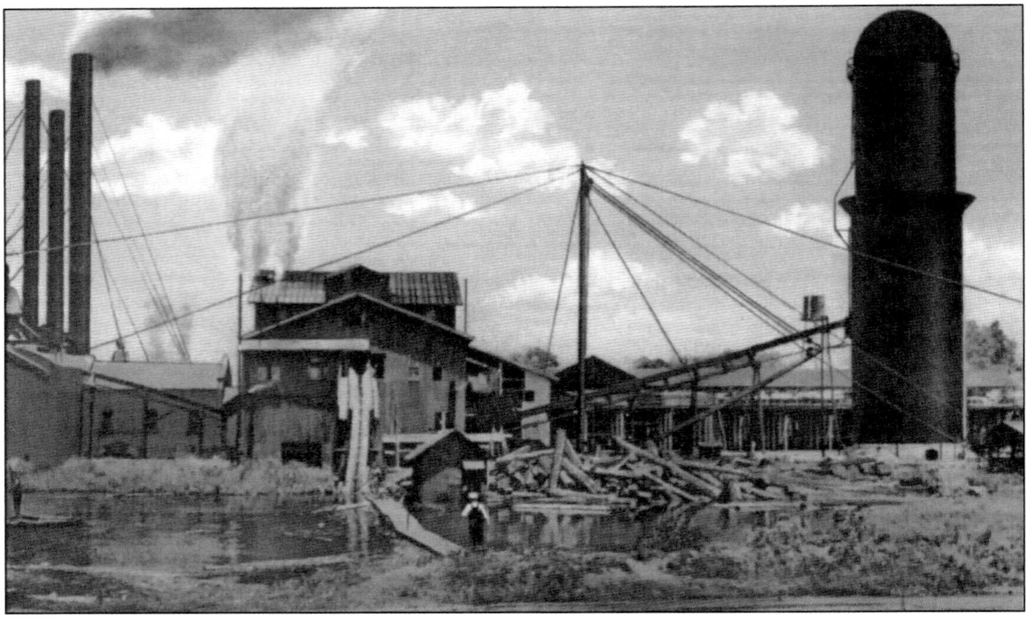

The long-running Frost-Johnson Lumber Company at Nacogdoches was featured on this promotional postcard published in the 1940s. The company was chartered in 1910 to purchase the properties of the Hayward Lumber Company, which had just rebuilt its mill after a fire destroyed it on March 24, 1909. The purchase included the 14-mile Nacogdoches & Southeastern Railway and several more miles of unincorporated tram line. (Courtesy Texas Transportation Archive.)

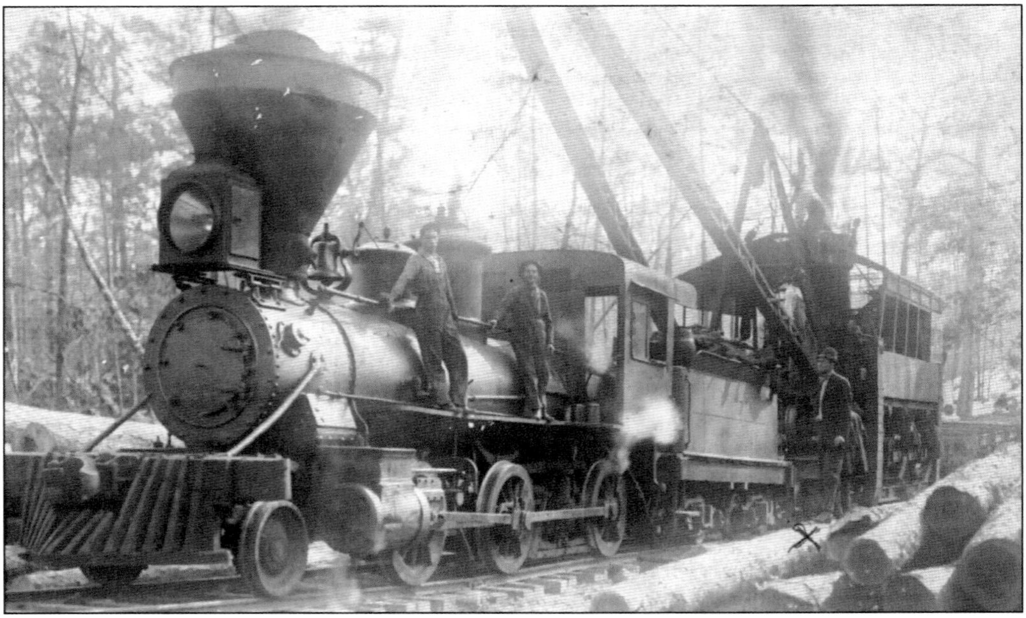

In 1905, Hayward Lumber decided to incorporate the main artery of its Nacogdoches County tram as the Nacogdoches & Southeastern Railway. The line reached from the Hayward Mill to Milepost 14, just beyond Oil Springs. In this view, an early Hayward train is seen at an unknown location around 1910.

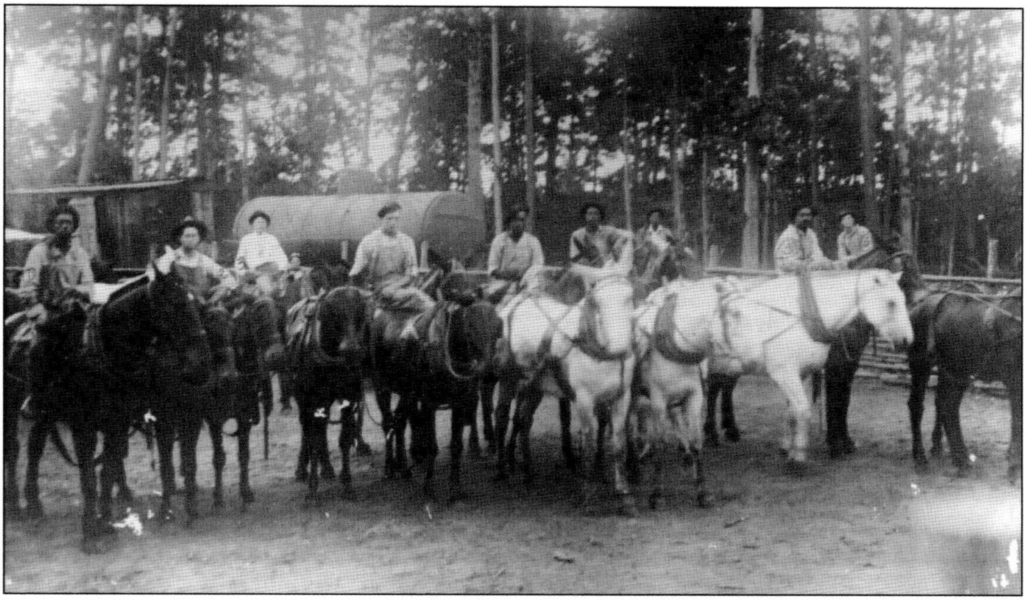

Frost-Johnson's Camp Dunham, 20 miles southeast of Nacogdoches, is pictured in 1916. It was one of five camps that the company operated over its 43-year history. Dunham was a large and busy camp, as evidenced by the Nacogdoches & Southeastern Railway's 1913 employee timetable, which warned its engineers to approach Dunham "under full control" and to "expect to find logging engines on the track." (Courtesy Pyrtle Teutsch.)

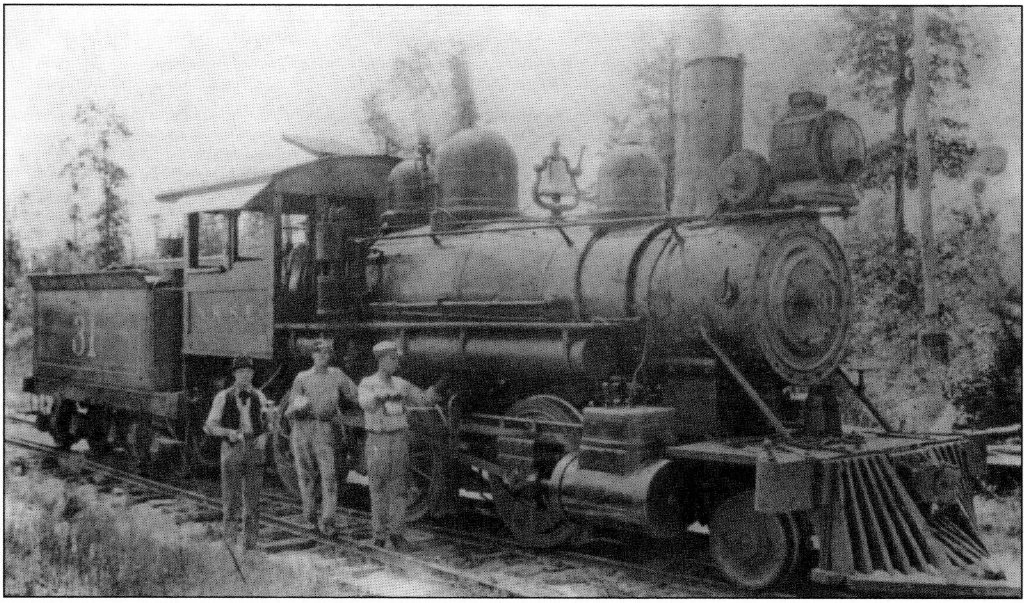

Hayward Lumber Company incorporated its tram in 1904 as the Nacogdoches & Southeastern Railway. The Nacogdoches & Southeastern built only 14 of its own miles but had trackage rights over the entire tram system. In 1912, No. 31 and its crew are pictured at Dockville, a siding located two miles south of Woden at Milepost 12. (Courtesy Pyrtle Teutsch.)

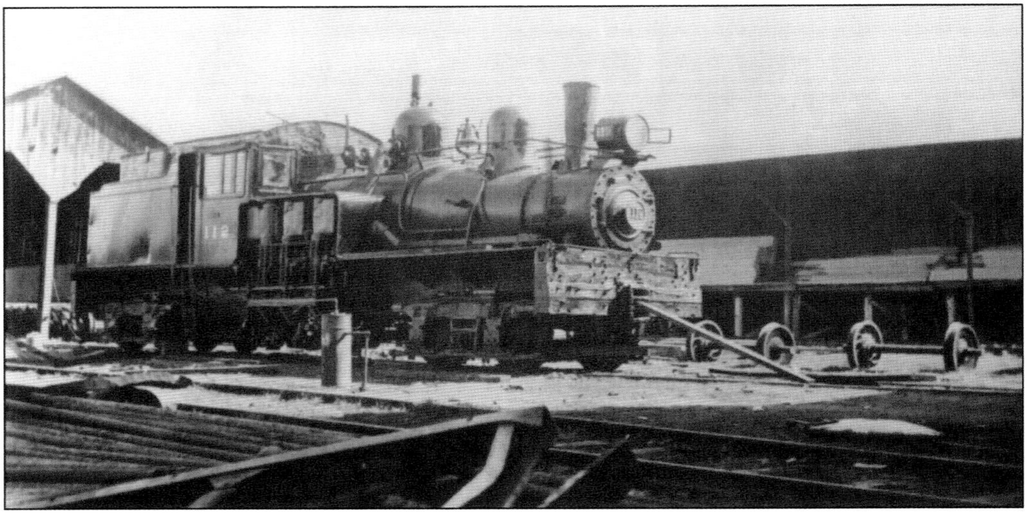

Powerful Shay No. 112 was built new for Frost-Johnson and operated at the company in Montrose, Louisiana, before being transferred to Nacogdoches. In this view, the No. 112 is outside the locomotive shed at Nacogdoches in March 1938. (Courtesy Richard W. Keeling Collection.)

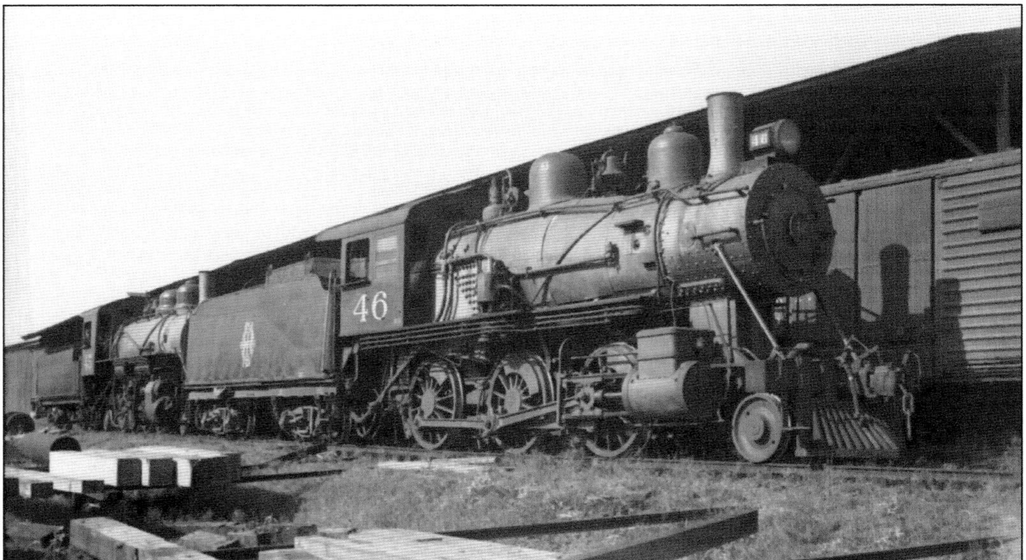

Frost-Johnson's Locomotive No. 46 rests in storage at the mill's machine shop in Nacogdoches on August 23, 1949. The No. 46 was purchased from the Missouri-Kansas-Texas Railway in 1926 and was later sold to the Kirby Lumber Company. (Courtesy Richard W. Keeling Collection.)

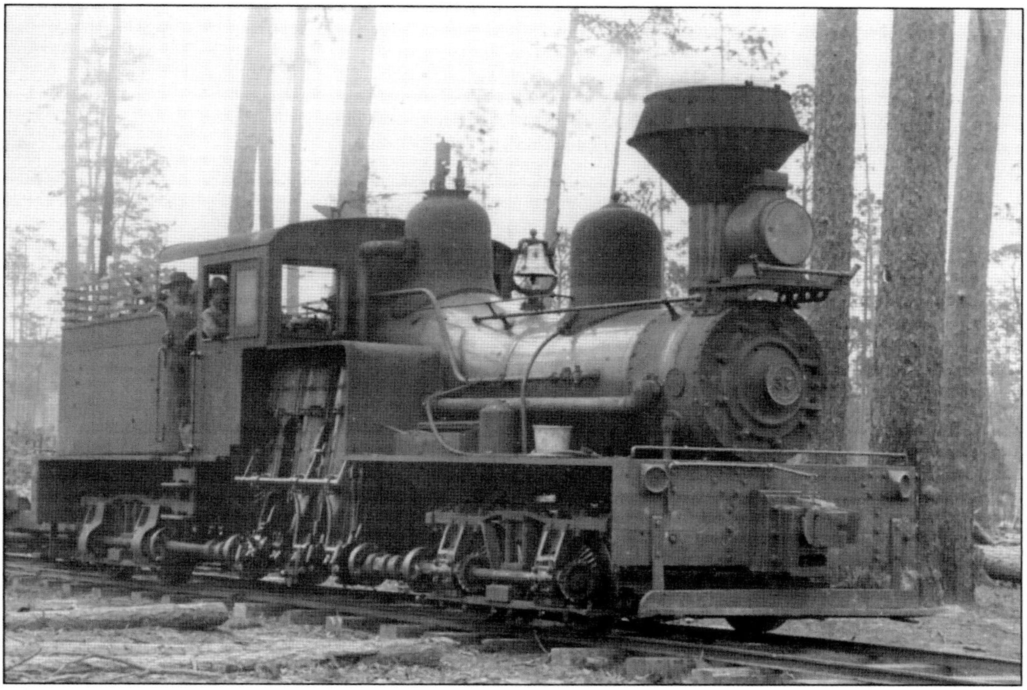

The northernmost of Kirby Lumber Company's two dozen mills was at Bronson on the Gulf, Colorado, & Santa Fe Railway, which is often referred to as simply the Santa Fe. The company harvested timber to the east and west of town using Shay locomotives like the No. 37, which is seen here near Bronson in 1904. (Courtesy Richard W. Keeling Collection.)

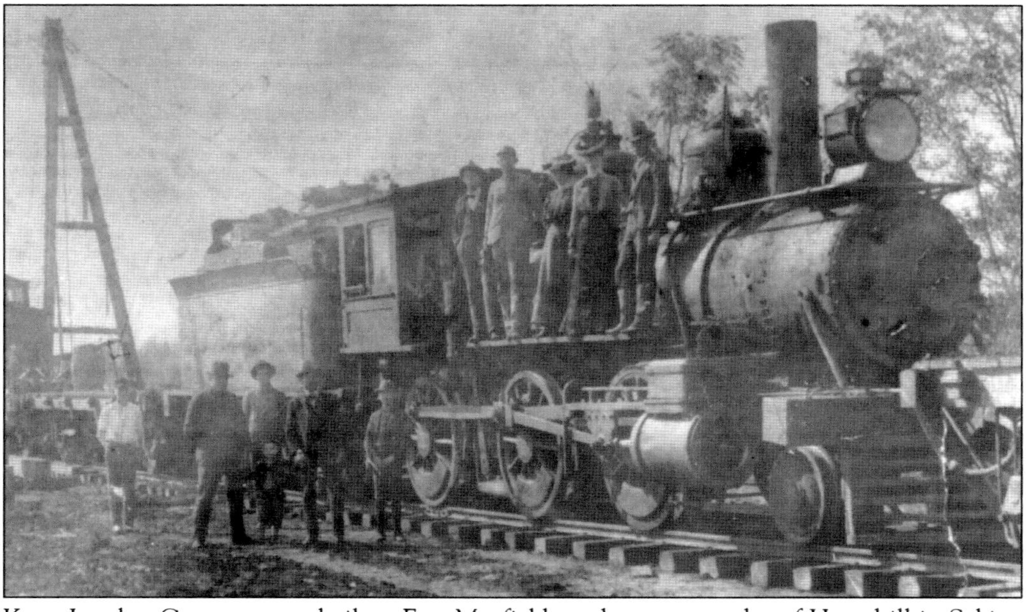

Knox Lumber Company was built at East Mayfield on the western edge of Hemphill in Sabine County. The short-line Lufkin, Hemphill & Gulf Railway was also built to connect with the Santa Fe at Bronson. This is a rare view of a Knox Lumber train around the 1910s. The Knox properties were sold to Temple in 1921. (Courtesy Richard W. Keeling Collection.)

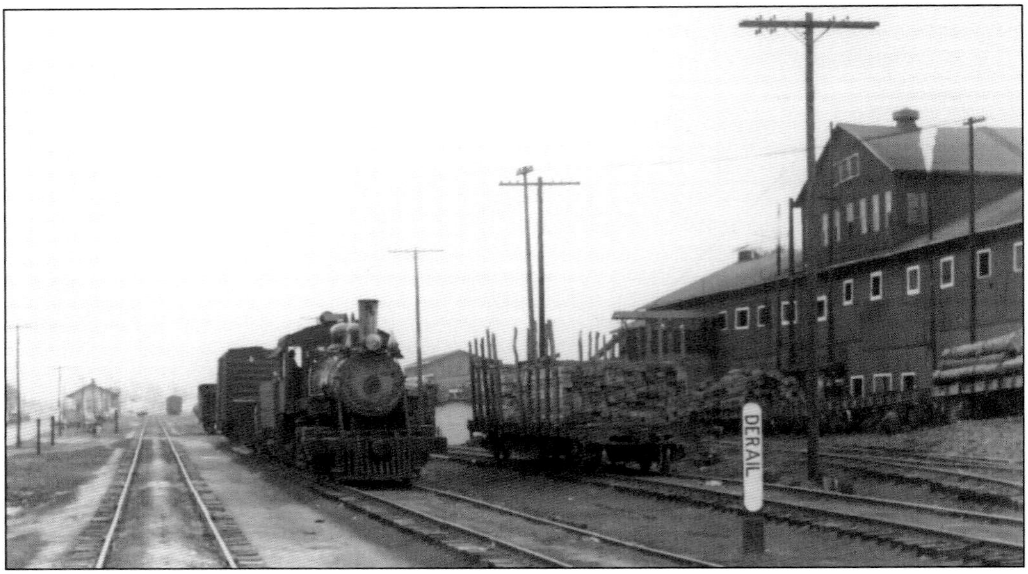

By far, the largest Sabine County operation was the Temple Lumber Company at Pineland, which took over the Garrison-Norton mill in 1910 and operated trams in eastern Sabine and northern Newton Counties into the 1950s. Here, Temple Lumber No. 18, built new in 1922, switches the Pineland mill in March 1948. (Courtesy Richard W. Keeling Collection.)

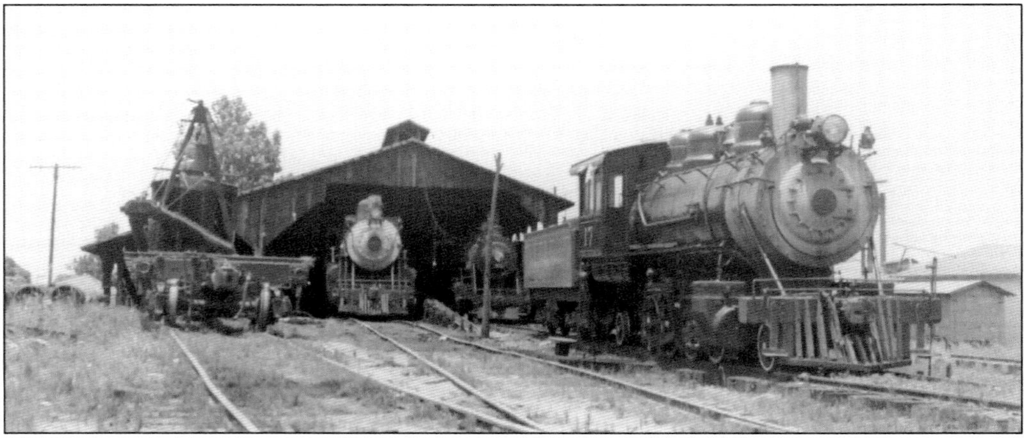

At the Pineland shops, several locomotives sit in the hot August sun in 1954. From left to right are ex–Santa Fe's (now Temple's) No. 1140, No. 20, and No. 17 (in the foreground). The No. 20 was built new for Temple in 1930 and was the last logging engine to be manufactured new for a Texas lumber carrier. (Courtesy Richard W. Keeling Collection.)

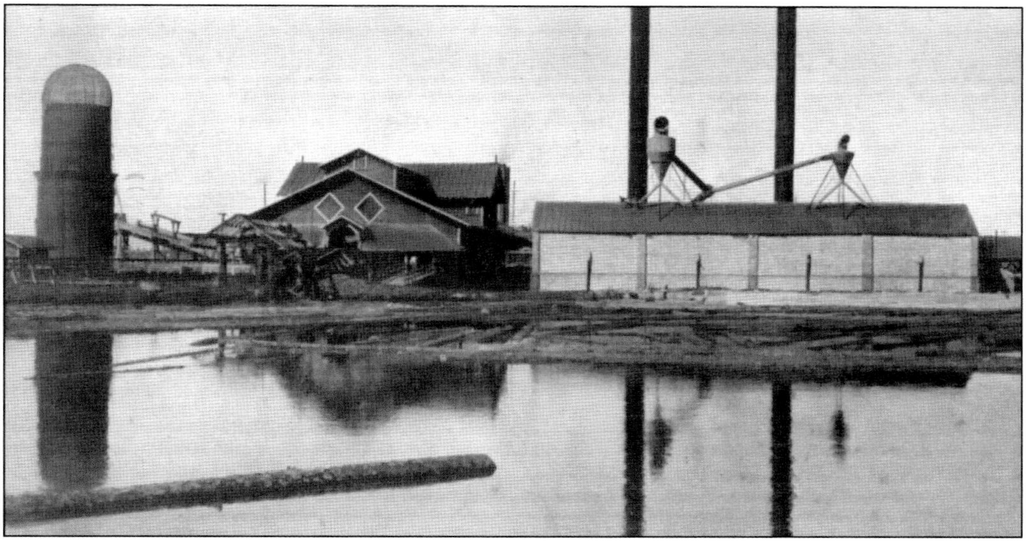

At Groveton in Trinity County, the aptly named Trinity County Lumber Company erected a mill in 1882 and operated an eight-mile tram by 1890. A larger mill built in 1904 burned the same year, followed by the mill seen in the above 1910 postcard view. At its peak, the company cut a massive 300,000 board feet per day. The last log was cut on December 31, 1930, and much of the timberlands were used to help form the Davy Crockett National Forest. Below, trams extend north and south from Groveton, totaling 20 miles by 1910 and reaching up to 35 miles in the peak years of the 1920s. (Both, courtesy Texas Transportation Archive.)

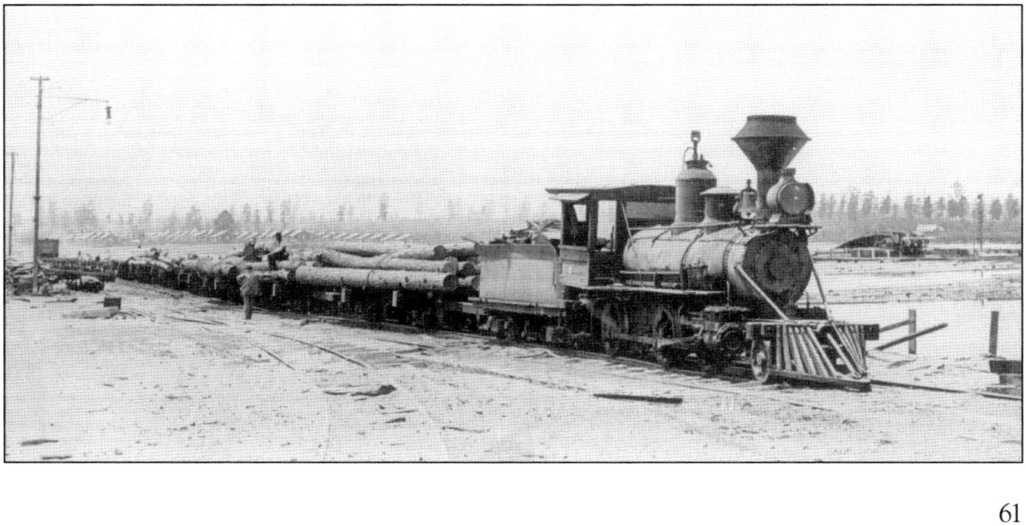

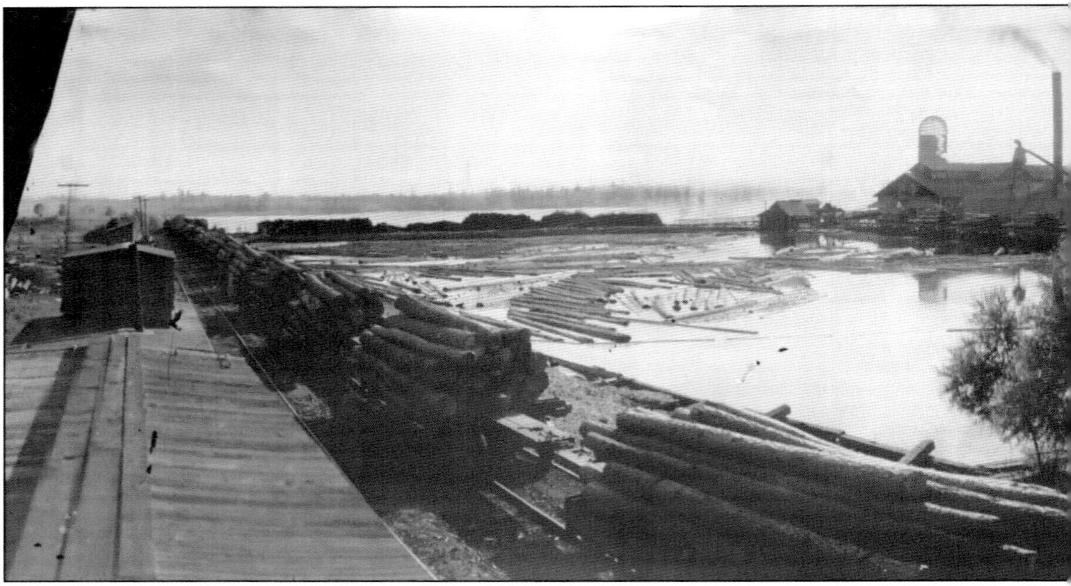

On July 24, 1916, attempting to convey in one panorama the massive mill complex of the Trinity County Lumber Company, Houston photographer Frank J. Schlueter created a glass plate negative that was 57 inches long. This is the entire panorama, divided and stacked in order to include the image in its entirety. Schlueter took several panoramas in July 1916, showing the

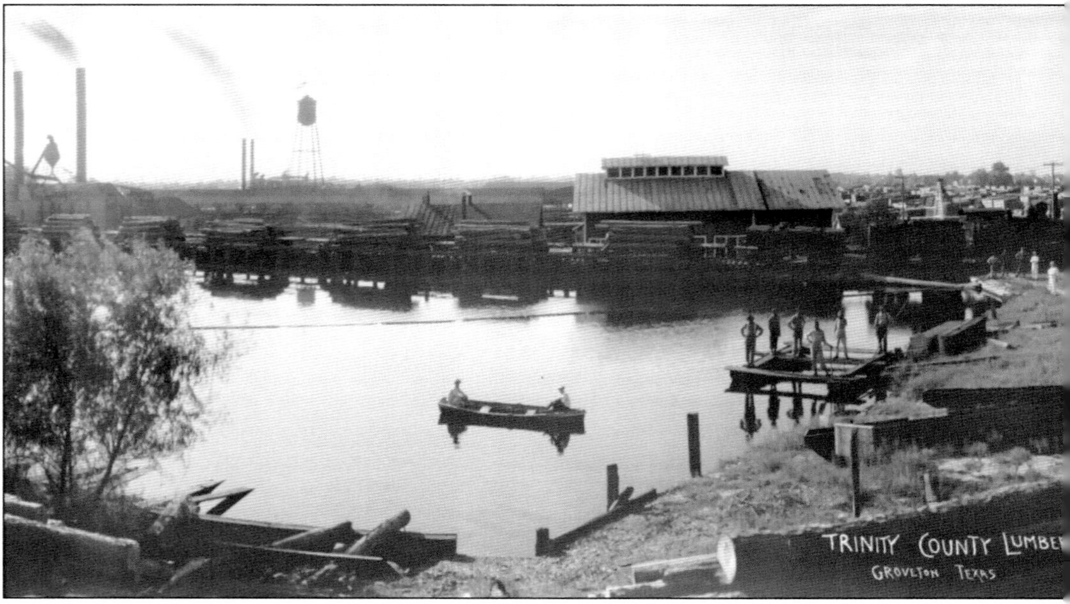

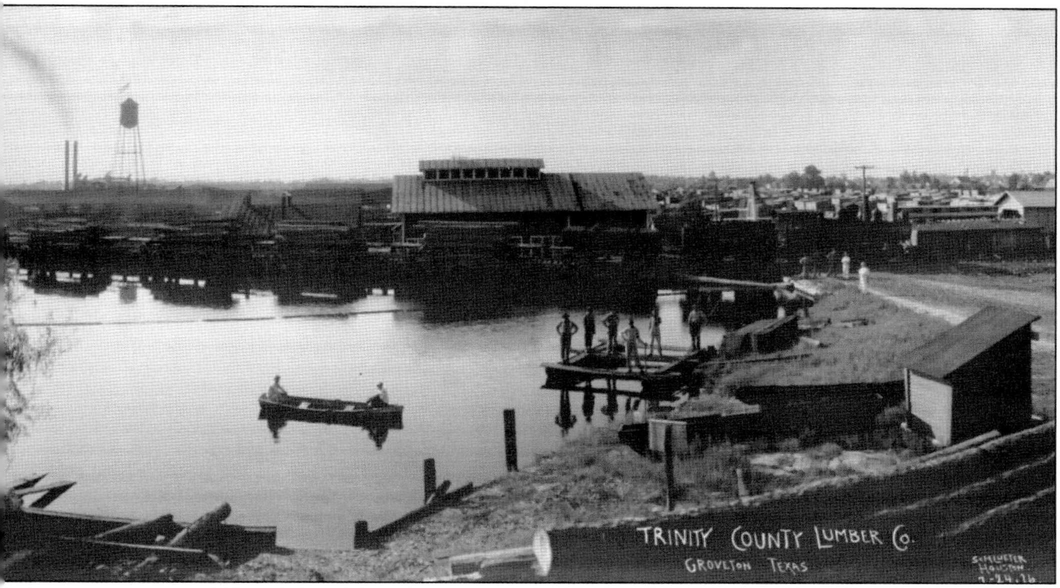

mill in peak production, when the company was sawing at 300,000 board feet per day. The mill was fed by several log camps, which moved multiple log trains over 20 miles of trams, including its own Groveton, Lufkin & Northern Railway. (Courtesy Houston Metropolitan Research Center, Image MSS 0223p-0081.)

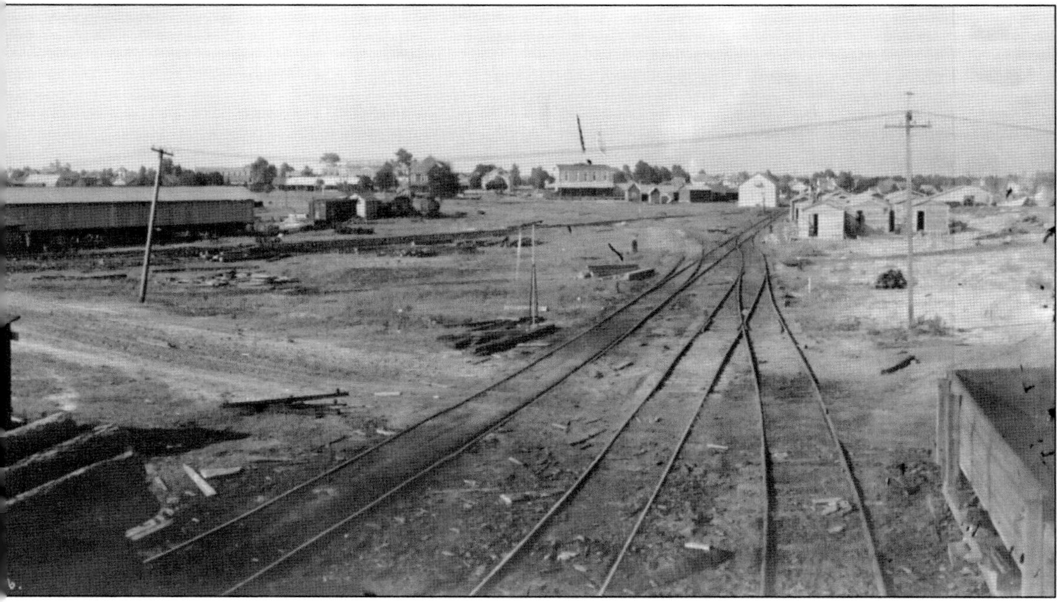

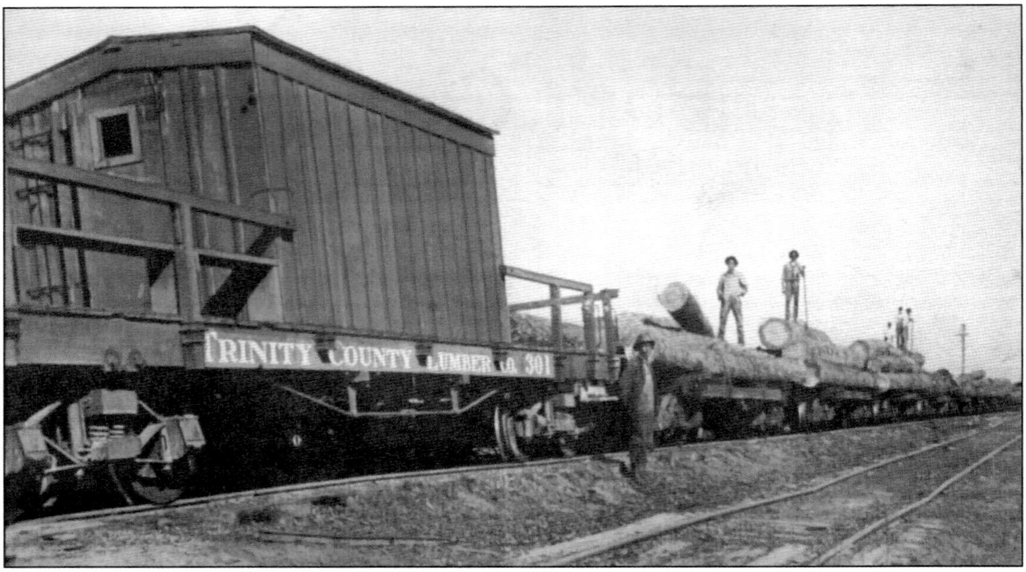

Trinity County Lumber Company's Caboose No. 301 began life as a common wooden flatcar that was modified by carpenters at the Groveton car shop. Trinity County Lumber maintained a fully equipped shop with the means to build a wide range of logging equipment—from common log cars to residential camp cars to rolling stock such as this caboose. (Courtesy Texas Transportation Archive.)

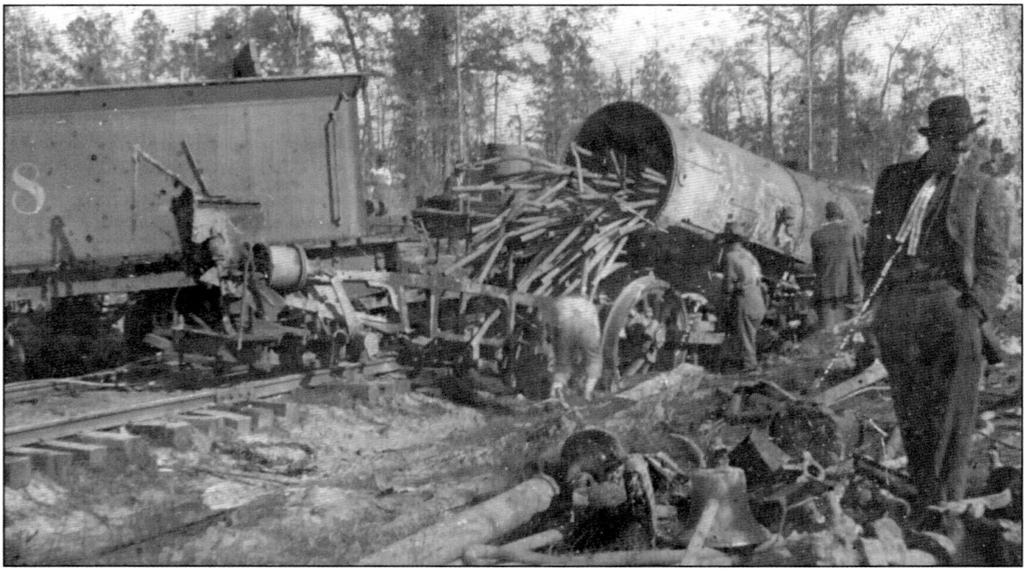

On the evening of November 27, 1912, locomotive engineer Aaron Norsworthy and fireman Joe Shepherd were inbound to Groveton with Engine No. 8 and a loaded log train when low water in the boiler led to a crown sheet failure and a violent boiler explosion. Both crewmen were killed instantly, and the locomotive was destroyed. This photograph shows the rear of the boiler where the cab once was and the missing backhead, now a twisted tangle of flues. (Courtesy History Center at Diboll.)

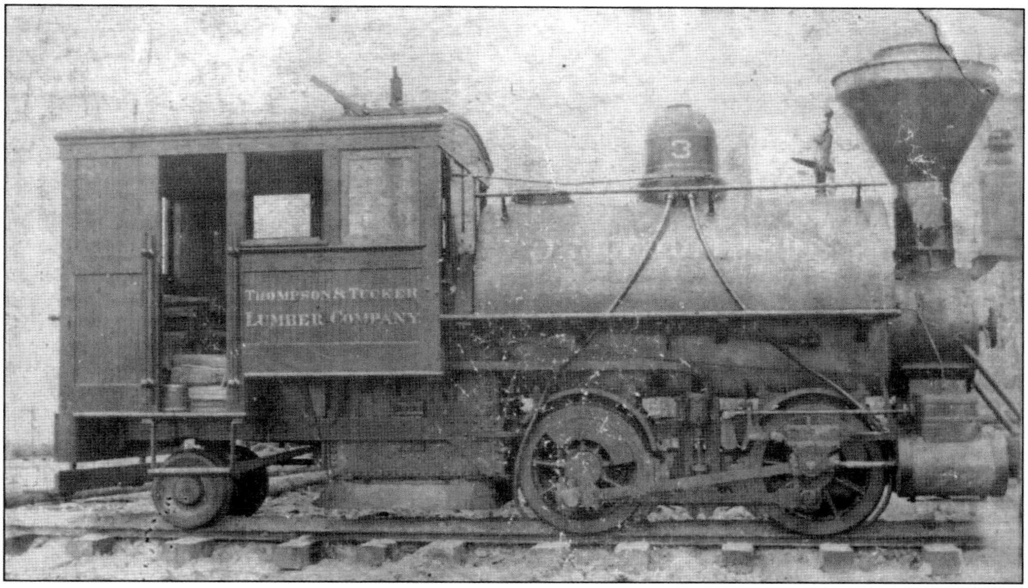

John M. Thompson and Henry Tucker began milling in 1882 at Willard, about six miles west of Groveton on the Trinity & Sabine Railway. The mill properties grew in capacity and timber holdings, and two other large mills were established at Trinity and New Willard. Between the three mills, there was a total of 81 miles of railroad, 19 locomotives, and 260 log cars. Above, Porter locomotive No. 3 pauses under steam at Willard in the early 1900s. No. 4, pictured below, was a heavier Porter locomotive, built new for Thompson-Tucker in 1909, about a year before the mill closed and operations moved to New Willard. (Both, courtesy Texas Transportation Archive.)

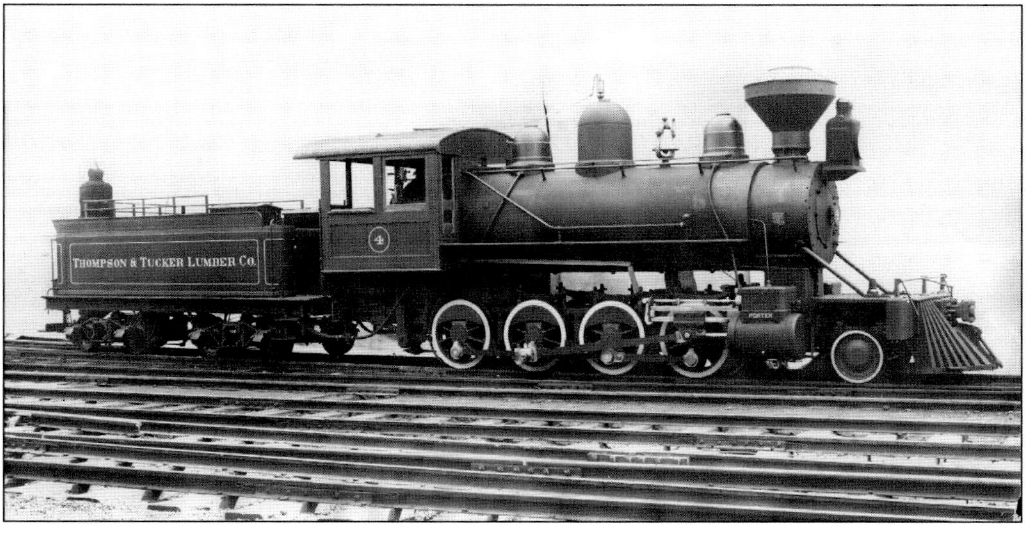

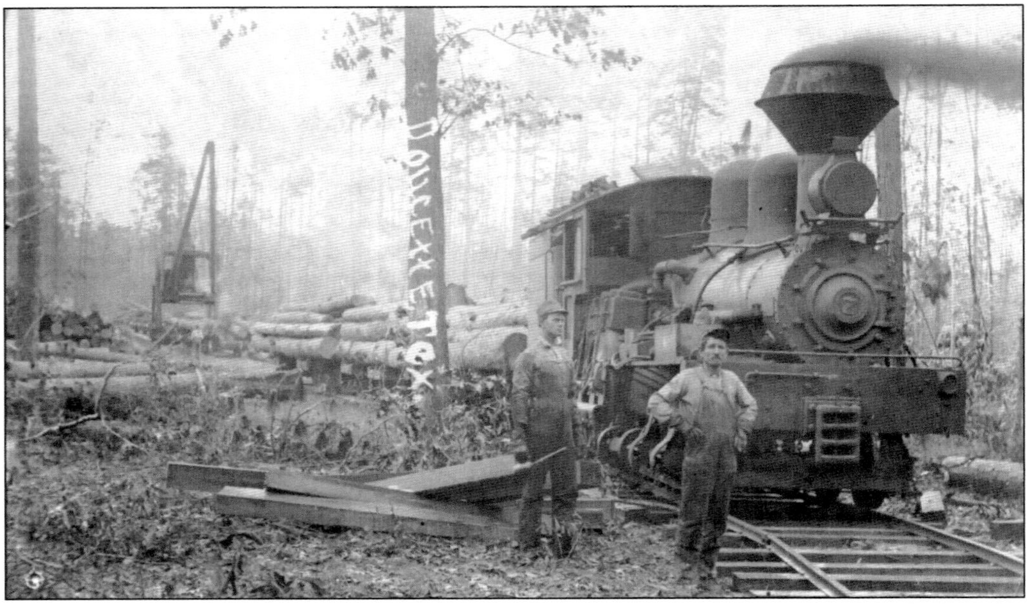

Another Thompson lumber interest was the Thompson Brothers Lumber Company, which built a mill in 1906 at Doucette in Tyler County, about seven miles south of Colmesneil on the Houston East & West Texas Railway. In this view, Shay No. 7 poses with the train crew at the company's log front around 1910. (Courtesy Texas Transportation Archive.)

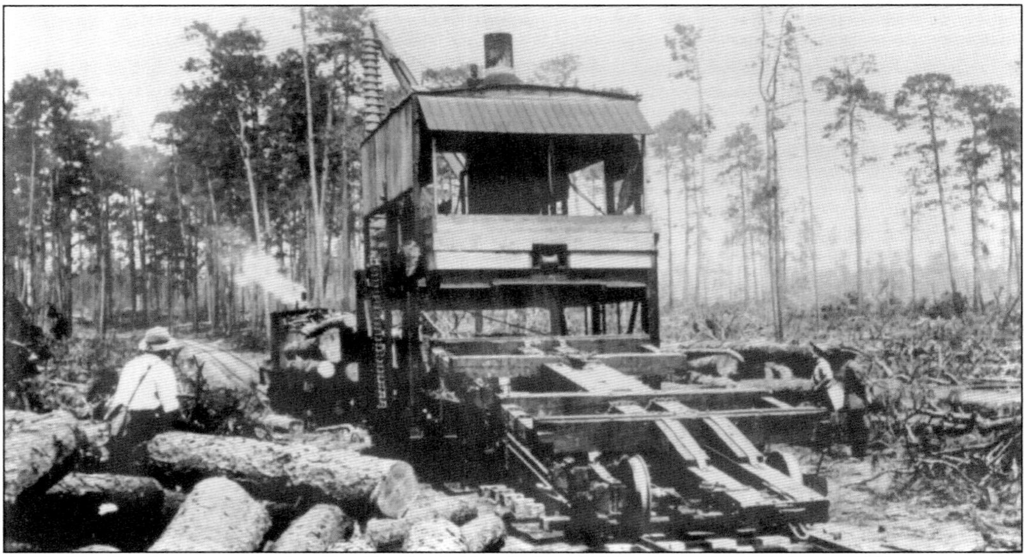

The Thompson Brother loader is working in the woods near Doucette around 1910. In a year, the Long-Bell Lumber Company would take over the former Thompson Brother properties, and Doucette would enjoy years of prosperity under its management. (Courtesy Richard W. Keeling Collection.)

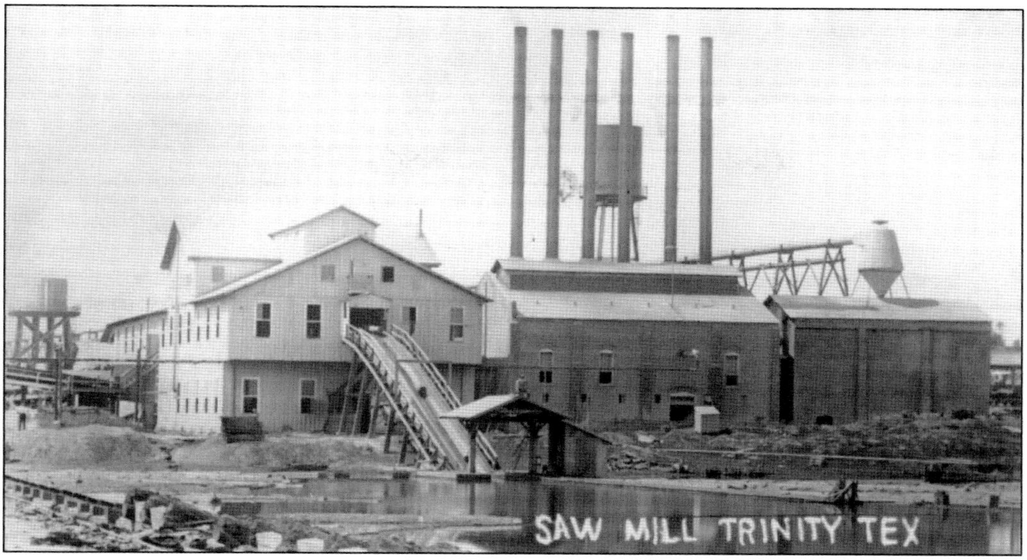

In the 1910s, the Thompson family reorganized, creating multiple companies to deal with cattle, farming, real estate, oil and mineral leases, and lumber on its vast timber holdings in Trinity, Houston, and Polk Counties. Lumber operations were assigned to the Rock Creek Lumber Company and the Texas Long Leaf Lumber Company at Trinity, Oakhurst, and New Willard. Above is the big mill at Trinity as it looked in the 1910s. Below, a Rock Creek Lumber engine sits outside the shop area at Trinity in July 1935. (Both, courtesy Texas Transportation Archive.)

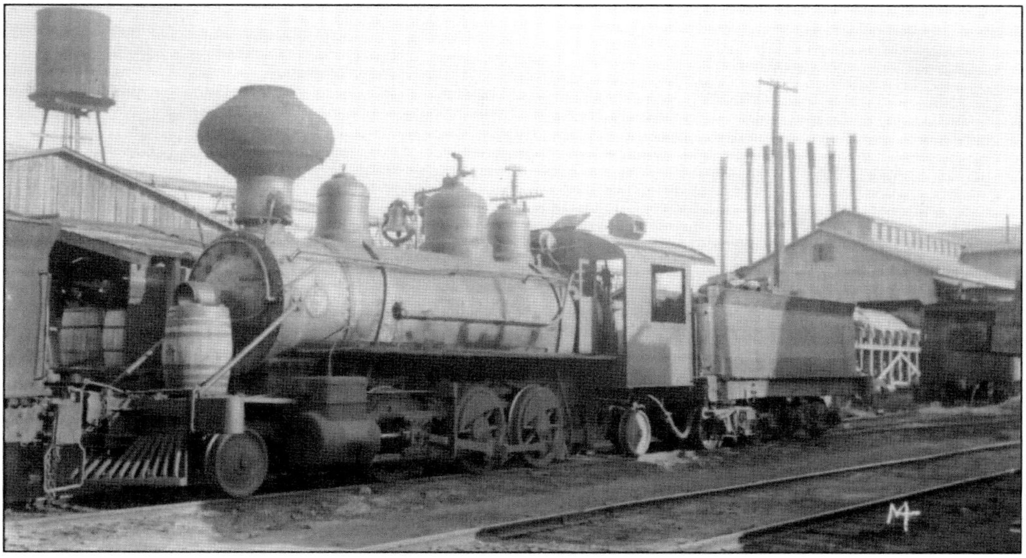

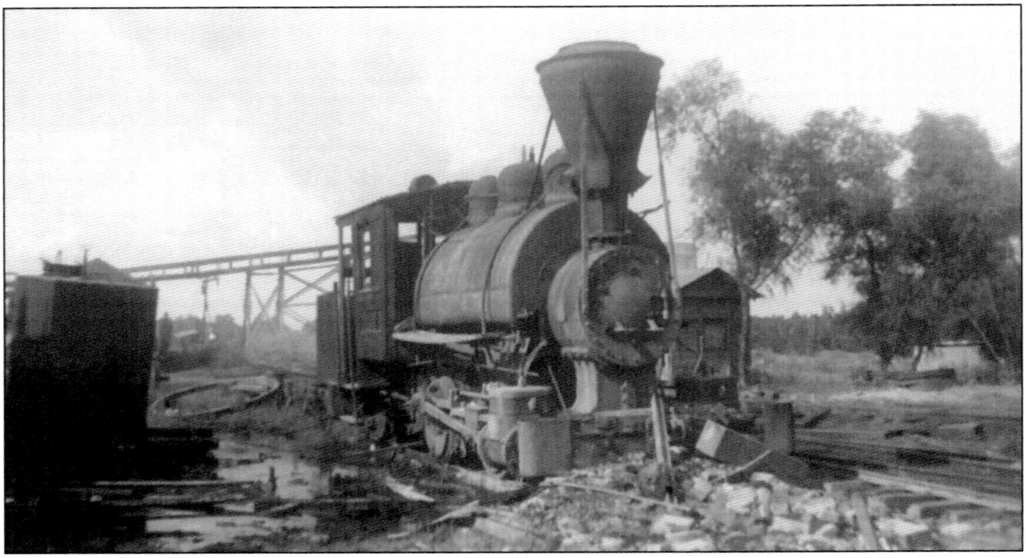
Rock Creek's little Porter Locomotive No. 9 was known as "the Goat." The No. 9 was used exclusively for shuttling cars and never traveled beyond the mill's yard trackage. In this photograph, the No. 9 sits idle at Trinity on August 26, 1937. (Courtesy Texas Transportation Archive.)

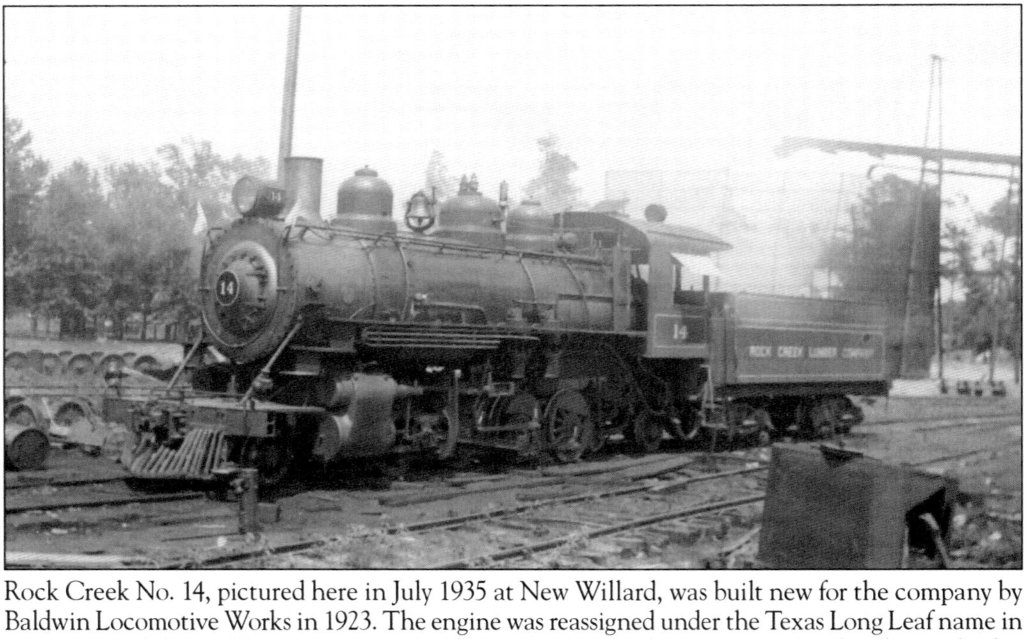

Rock Creek No. 14, pictured here in July 1935 at New Willard, was built new for the company by Baldwin Locomotive Works in 1923. The engine was reassigned under the Texas Long Leaf name in the 1930s and then sold to W.T. Carter in 1940 as its No. 14. The engine survived and is on display today near the former Carter mill at Camden. (Courtesy Richard W. Keeling Collection.)

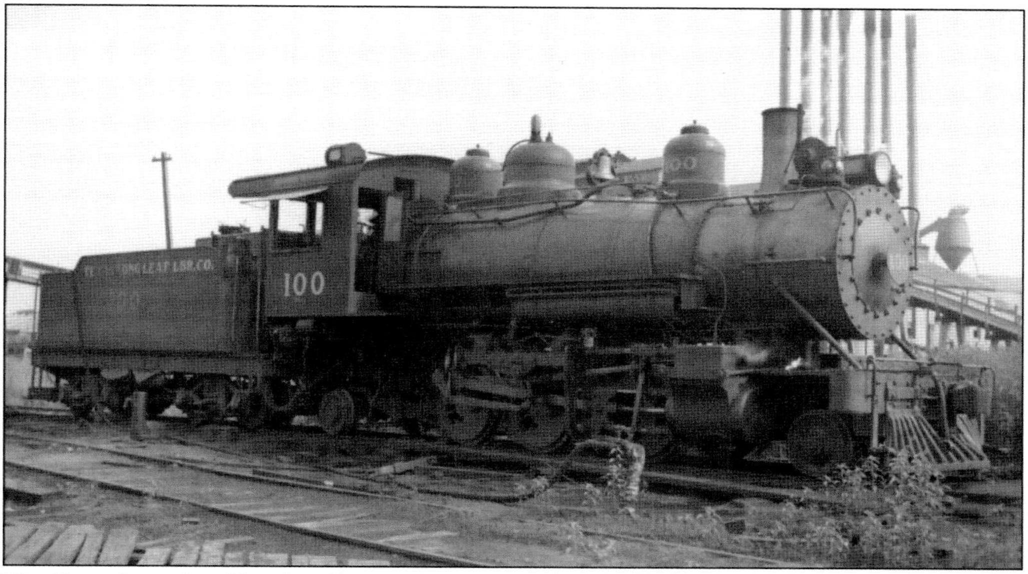

The Texas Long Leaf Lumber Company maintained a sizeable locomotive fleet to deal with the many cutting areas that dotted its lands in Trinity, Houston, Polk, and San Jacinto Counties. In this photograph, Engine No. 100 sits at New Willard on July 14, 1937. (Courtesy Texas Transportation Archive.)

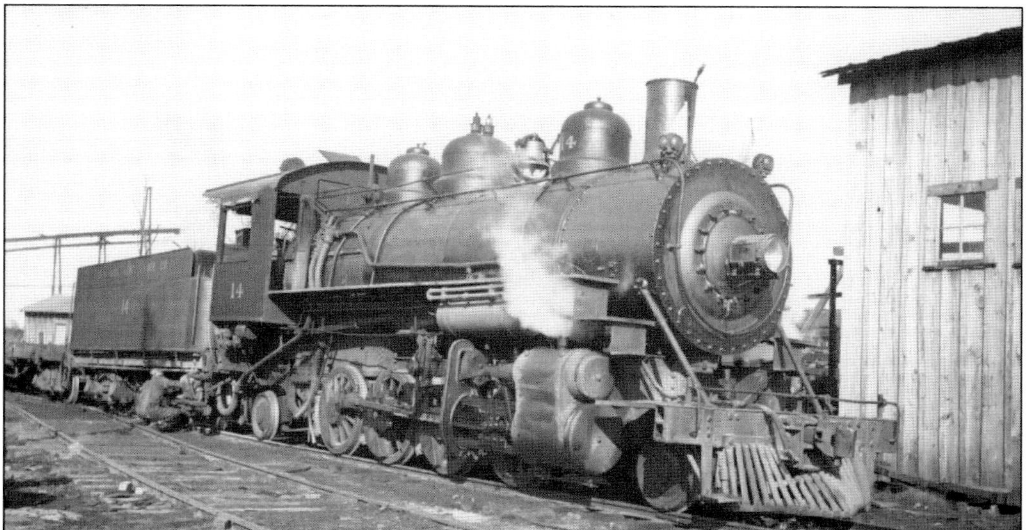

Texas Long Leaf Lumber No. 14 sits under steam at Trinity on November 28, 1938. The No. 14 was sold to the W.T. Carter Company at Camden two years after this photograph was taken. Today, the engine is on display at Camden. (Courtesy Texas Transportation Archive.)

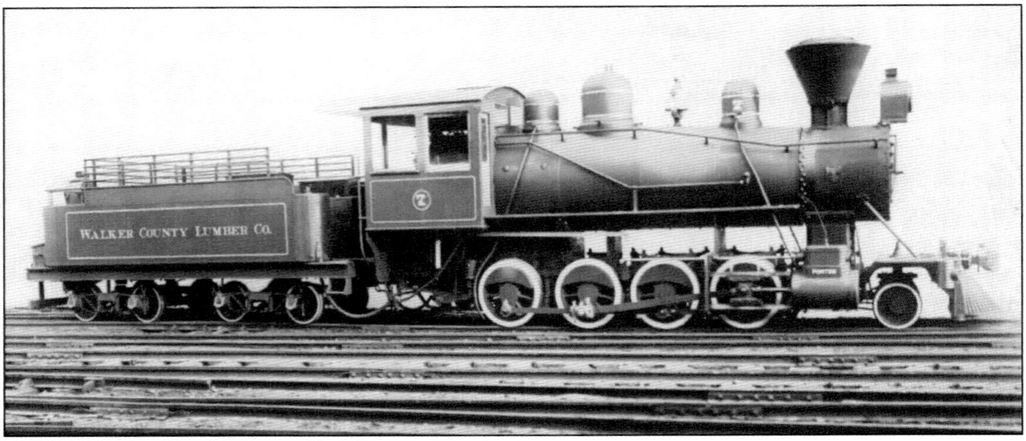

Walker County Lumber Company erected a mill at Elmina in Walker County in 1902 and began building a network of narrow-gauge trams that was incorporated in 1904 as the Elmina & Eastern Transportation Company (E&ET). The line operated three locomotives, 48 log cars, and two cabooses over 24 miles of tram line to the logging camp communities of Seaman, Lick Skillet, and Clint. In 1910, the E&ET was dissolved and its properties were consolidated back under the Walker Lumber name. Above, newly constructed Engine No. 7 poses for the factory photographer at the H.K. Porter Company in 1915. Below, Walker County Lumber Company No. 8, which began its career in Colorado as the Denver & Rio Grande Railroad's No. 289, sits outside the company's shops in the 1920s. The company and its railroad concluded operations after the Elmina mill suffered a catastrophic fire in 1931. (Both, courtesy Texas Transportation Archive.)

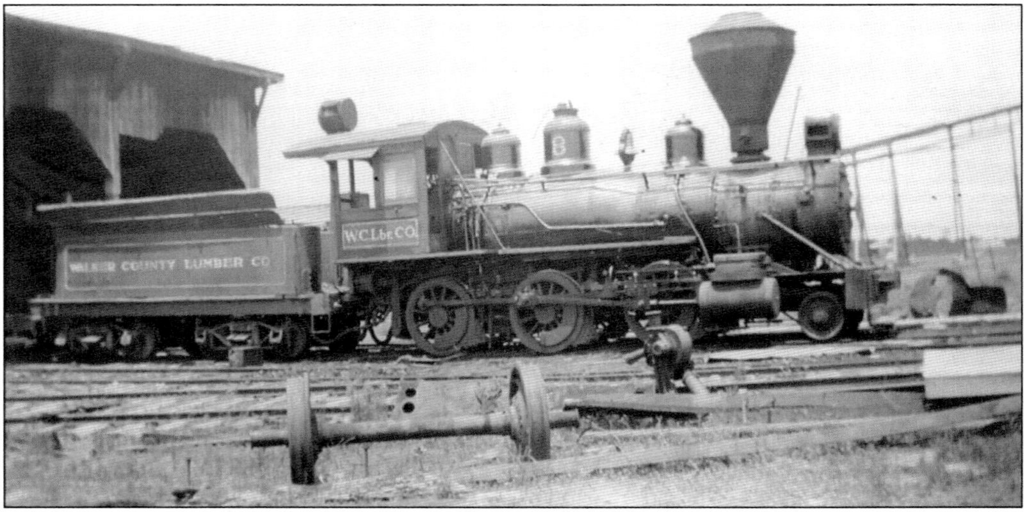

Four

Logging in the Big Thicket Region

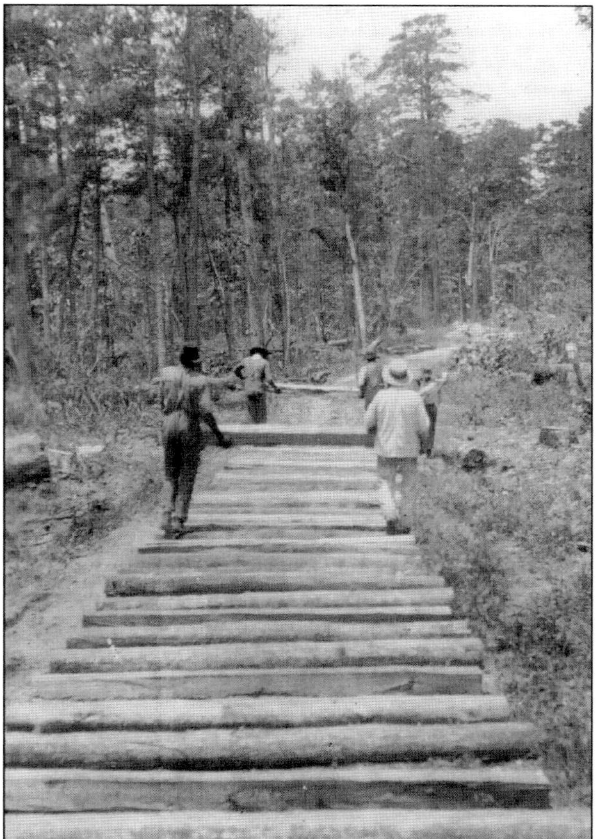

The "Big Thicket" is a heavily forested area spread across the five counties of Hardin, Liberty, Tyler, San Jacinto, and Polk. In this Hardin County scene from the 1910s, a Kirby Lumber Company tram crew has performed the clearing and earthwork and will soon lay the rails that will give railroad access to millions of board feet worth of timber in the forest beyond. Such a scene repeated itself countless times during the heyday of the Texas lumber industry. (Courtesy Richard W. Keeling Collection.)

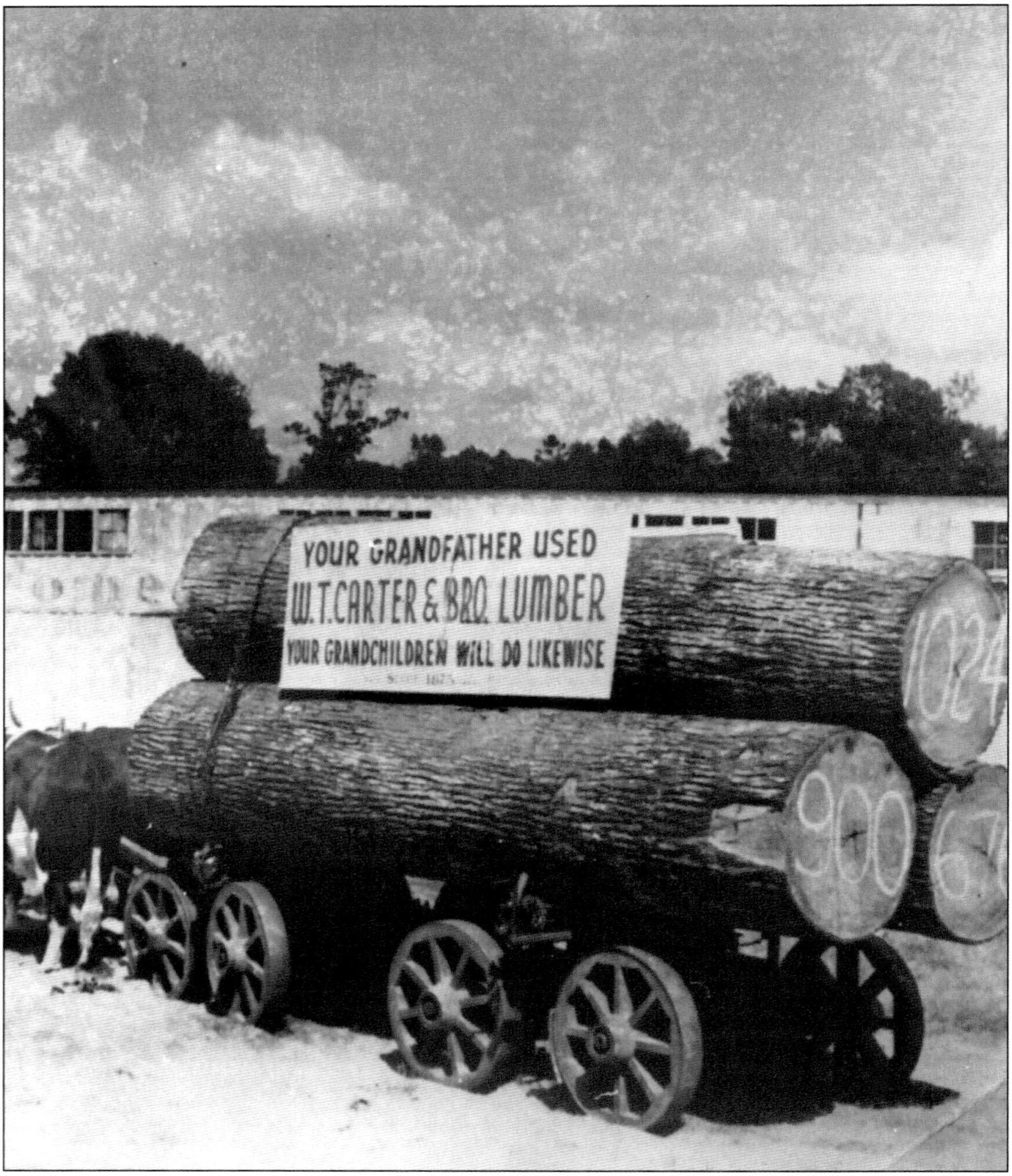

A Lindsey eight-wheel log wagon—a common tool of timber haulers in the old East Texas woods—is fitted with a parade banner that reads, "Your Grandfather Used W.T. Carter & Bro. Lumber, Your Grandchildren Will Do Likewise." One of the longest-running operations in the history of the East Texas industry, W.T. Carter & Brother Lumber began when brothers William T. and Earnest A. Carter began milling at Barnum in Polk County in 1885 using mule power and a crude wooden-railed tram. In 1898, a mill fire prompted a move to what would become a 70-year stay at Camden, Texas. A common carrier short-line, the Moscow, Camden & San Augustine Railroad (MC&SA), was built to provide a freight and passenger connection with the Houston East & West Texas Railway at Moscow. The MC&SA would live to see the 21st century, and at the time of this writing, continues to move wood products along a route that has remained unchanged since 1898. (Courtesy Lester Haines.)

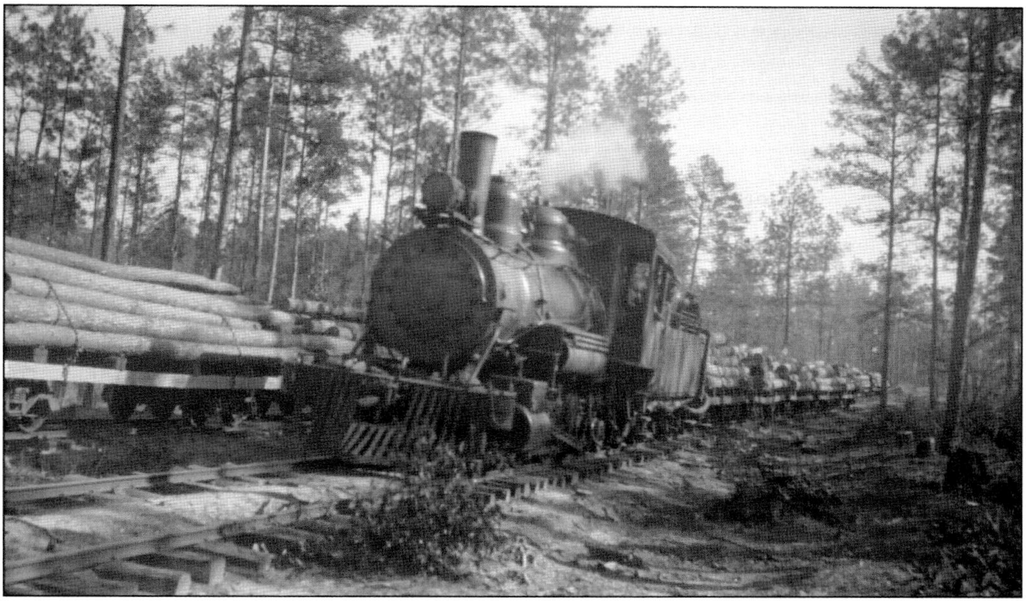

W.T. Carter's No. 4 moves past another log train toward Camden in 1955. The No. 4 survived and is preserved at the Eureka Springs Museum in Arkansas. (Courtesy Richard W. Keeling Collection.)

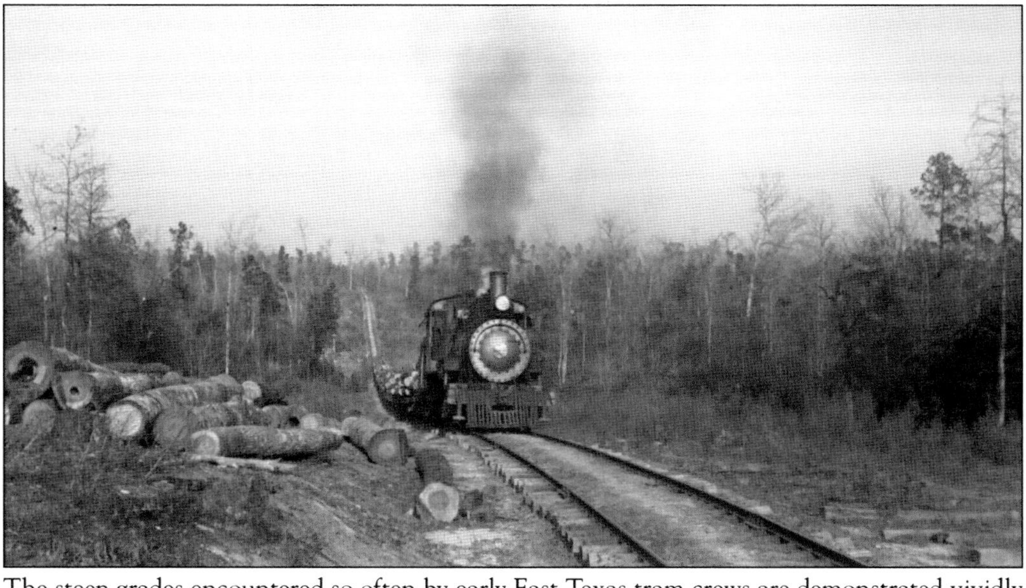

The steep grades encountered so often by early East Texas tram crews are demonstrated vividly in this view of W.T. Carter's Engine No. 4 as it fights its way up a steep grade on the tram east of Camden in 1955. (Courtesy Richard W. Keeling Collection.)

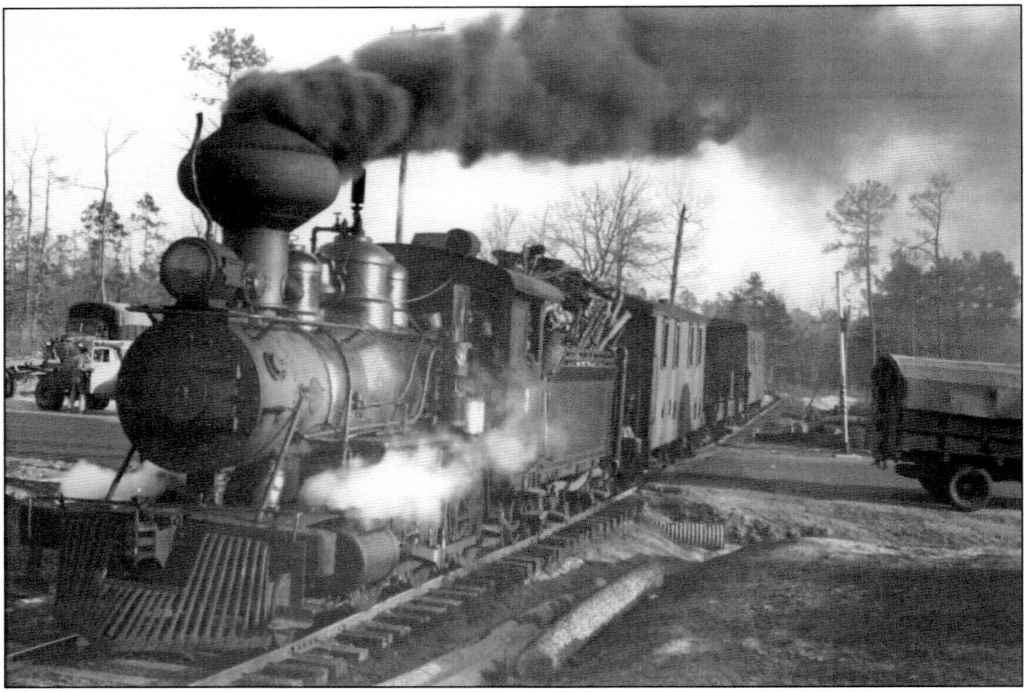

No. 3 pulls into the W.T. Carter loading area with two crew cars and a flatcar in 1955. These sorts of camp cars were used to transport woods workers between the forest and their homes. (Courtesy Richard W. Keeling Collection.)

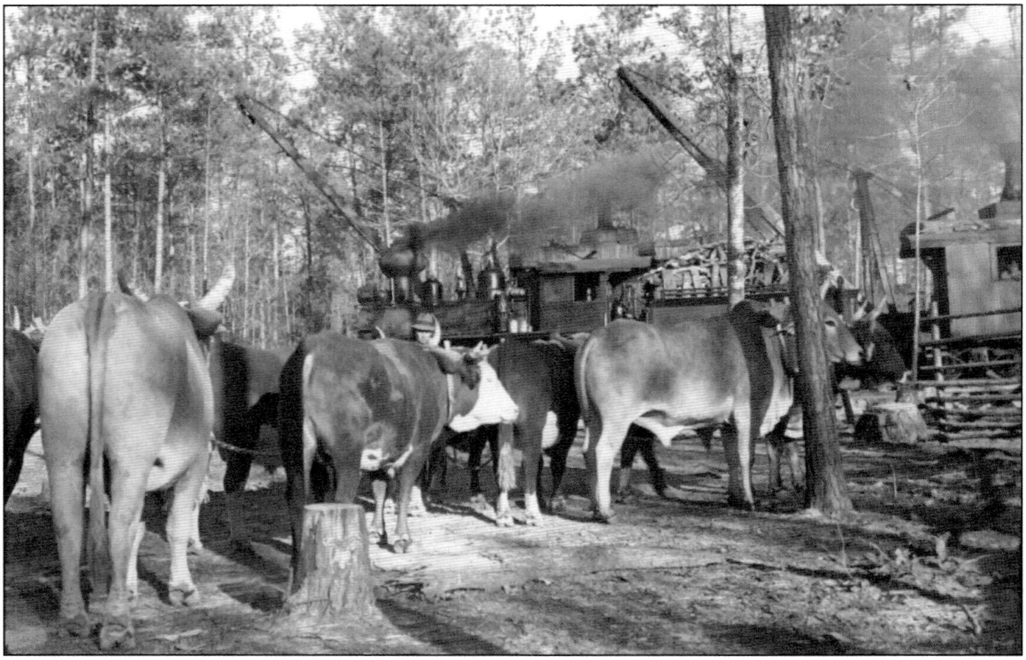

On the W.T. Carter trams were tributary camps known as "mule corrals," where animals were picketed and tended to by woods workers. In this 1955 view, one such worker looks out over the backs of several beasts of burden as Carter Engine No. 3 with its crew train steams in the background. (Courtesy Richard W. Keeling Collection.)

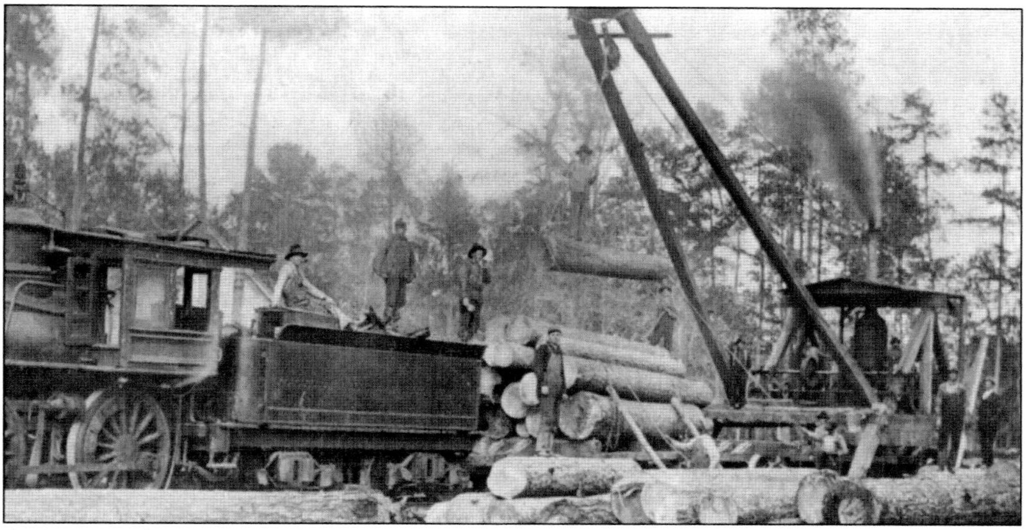

A Knox Lumber Company log train works the Knox tram in Polk County. Hiram Knox built a mill seven miles east of Livingston at Soda in 1902, laying a tram that extended from Livingston to the Knox lands three miles beyond the mill. The tram was incorporated as the Livingston & Southeastern Railway and operated until 1913, when the mill closed and Knox moved to Sabine County. (Courtesy Texas Transportation Archive.)

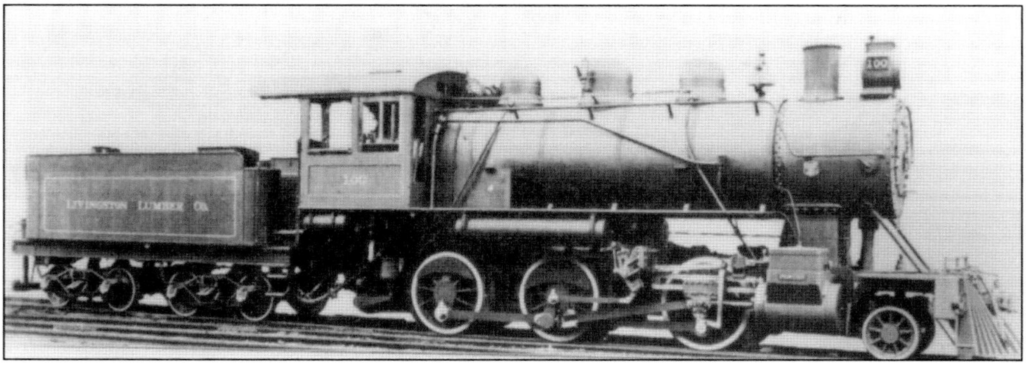

Just north of Livingston on the Houston East & West Texas Railway at Buck, the Livingston Lumber Company started operating its mill in 1902, logging over a 10-mile tram. This engine was built new for the company by Porter in 1914 and was known to the mill residents as "Old One Hundred." The company ceased operations in 1918. (Courtesy Texas Transportation Archive.)

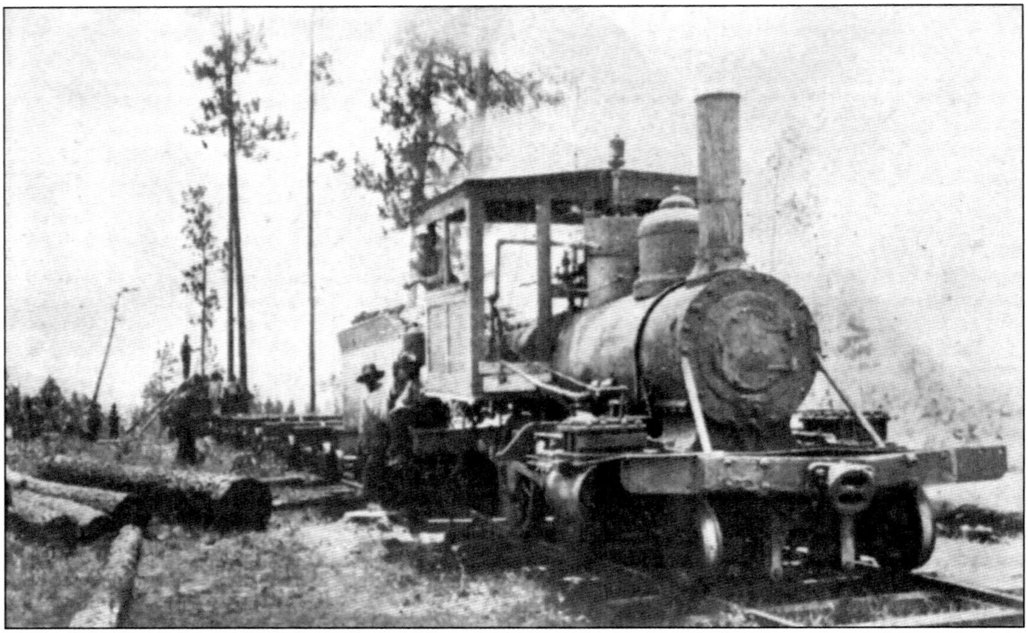

Davidson-Ingram Lumber Company incorporated in 1907 to purchase mills at Benford and Potomac from J.M. West. The company operated trams at Benford, Laurelia, and Potomac—all in Polk County. The name changed again in 1909 to the Benford Lumber Company. At Benford, several locomotives were operated on its trams, including this teakettle of a locomotive pictured in 1907. (Courtesy Texas Transportation Archive.)

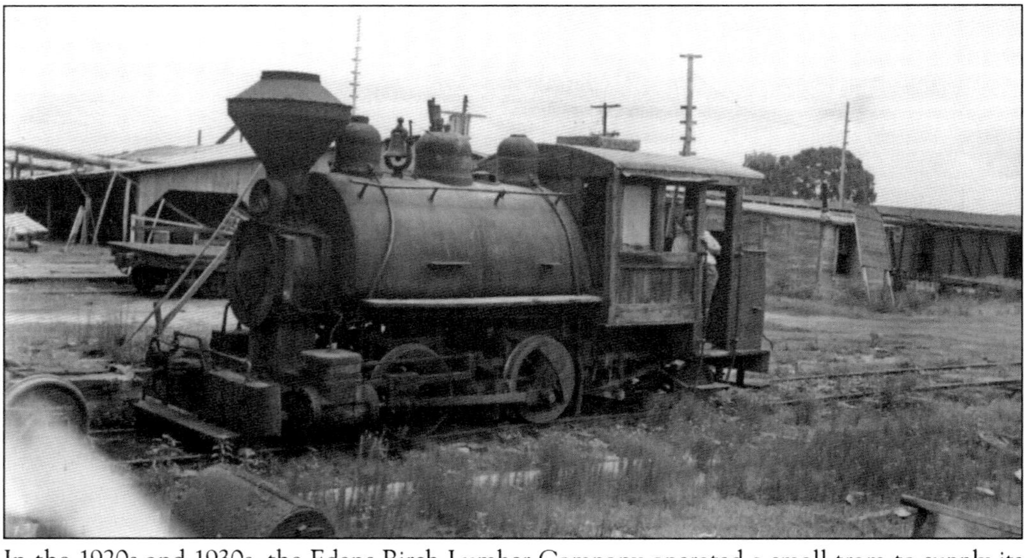

In the 1920s and 1930s, the Edens-Birch Lumber Company operated a small tram to supply its mill at Corrigan in Polk County. The company used two locomotives, including its No. 5, which was purchased from Texas Long Leaf. Here, the No. 5 sits static at the Edens-Birch property on March 17, 1938. (Courtesy Texas Transportation Archive.)

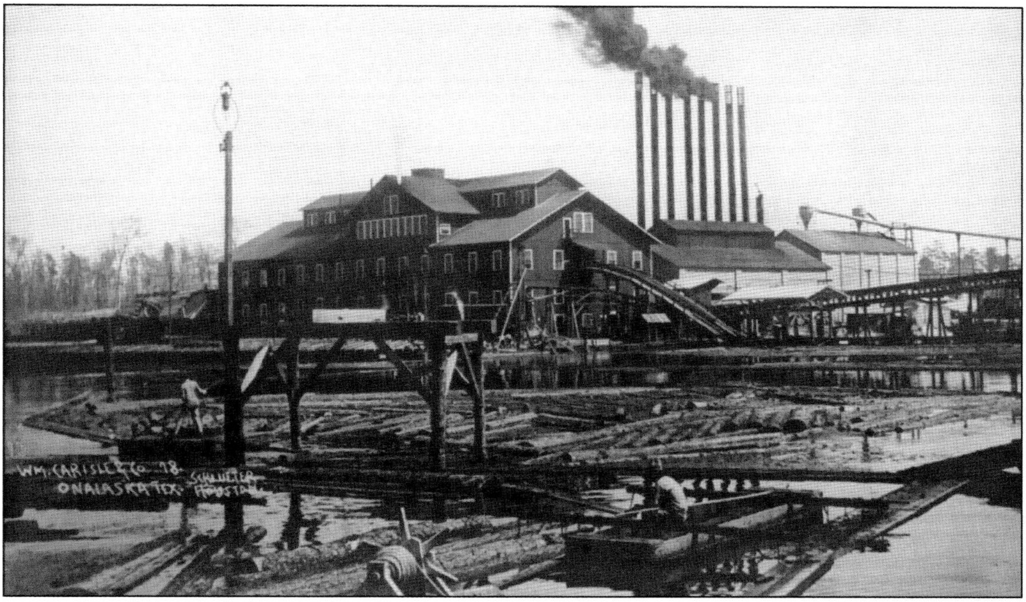

In 1905, William Carlisle completed his big mill at Onalaska and organized the 33-mile Beaumont & Great Northern Railroad (B&GN) to provide rail outlets with Trinity to the north and Livingston to the south. Carlisle famously built four towns named Onalaska—in Wisconsin, Arkansas, Texas, and Washington. At a combined capacity of 225,000 board feet, the Texas mill was one of the largest in its time. (Courtesy Texas Transportation Archive.)

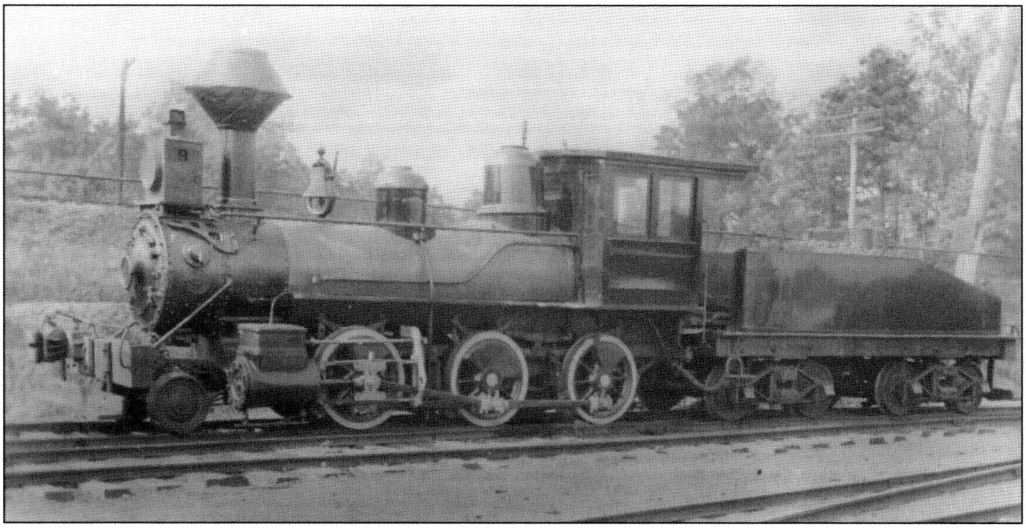

Carlisle's trams branched off the B&GN using updated locomotives that could legally move log trains over the common carrier B&GN. In 1909, the Onalaska properties were purchased by the West Lumber Company, which expanded operations with the purchase of additional equipment, including Engine No. 9, seen here at reseller Southern Iron & Equipment in September 1918. (Courtesy Texas Transportation Archive.)

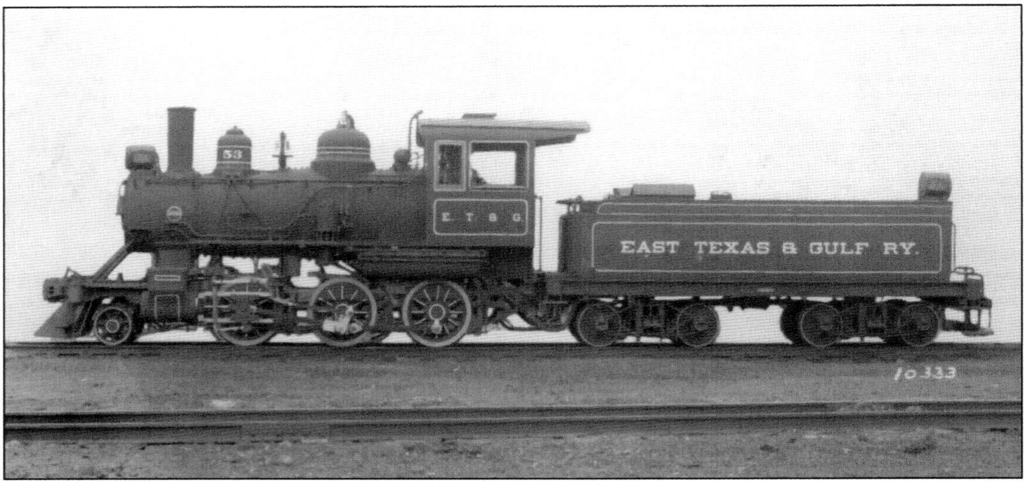

In 1917, Lodwick Lumber Company built at Hicksbaugh, four miles south of Warren in Tyler County. Lodwick incorporated the East Texas & Gulf Railway as a common carrier link to the Texas & New Orleans at Hyatt, while six miles of unincorporated tram was extended south of the mill into the timber. Locomotive No. 53, pictured here, was delivered new in 1929. The mill and its railroads were dismantled in 1934. (Courtesy Texas Transportation Archive.)

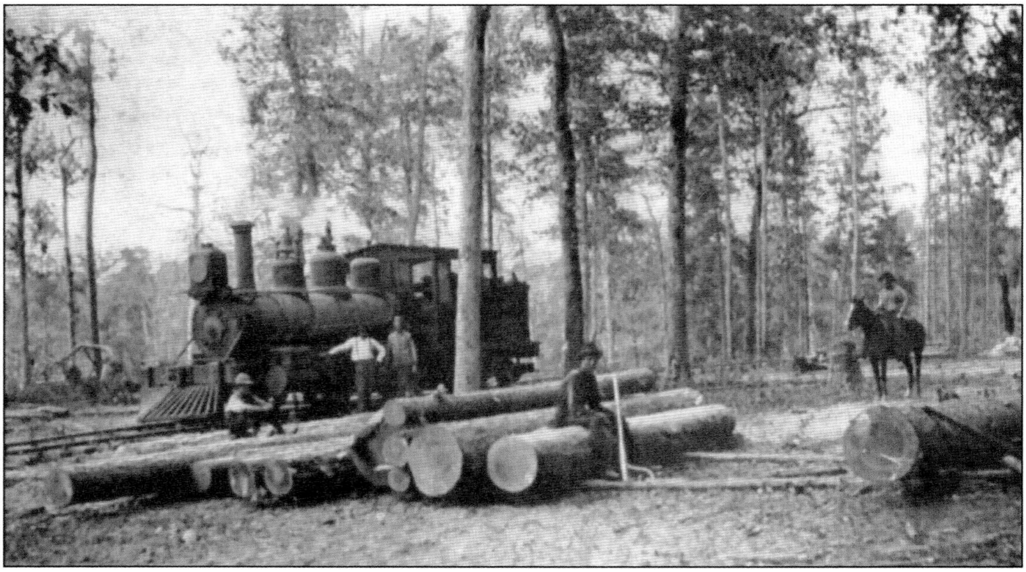

In 1901, Kirby Lumber Company purchased and enlarged an existing mill at Woodville in Tyler County. The tram was linked into a tram network operated by Camp 12, which also logged for the Kirby mills at Village and Silsbee. By 1911, the mill was idle and no longer mentioned in company correspondence. This view shows a Kirby engine on the Woodville tram in 1902. (Courtesy Texas Transportation Archive.)

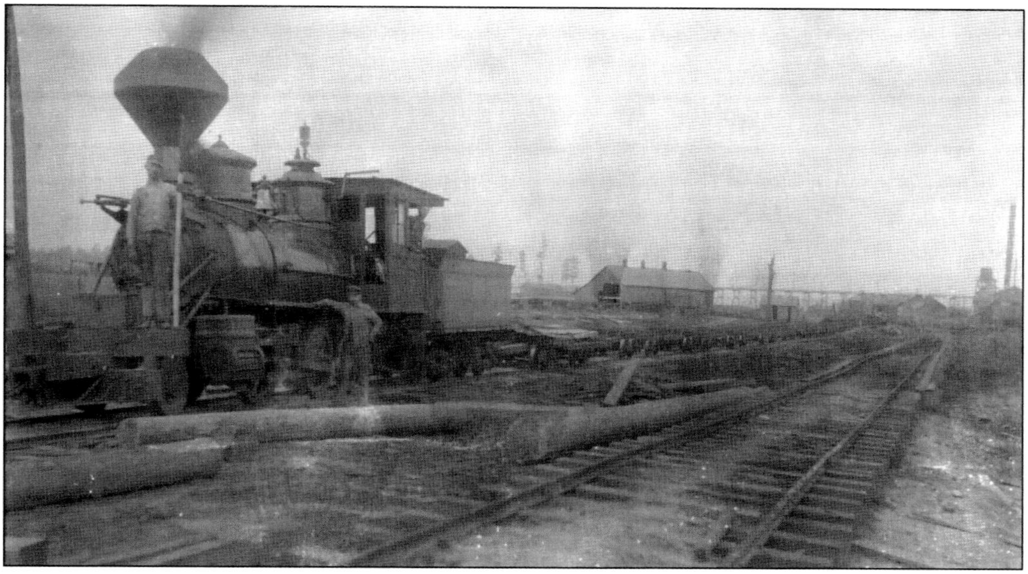

In 1897, the Texas Yellow Pine Lumber Company purchased the Warren Lumber Company, which had been operating a 10-mile tram west of town. The old tram was incorporated as the Warren & Corsicana Pacific Railroad (W&CP) in 1899 and extended to a point called Campwood, 18 miles from the Warren mill in eastern Polk County. Depots were built at Warren and Stutts, and mixed-train service was established. In the above view, W&CP Engine No. 6 prepares to leave Warren with a train of empty log cars. Below, Engine No. 6 pauses for the photographer at Campwood before returning to Warren. (Both, courtesy Prints and Photographs Collection, Texas State Library and Archives Commission.)

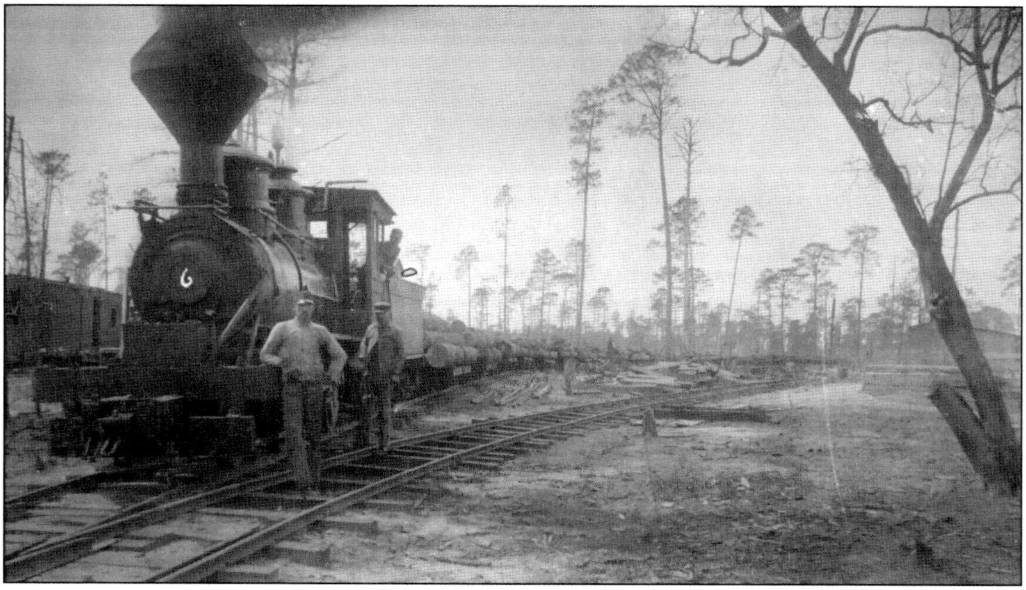

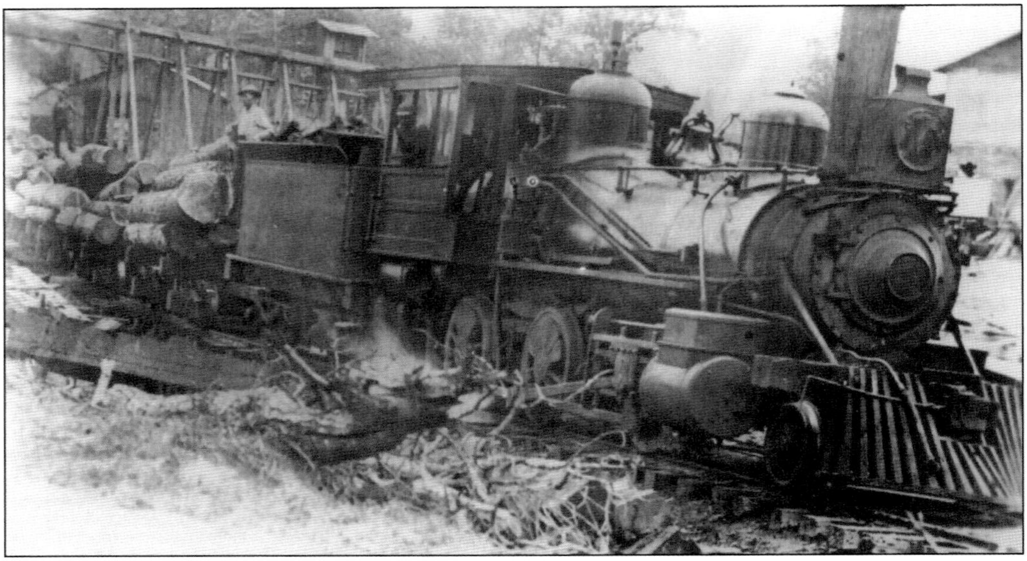

In 1923 at Oakhurst in San Jacinto County, the Oakhurst Lumber Company consolidated the former Palmetto and Columbia Lumber Companies. Included in the sale were two mills, over 20 miles of tram, the Snowtown and Pinedale log camps, and the Trinity Valley Southern Railway, which linked Oakhurst with the International–Great Northern at Dodge. In this 1920s view, a log train arrives at the Oakhurst pond. (Courtesy Texas Transportation Archive.)

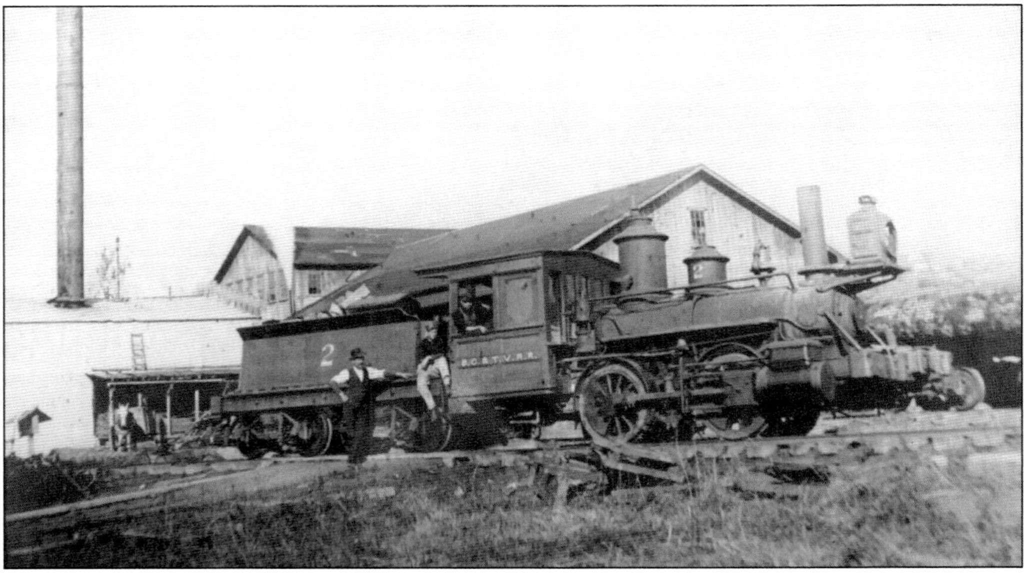

From 1906 until the late 1910s, the Liberty Hardwood Company logged hardwood along the Trinity River bottoms over an eight-mile tram known as Big Creek & Trinity Valley Railroad. In this 1908 view, Big Creek & Trinity Valley Engine No. 2 stops for a portrait. (Courtesy Texas Transportation Archive.)

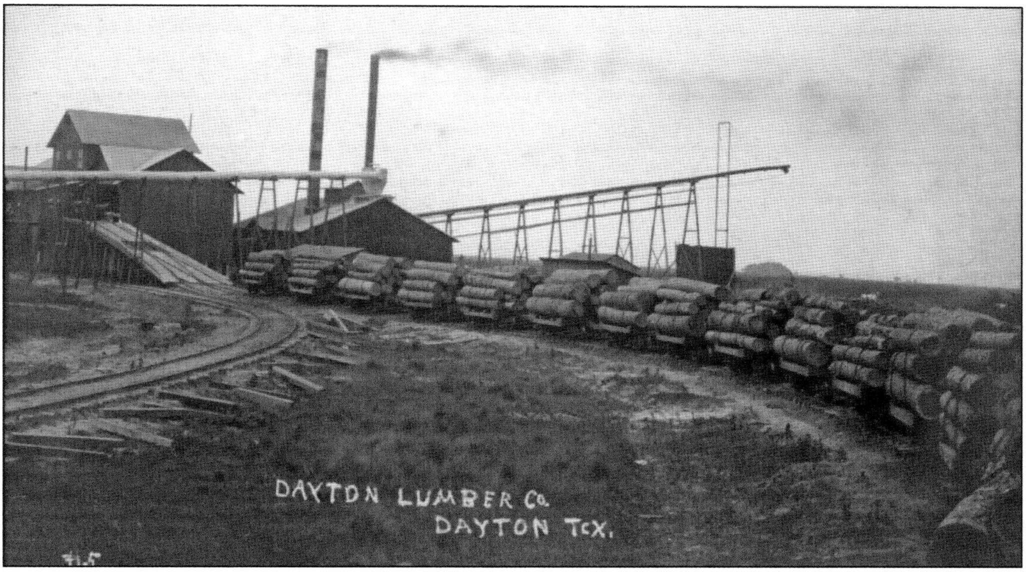

In 1906, the Dayton Lumber Company built its mill one half mile north of the Texas & New Orleans Railroad at Dayton in Liberty County. The company also incorporated and built the 10-mile Trinity Valley & Northern Railway (TV&N) to serve as a main logging route and to provide passenger and mail service to the various communities along its line. Above, a log train has arrived at the mill around 1907. Below, Dayton Lumber's Engine No. 2 was purchased in 1907 after having spent more than two decades in commuter train service in New York City. After 1920, the Dayton mill was operated by the South Texas Hardwood Company, while the TV&N continued as a separate company. The TV&N was finally abandoned when lumber operations ceased in 1931. (Both, courtesy Texas Transportation Archive.)

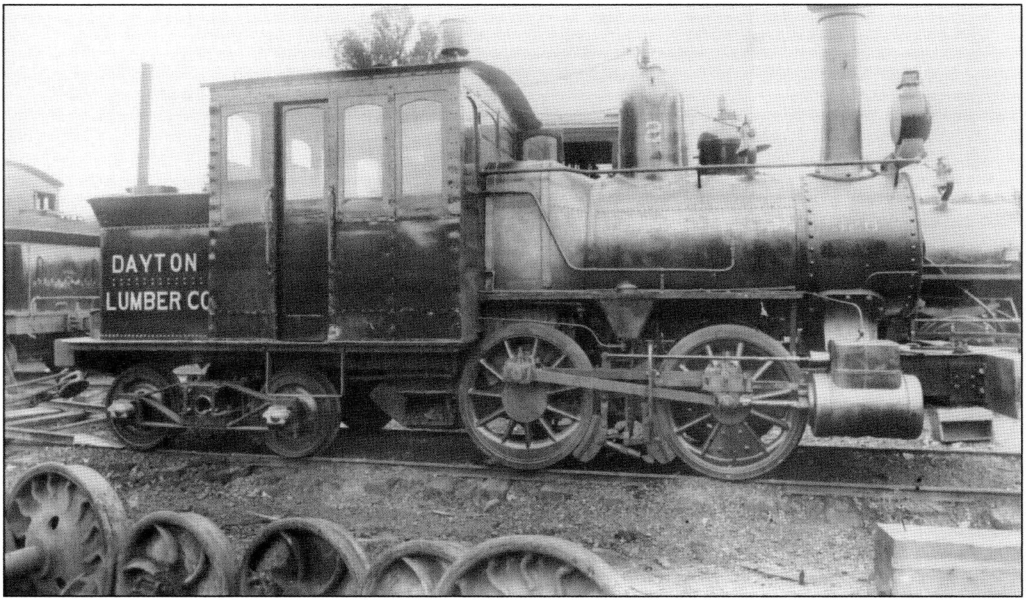

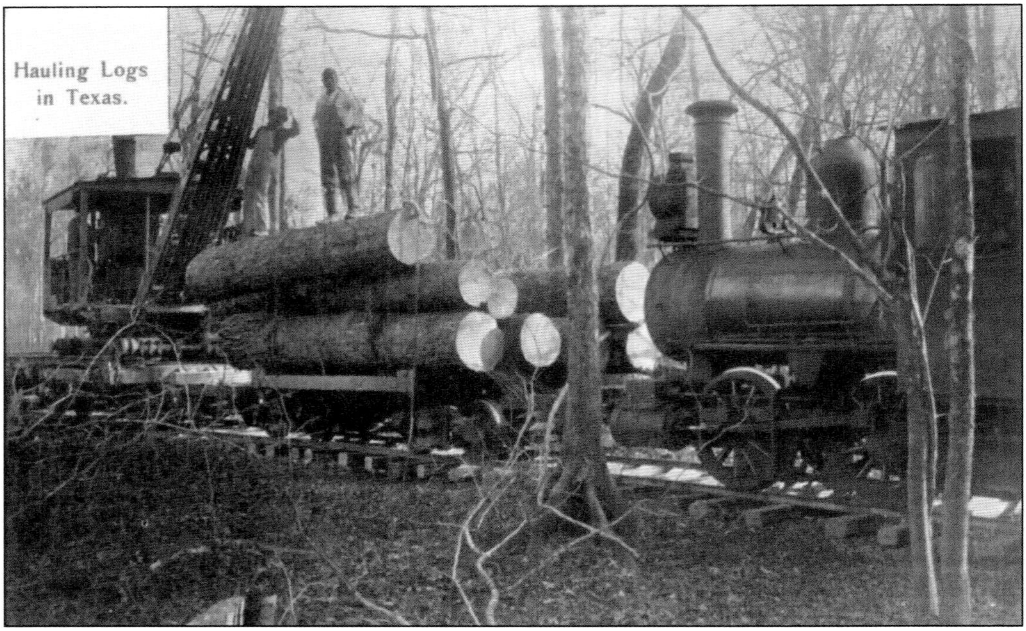

"Hauling Logs in Texas" is the apt title for this souvenir postcard from around 1909. Dayton Engine No. 2 noses up to a log car at a loading front somewhere in the woods north of Dayton. (Courtesy Texas Transportation Archive.)

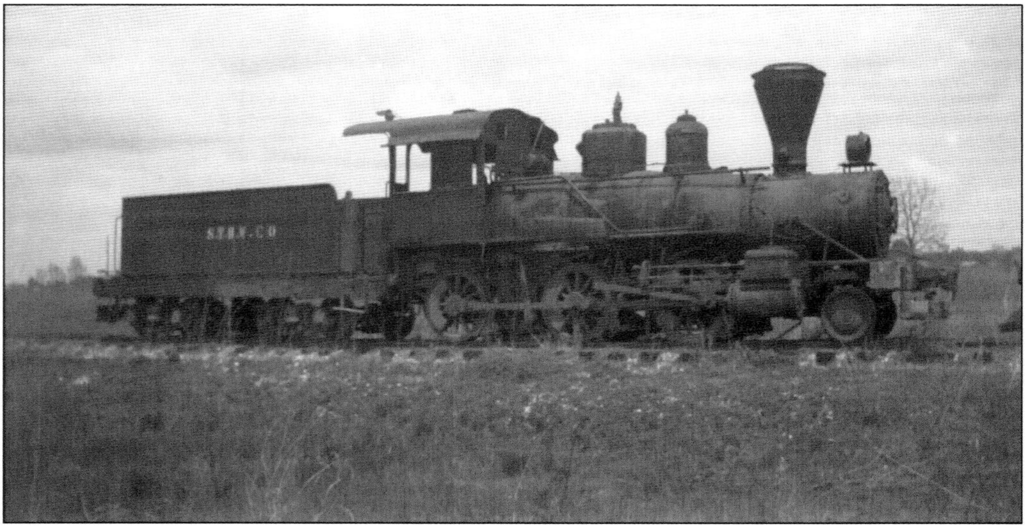

The South Texas Hardwood Company purchased the Dayton Lumber Company in 1920 and used the old Dayton trams to log the mill until operations ceased in 1931. This photograph taken in the mid-1930s shows one of several locomotives that were stored at the former mill site at Dayton before they were finally scrapped. (Courtesy Texas Transportation Archive.)

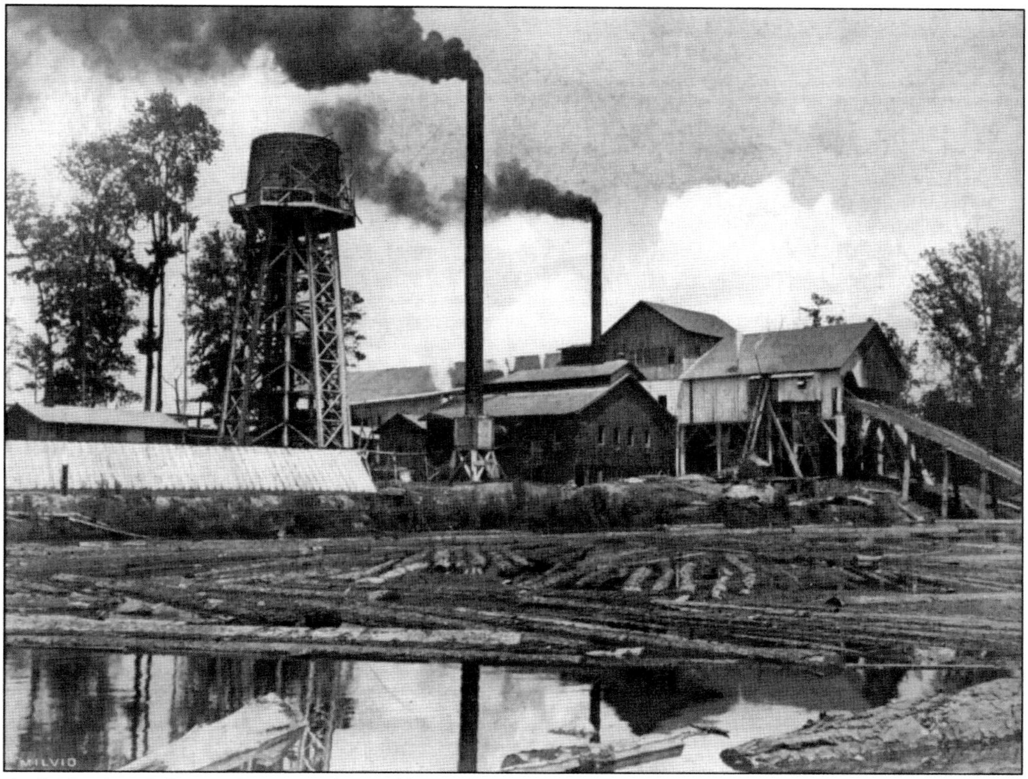

At Milvid in Liberty County, the Miller-Vidor Lumber Company built a 12-mile tram known as the Riverside & Gulf Railroad (R&G) to serve the above mill. The company hoped to build the R&G to Galveston Bay on the south and to Livingston on the north, but the line never extended beyond its original mileage. The fate of the tram is unclear, though there is reason to believe that West Lumber Company, which purchased the Milvid operation in 1915, operated the mill and its tram until it ceased operations at Milvid in 1928. Below, R&G's little 0-6-0 Engine No. 1 is pictured with its crew in 1910. (Both, courtesy Texas Transportation Archive.)

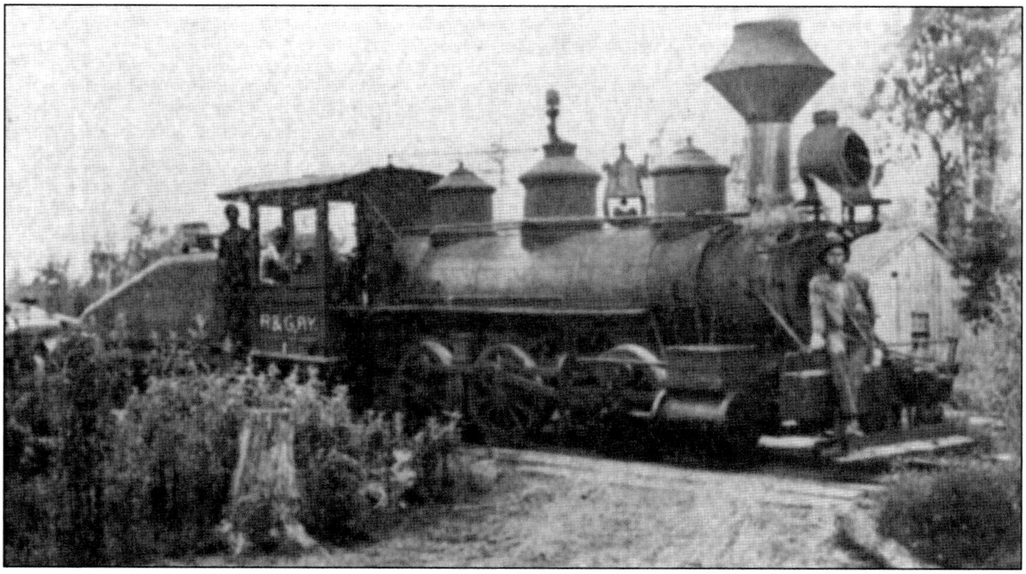

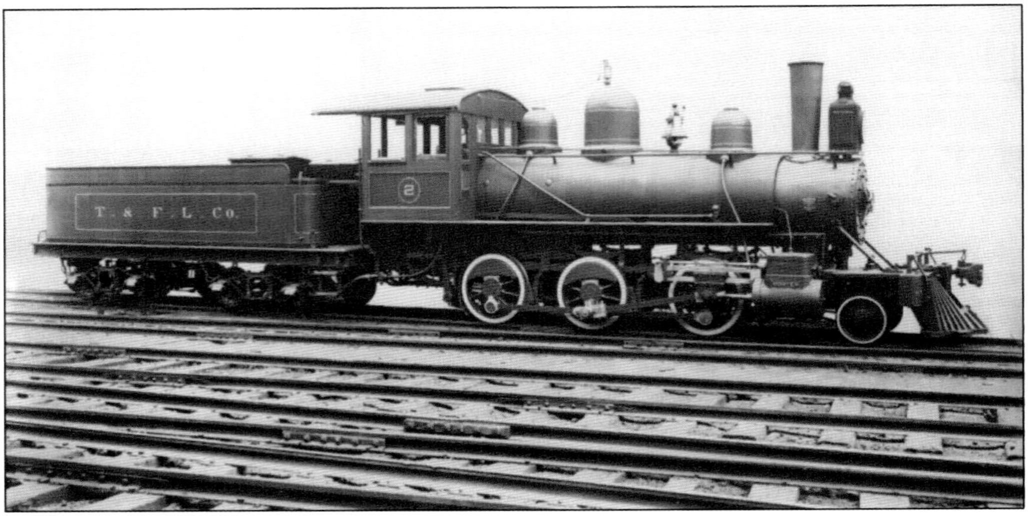

In 1907, the Thompson & Ford Lumber Company built a large mill at Grayburg, two miles south of Sour Lake in Hardin County. Tram mileage was 12 miles initially, extending to 20 miles as production increased in the 1920s. This photograph shows Thompson & Ford Engine No. 2 as it looked just prior to delivery to the company in May 1909. Thompson & Ford ceased operations at Grayburg in 1928. (Courtesy Texas Transportation Archive.)

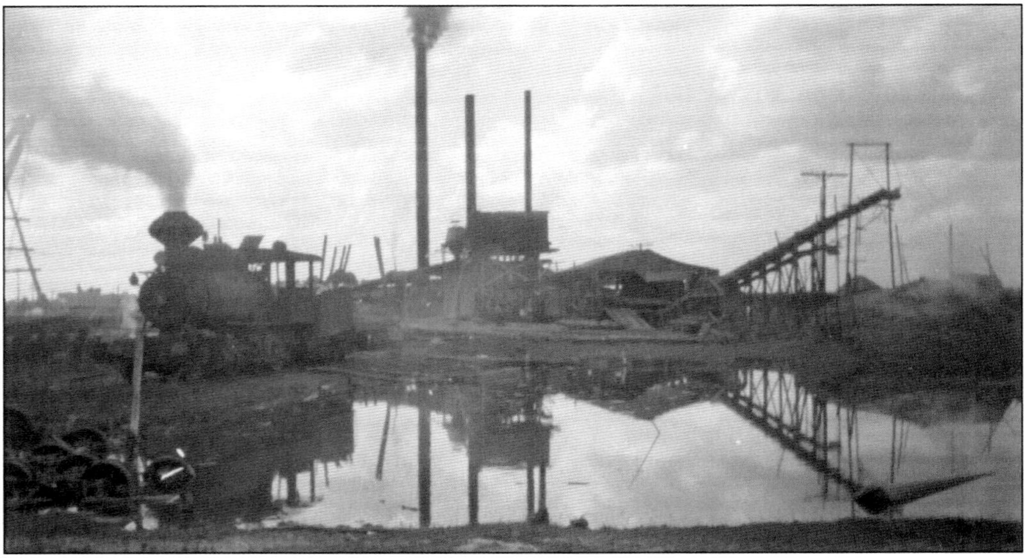

On June 7, 1934, rail photographer H.J. Heaney was at Kountze in Hardin County photographing the mill of Marshall-Sweeney Lumber Company. A Porter engine that carried the number 5 was moving around the millyard. Little is known about the operation, except that the Porter's number matches that of the Nona-Fletcher Lumber Company, which also operated at Kountze in the 1930s and into the 1940s. (Courtesy Richard W. Keeling Collection.)

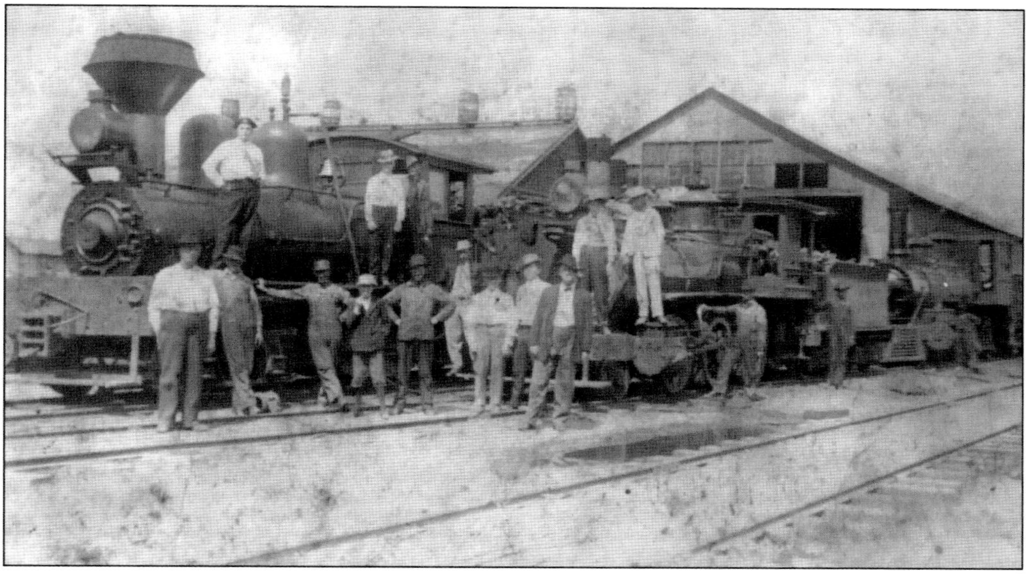

Kirby Lumber Company's Silsbee mill was the longest-running of all the Kirby mills. This view from around the 1910s reveals the variety of motive power used by the company in the early years on the Silsbee trams. (Courtesy Richard W. Keeling Collection.)

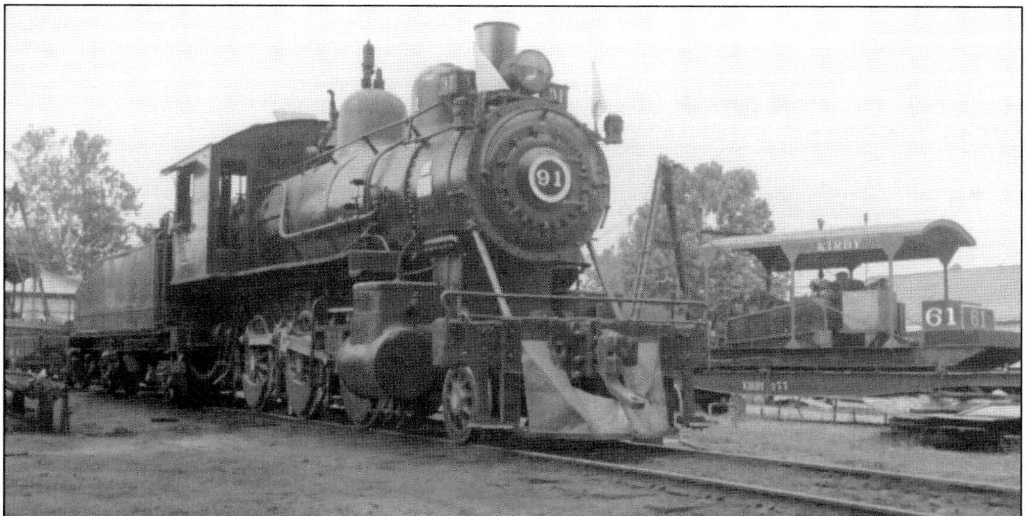

Moving the clock forward to 1951, No. 91 and various loaders—including loader No. 61, visible in the background—used Silsbee as a home base for working trams that branched off the Santa Fe east of town. (Courtesy Texas Transportation Archive.)

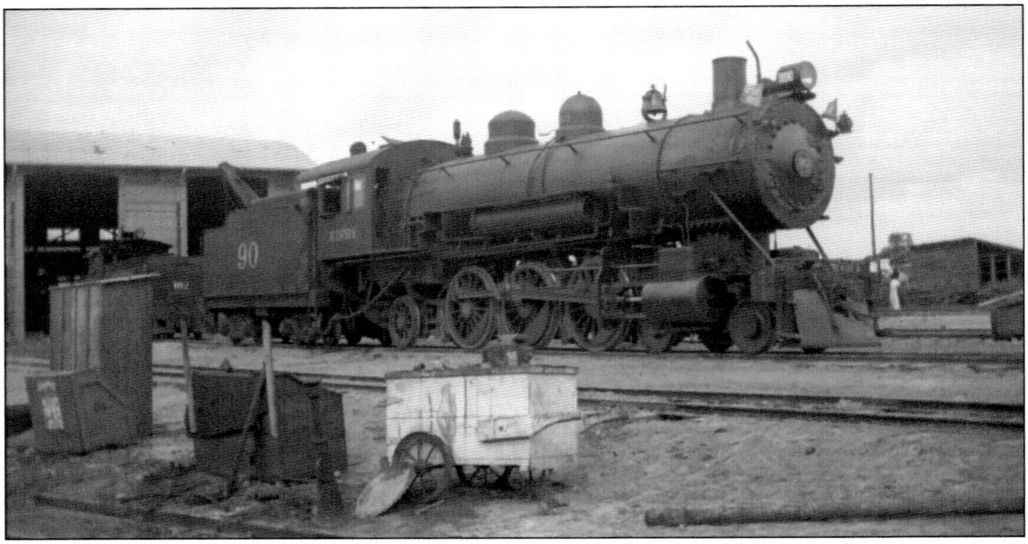

Kirby's most powerful engine was the No. 90, a 1903 Baldwin locomotive that pulled passenger trains on the El Paso & Southwestern before it came to Kirby in 1924. The No. 90 is pictured above on the Silsbee tram in the 1940s. In 1928, a Santa Fe flagman charged with protecting a bridge crew doing major work at Nichols Creek fell asleep and allowed the No. 90 to pass by with no warning as to what lay ahead. Unable to stop, the Kirby trainmen leapt out of the cab, and the No. 90 came to rest upside-down in the creek, as seen below. The Santa Fe rebuilt the engine, and the No. 90 operated for Kirby for many more years before it was finally scrapped in 1950. (Both, courtesy Richard W. Keeling Collection.)

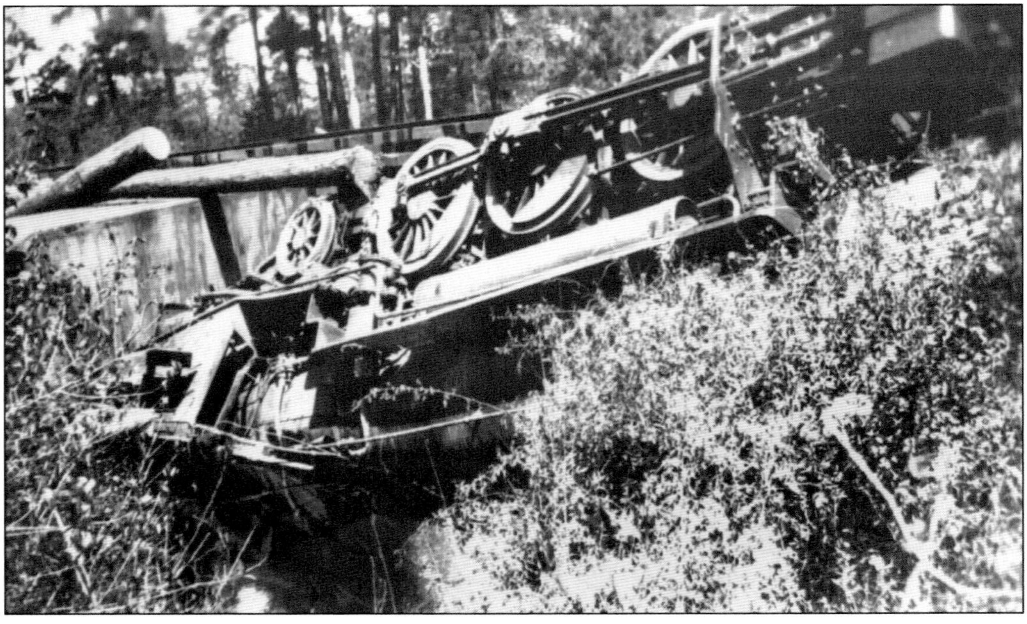

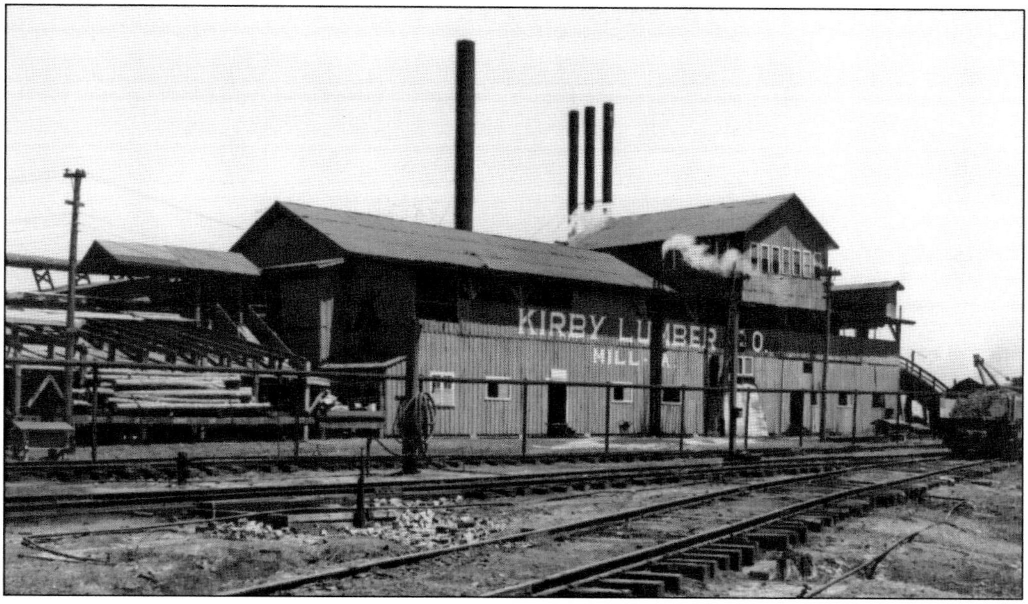

R.A. Myer's mill at Honey Island, pictured above, was purchased by Kirby in 1929, becoming a fairly late addition to the Kirby empire. The mill was logged after 1934 by Camp Seale, which sent several trains daily over the 20-mile tram. Camp Seale closed in 1948, and its residents were transferred to Honey Island. Below, Kirby Lumber Company No. 32 waits outside the machine shop at Honey Island in April 1934. (Above, courtesy Texas Forestry Museum; below, courtesy Texas Transportation Archive.)

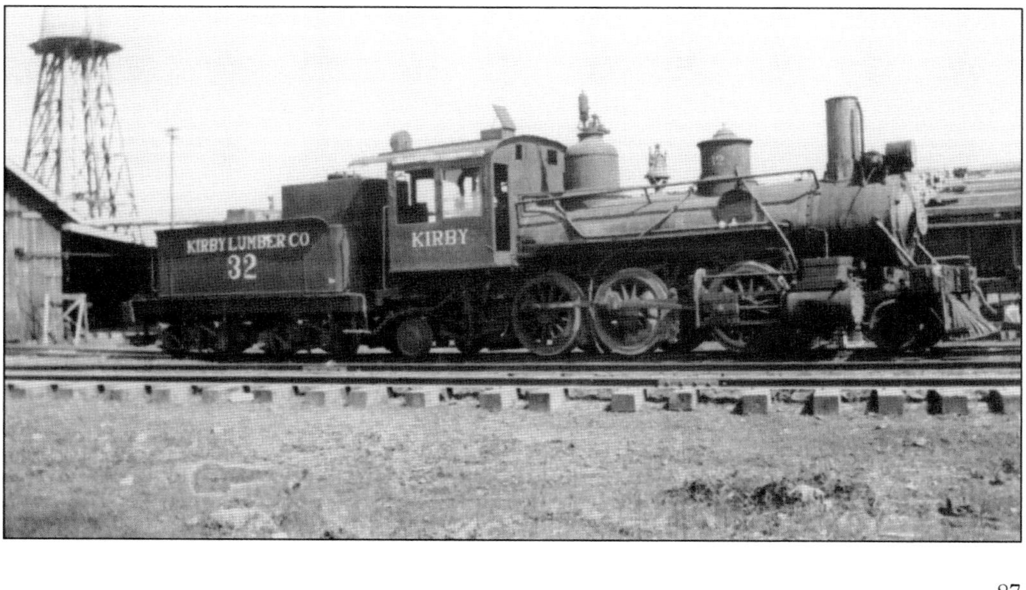

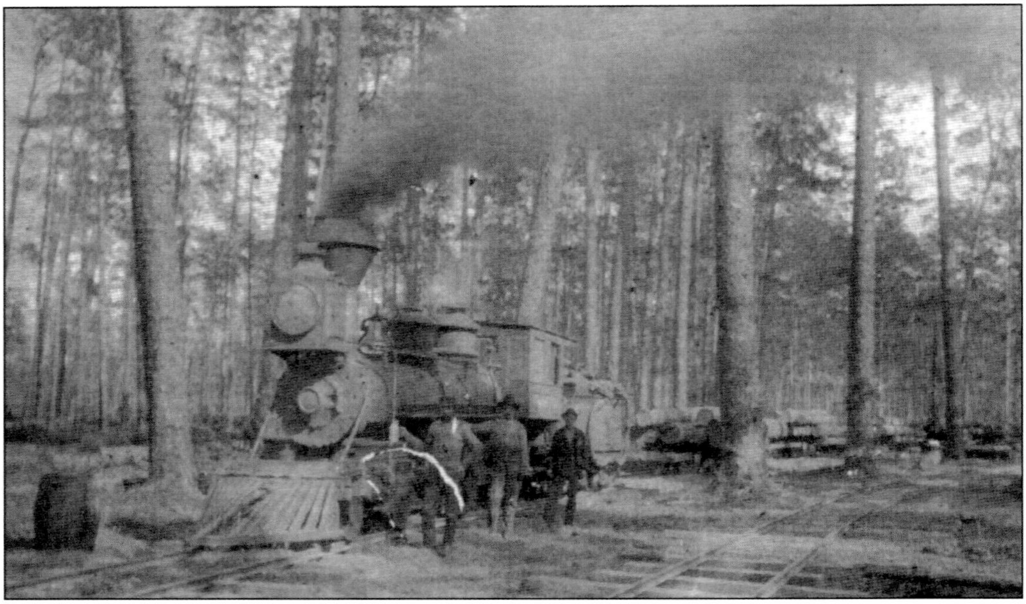

At Village Station on the Texas & New Orleans Railroad in Hardin County, the Texas Tram & Lumber Company had operated a mill since 1883. In 1901, the Kirby Lumber Company purchased the property, which included a 21-mile narrow-gauge tram that Kirby would later widen to standard gauge. The above view captures tram operations shortly after Kirby took over. Below, a Kirby engine is seen in the woods near Village Mills around 1920. The mill remained highly productive, cutting mostly crossties until the late 1920s, when the timber was depleted and Kirby decided to conclude its operations at Village. Sawmilling ceased in 1931, and the mill was dismantled in 1933. (Both, courtesy Jack Langston.)

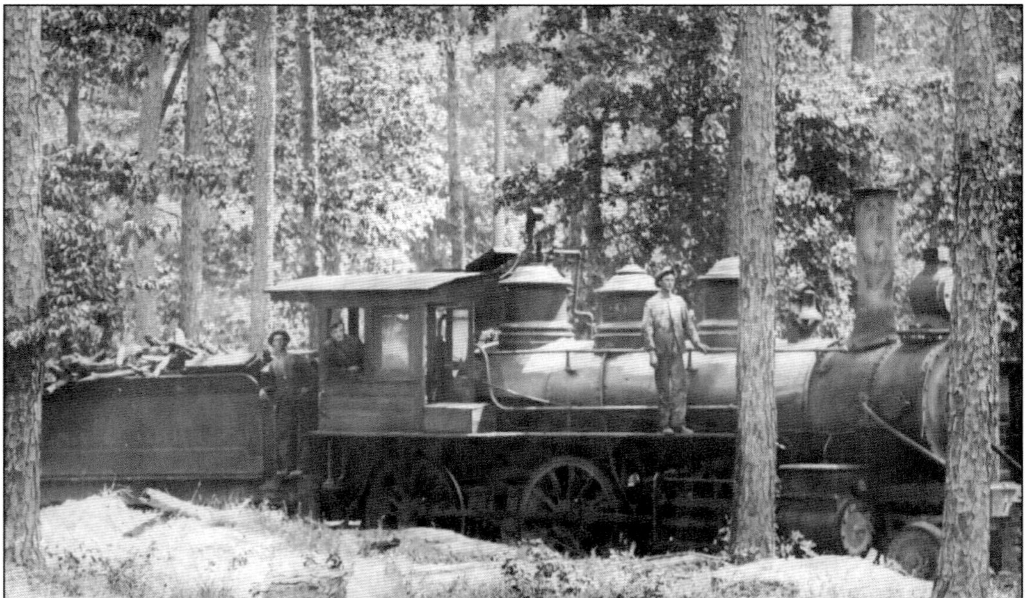

Five

Logging in the Deep South East Counties

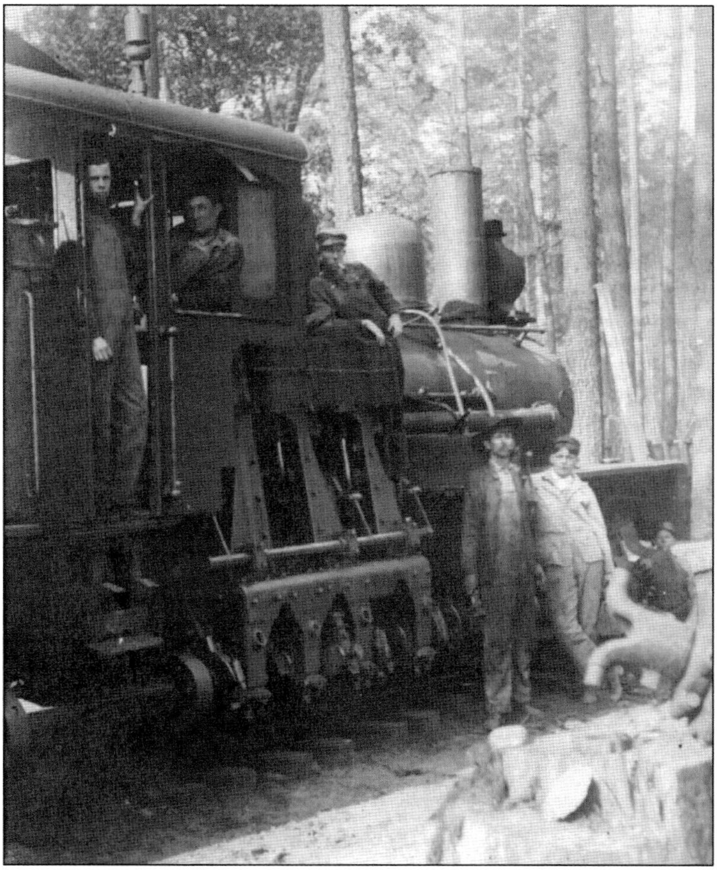

The greatest concentration of lumber companies in Texas was in the southeastern counties between 1902 and the 1950s. The Kirby Lumber Company operated more of those mills than any other single enterprise. Kirby labeled its mills according to the alphabet, from Mill A at Beaumont to Mill W at Voth, all fed by dozens of logging camps that came in and out of existence over its 85-year history. The last Kirby mill closed in 1987, ending one of the most extraordinary and enduring chapters in East Texas lumber history. Here, a Kirby train and woods crews pause along one of the many Kirby trams. (Courtesy Texas Transportation Archive.)

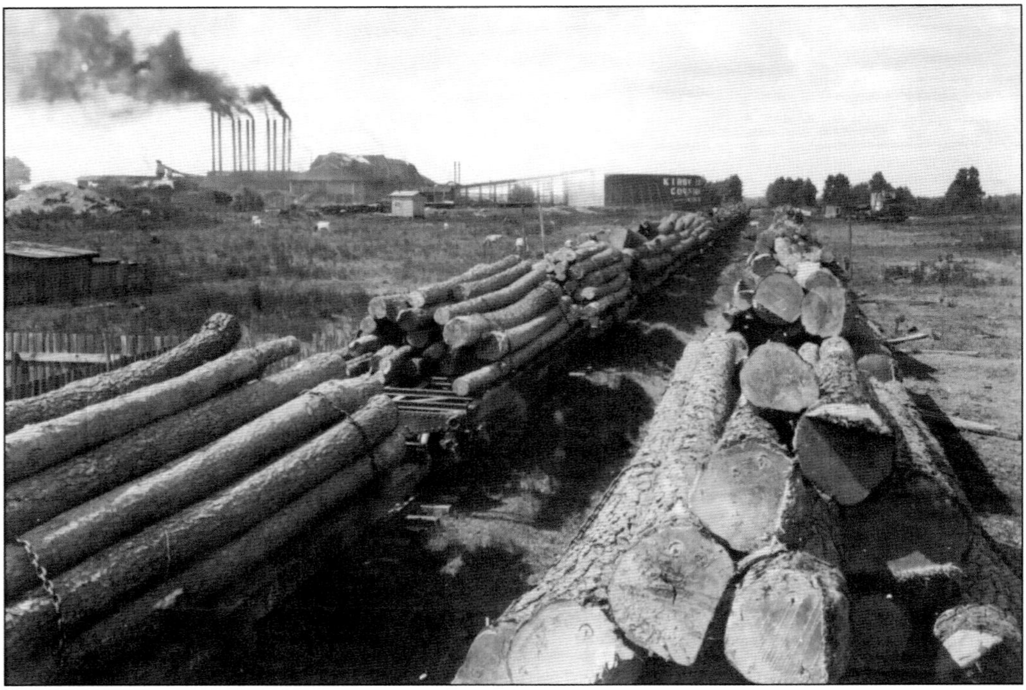

In Jasper County, Kirby Lumber Company's Bessmay mill fired 12 boilers to power its daily 250,000 board-feet capacity. To feed this giant, two log trains loaded to capacity are waiting to be unloaded into the millpond in 1939 (above). A devastating fire destroyed much of the mill complex on May 10, 1950, and Bessmay slowly became another Jasper County ghost town. Below, Kirby Engine No. 93 is steamed and readied in front of the company's large waste sawdust fence in this view from around 1940. (Courtesy Texas Transportation Archive.)

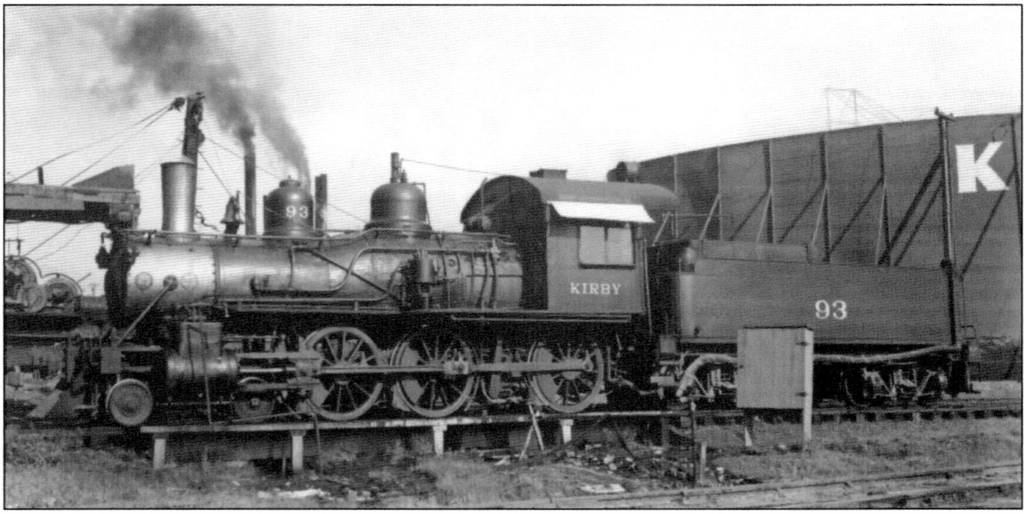

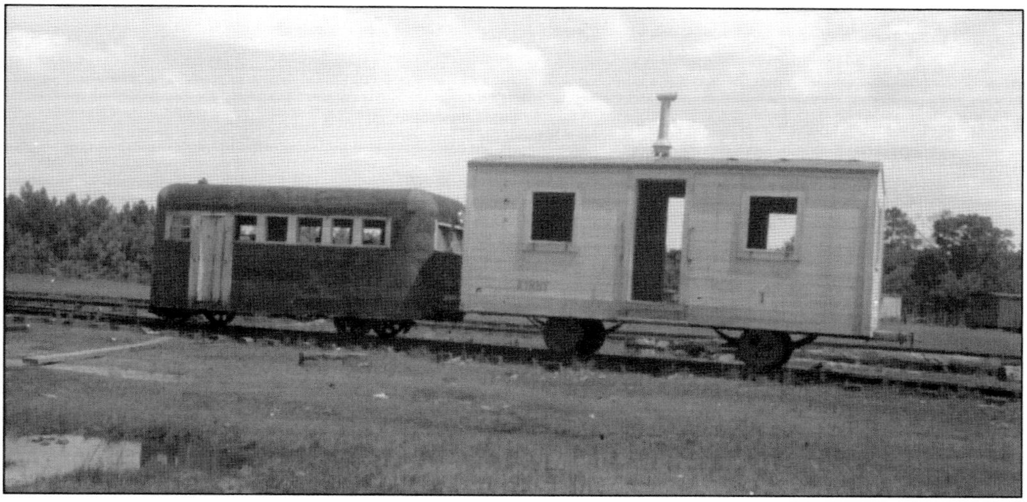

In the 1940s, as transportation of woods crews by steam locomotive became more and more costly, the Kirby Lumber Company devised this cost-cutting method at Evadale. A gasoline-powered passenger bus was fitted with flanged wheels, while a four-wheel trailer was built from scratch in the company's own shops. (Courtesy Richard W. Keeling Collection.)

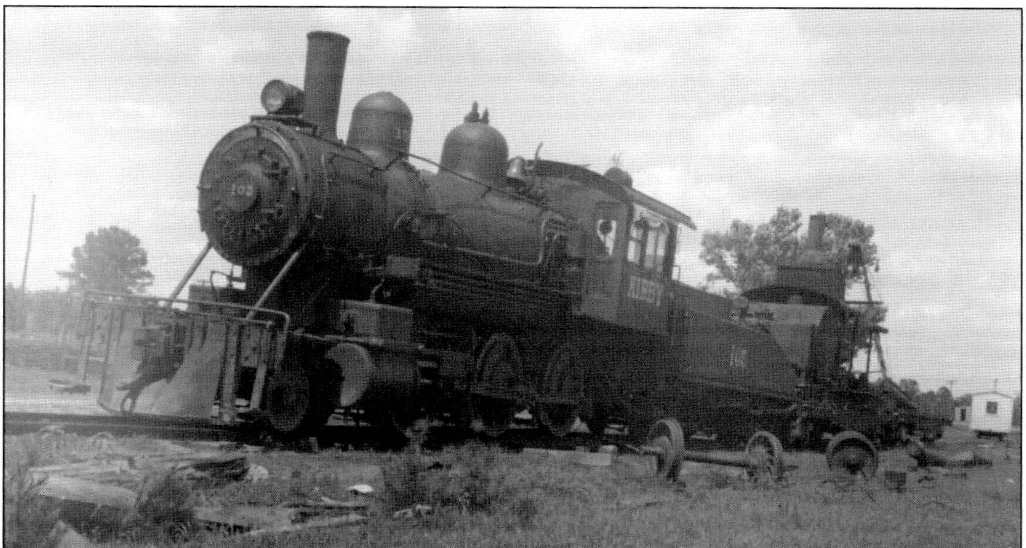

Engine No. 105 worked out of Evadale for many years. This photograph was taken on the same day as that of the Evadale railbus, sometime in the 1940s. The rear of the railbus can be seen in the distance. (Courtesy Texas Transportation Archive.)

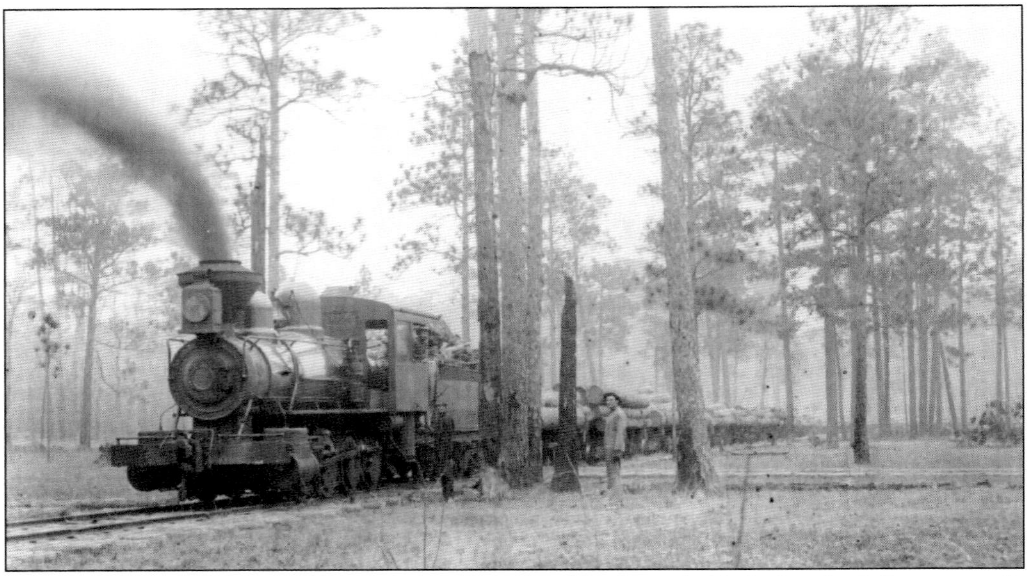

Buna was known as Camp No. 3 and was charged with logging for Kirby Lumber's Bessmay mill. At its peak, it employed 250 workers and operated a tram that, in 1918, had 11 miles in Newton County and 21 miles in Jasper County. Kirby's No. 41 is pictured in the pristine Jasper County woods in December 1903. (Courtesy Richard W. Keeling Collection.)

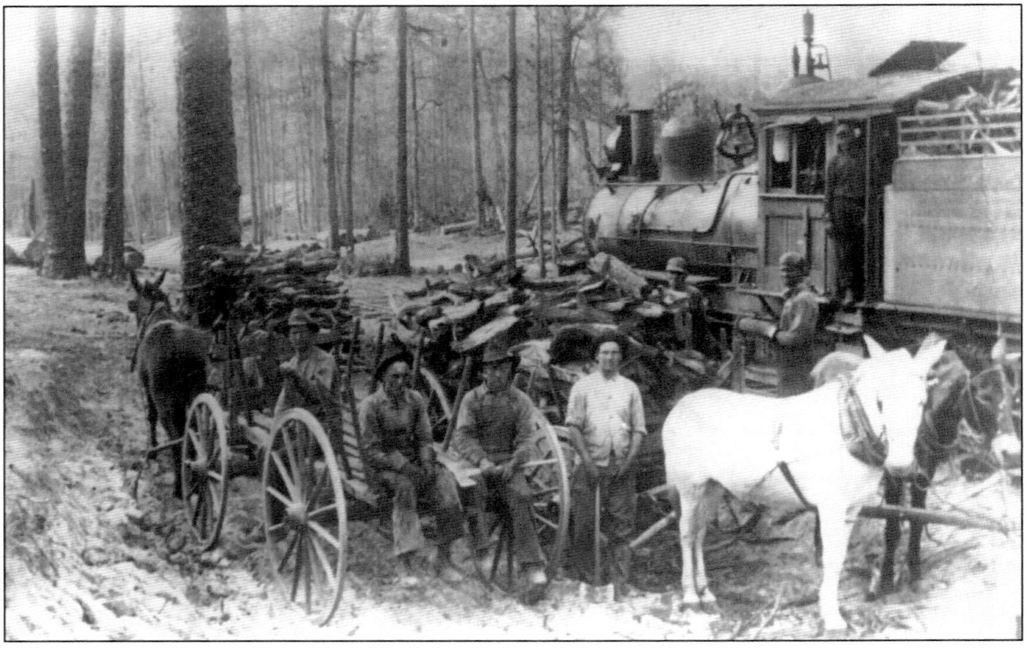

Harrisburg was a community 10 miles north of Jasper on the Gulf, Beaumont & Kansas City Railway. Logging was conducted by Kirby in the area in the 1910s. In this 1911 view, the Kirby train crew refuels the tram locomotive with pine knots that have been gathered and piled alongside the tram. (Courtesy Jasper County Museum.)

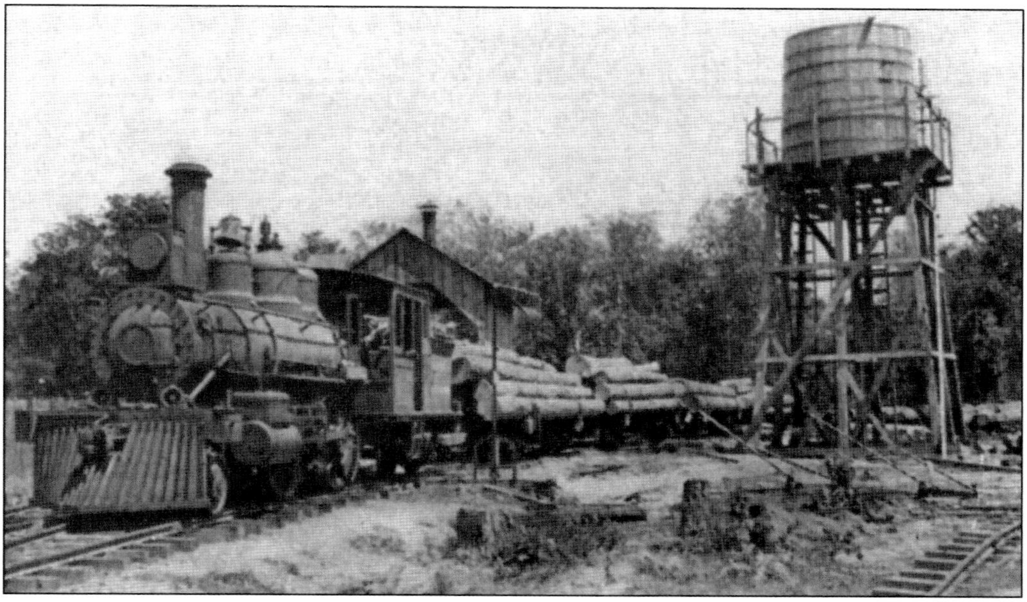

In 1912, Kirby Lumber Company reported to the *American Lumberman* magazine that it was operating 14 miles of trams at Roganville in east-central Jasper County. Images of Roganville are rare, but this view was published in 1902 by *American Lumberman* and gives a good view of the company's water tank, engine shed, and camp locomotive. (Courtesy Texas Transportation Archive.)

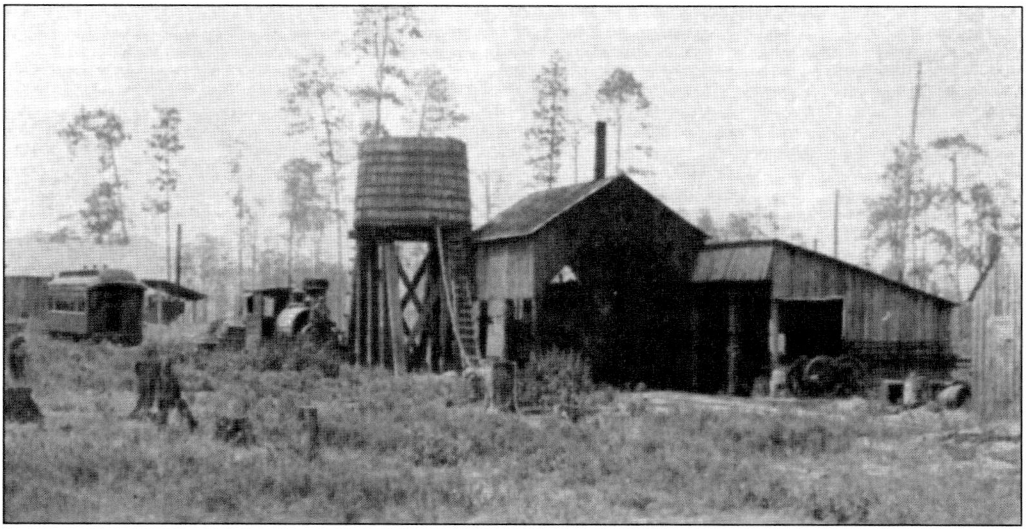

At Kirbyville, the extreme backwoods character of the engine shop area is vividly displayed in this 1902 view published by *American Lumberman*. In 1912, the same publication noted that Kirbyville was operating 20 miles of tram line. (Courtesy Texas Transportation Archive.)

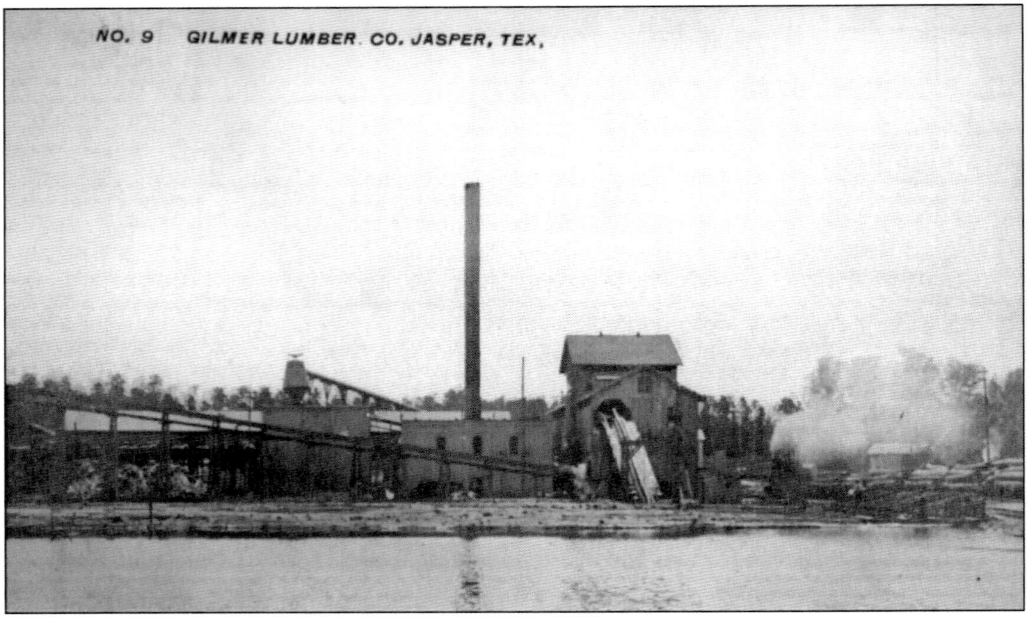

Alexander Gilmer's mill at Remlig (Gilmer spelled backwards) was located in Jasper County so close to where Sabine, Jasper, and Newton intersect that its mill whistle was heard in all three counties. In this 1907 view, a great deal of steam and smoke is put up by the log train that has just arrived at the millpond. The Remlig mill operated until 1926. (Courtesy Texas Transportation Archive.)

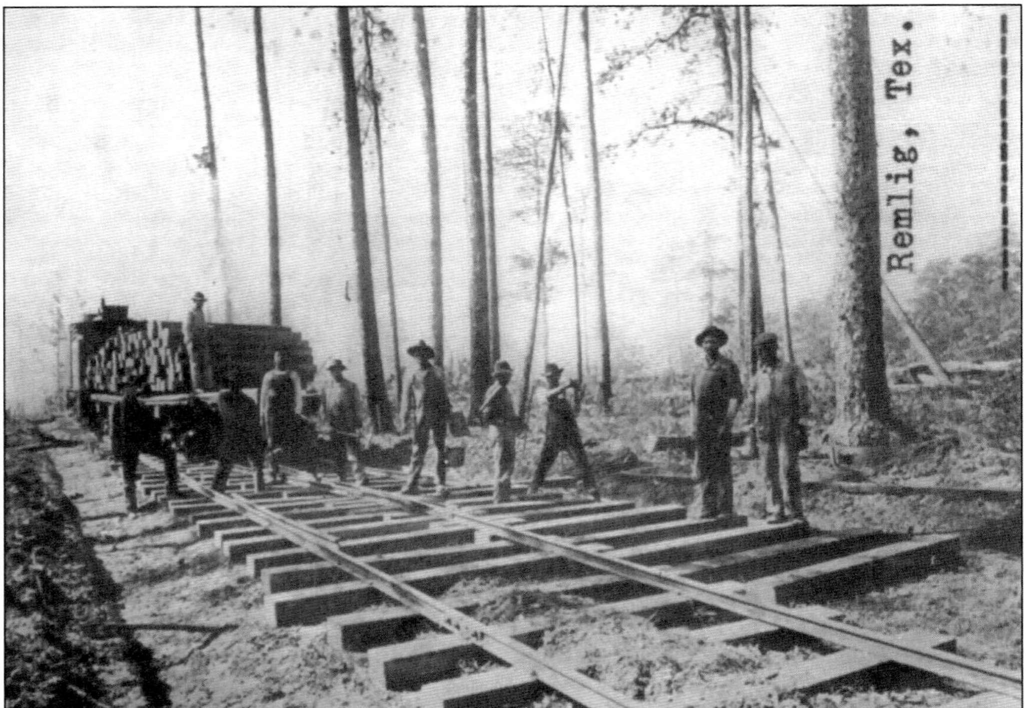

In the woods near Remlig, the "steel gang" for the Alexander Gilmer Lumber Company gathers on the main tram to send a new spur into uncut timber. This photograph was taken around 1907. (Courtesy Texas Transportation Archive.)

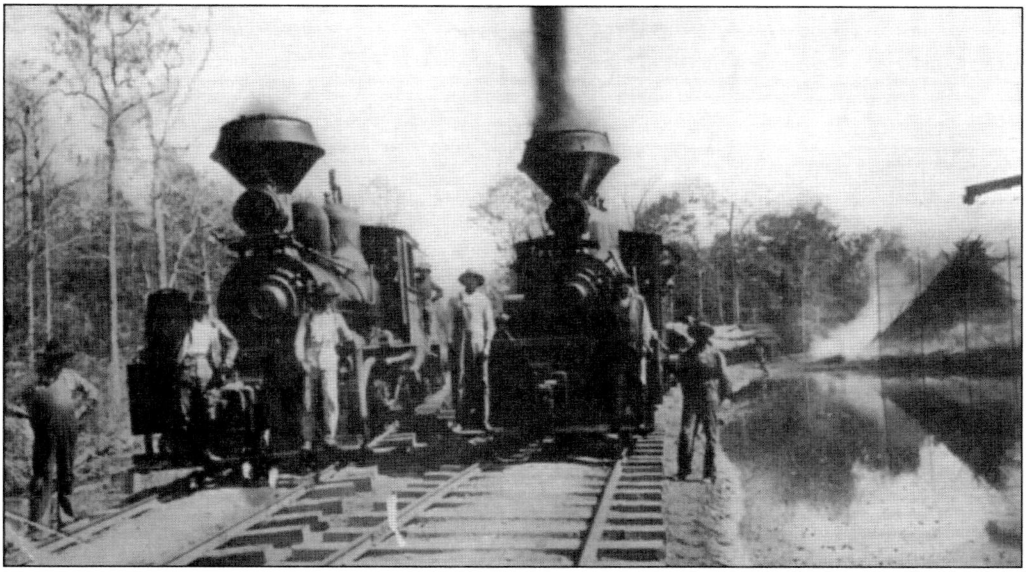

Alexander Gilmer Lumber Company's twin Shay locomotives are featured in a company portrait at the Remlig millpond around 1907. Both Shays were purchased new—the No. 1 in May 1905 and the No. 2 in June 1906. (Courtesy Texas Transportation Archive.)

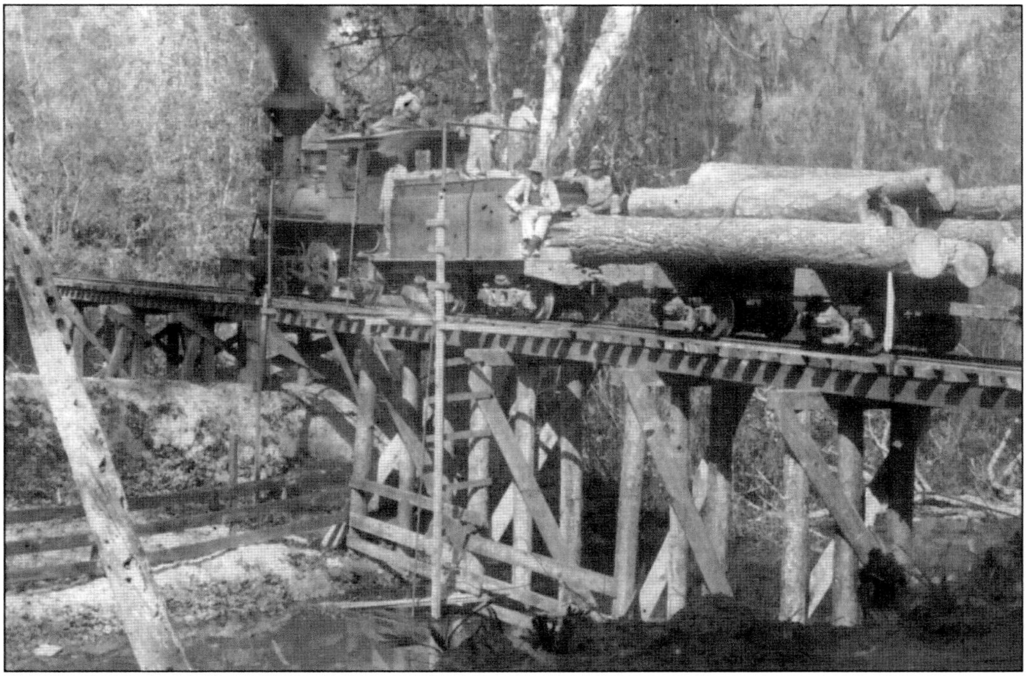

One of Gilmer Lumber Company's rod engines pauses over a creek in this photograph taken around 1910. Tram crews had to be proficient at building bridges strong enough to support the weight of a fully loaded log train. Many accidents were caused by heavy trains crossing weakened or poorly constructed bridges. (Courtesy Jasper County Museum.)

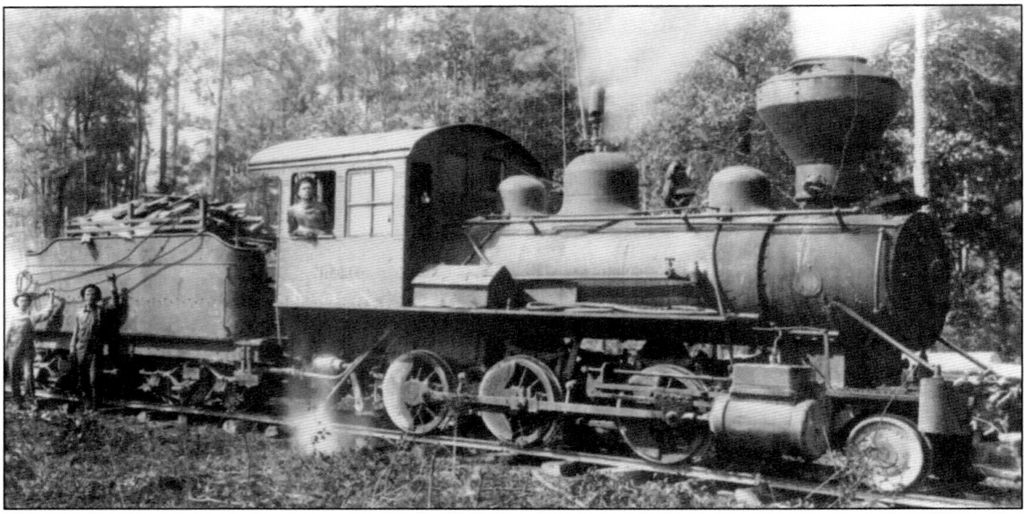

Grogan Manufacturing's No. 5, officially and affectionately known as "Mildred," was built by Vulcan in November 1915. Mildred operated over a tram that varied between seven and 15 miles long, providing good service to the company until the engine was scrapped around 1933. (Courtesy Texas Transportation Archive.)

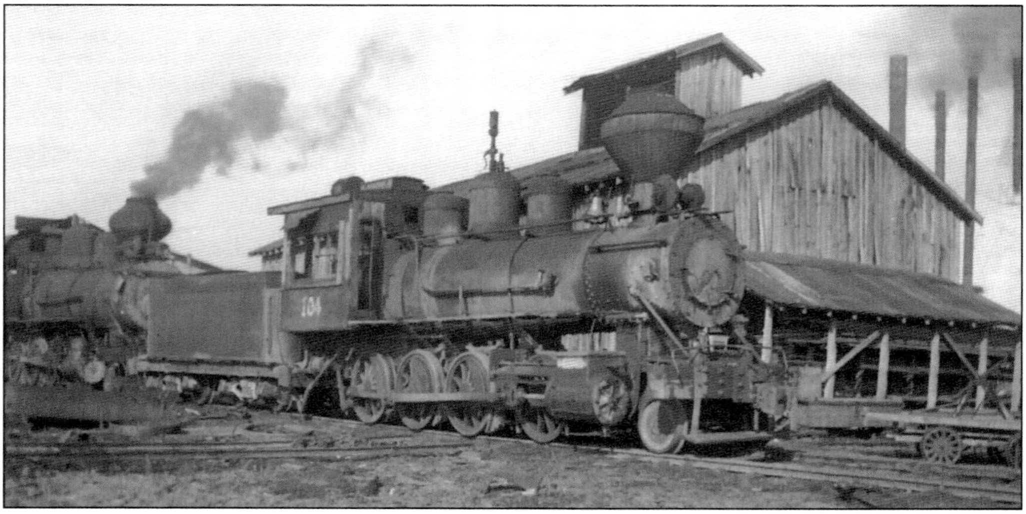

In later years, members of the Grogan family formed Grogan-Cochran at Magnolia on the International–Great Northern Railroad in Montgomery County. The mill operated at a capacity of 50,000 board feet, logged by a 15-mile tramline using several locomotives. In this photograph, Locomotive No. 110 steams up behind No. 104 at the Magnolia mill on December 29, 1938. Railroad logging at Magnolia probably continued into the 1940s. (Courtesy Texas Transportation Archive.)

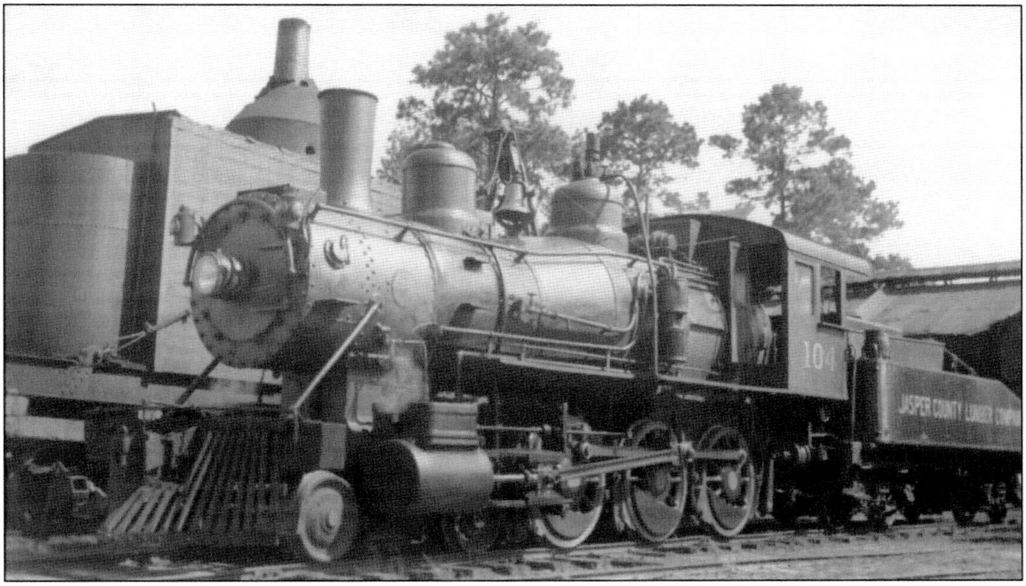

Another of Alexander Gilmer's mills was the Jasper County Lumber Company at Jasper, which began operations in 1909. It was sold to Frost Lumber Industries of Texas in 1923 and then to J.H. Kurth in 1946, who changed the name to Kurth Lumber Company. This photograph shows No. 104 at Jasper around 1940, when the mill was under Frost ownership. (Courtesy Texas Transportation Archive.)

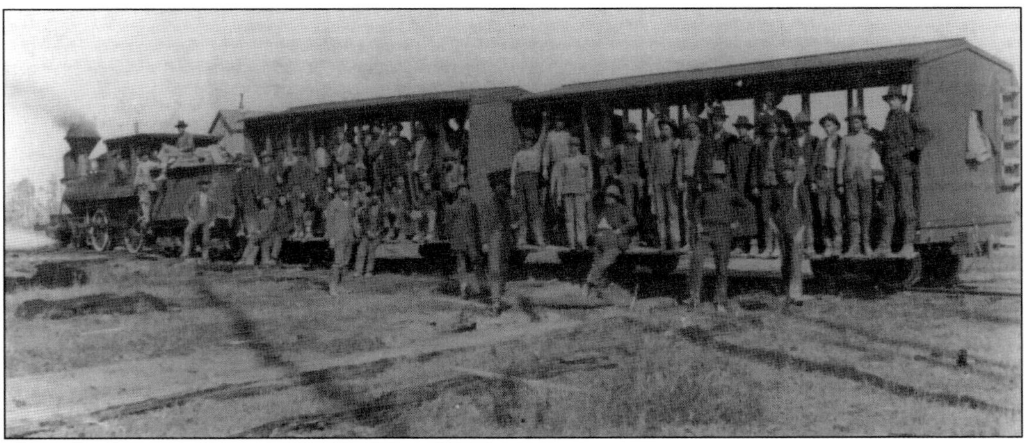

These tram cars were designed to move workers to and from the woods each day. Kirbyville historian D.T. Kent identifies this as the "Trotti tram near Salem," which would make this T.J. Trotti's Newton County Tram Company, which operated a 10-mile tram in the 1890s near Old Salem. Trotti sold the tram to the Kirby Lumber Company in 1901. (Courtesy Newton County Historical Center and Museum.)

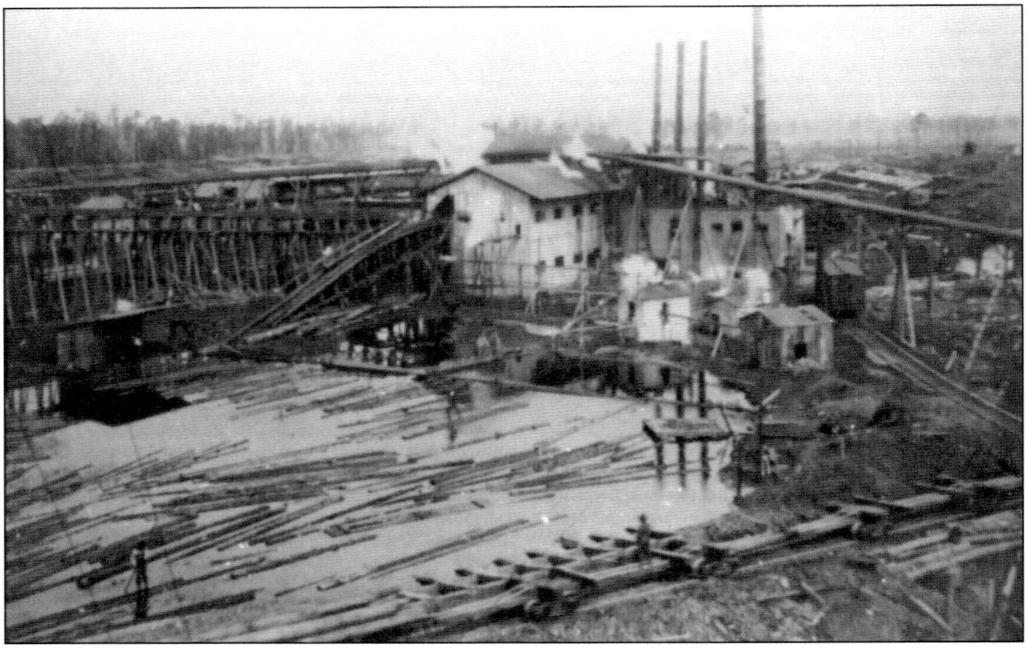

Kirby Lumber Company's big Call mill complex was located so far east in Newton County that its mill building actually stood in Jasper County. Kirby purchased the property from the Cow Creek Tram in 1901 and began an expansion program until Call was producing 175,000 board feet per day. This undated photograph conveys the sheer size and activity of Call at its peak. (Courtesy Kirbyville Public Library.)

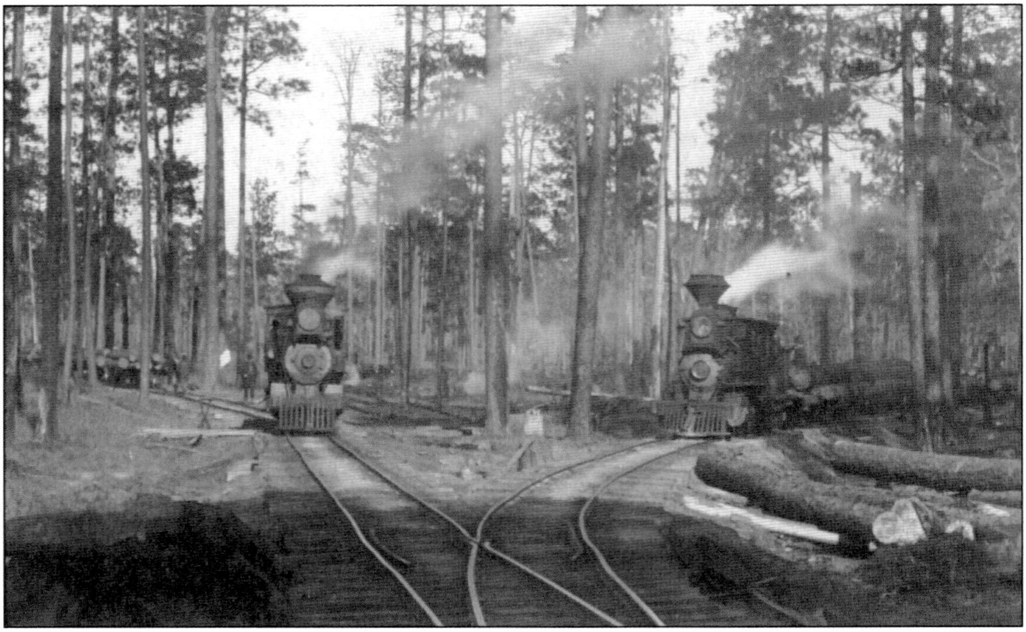

Kirby increased the old Cow Creek tram's original eight miles to 30 miles in Call's peak years. In this photograph taken around 1902, two log trains meet at a tram switch. (Courtesy Texas Transportation Archive.)

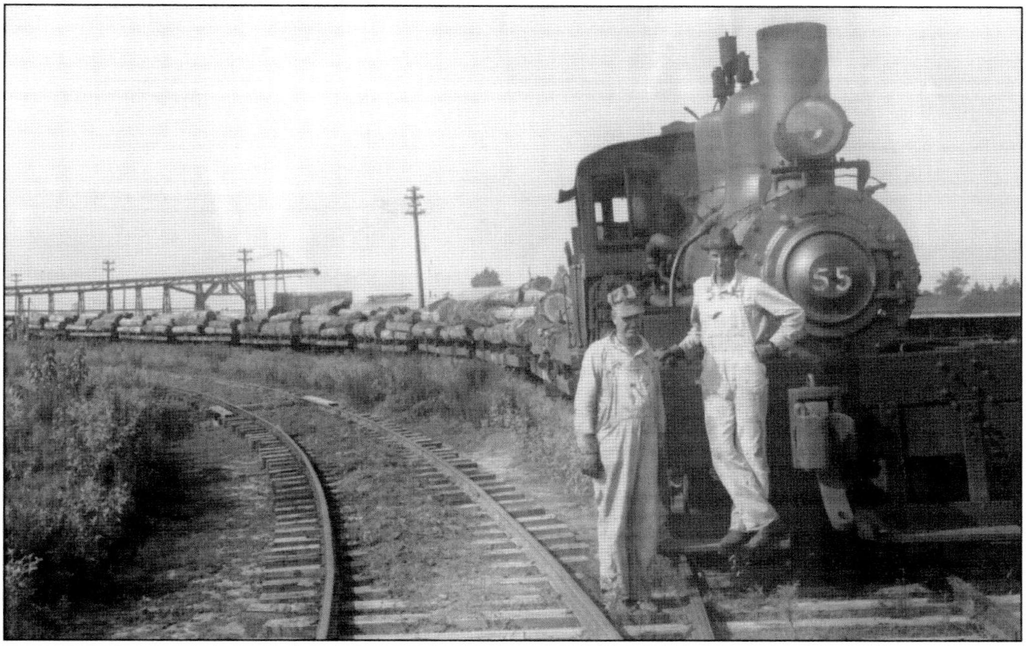

The Call log train enters the millyard on August 30, 1939. In the late 1930s, Kirby operated a well-built tram that extended east and then northeast of the mill for about 12 miles. (Courtesy Texas Forestry Museum.)

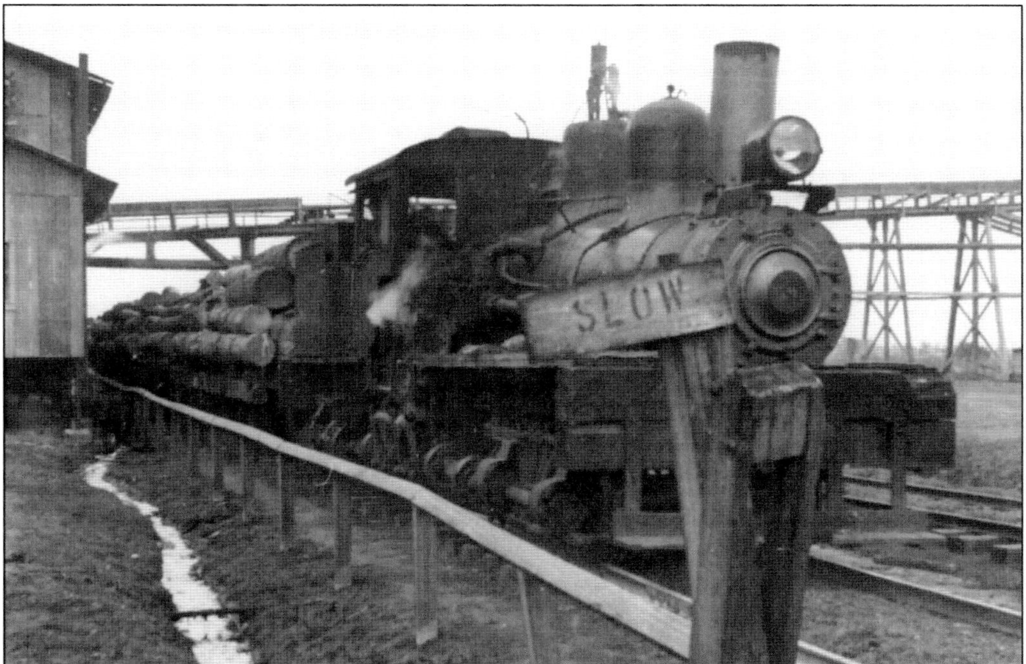

A simple wooden sign warns Kirby train crews to move with caution as they make their way around the Call millpond. Kirby operated its Call mill for a few more years until 1953, when the decision was made to close the Call mill and center all mill operations at Silsbee. (Courtesy Kirbyville Public Library.)

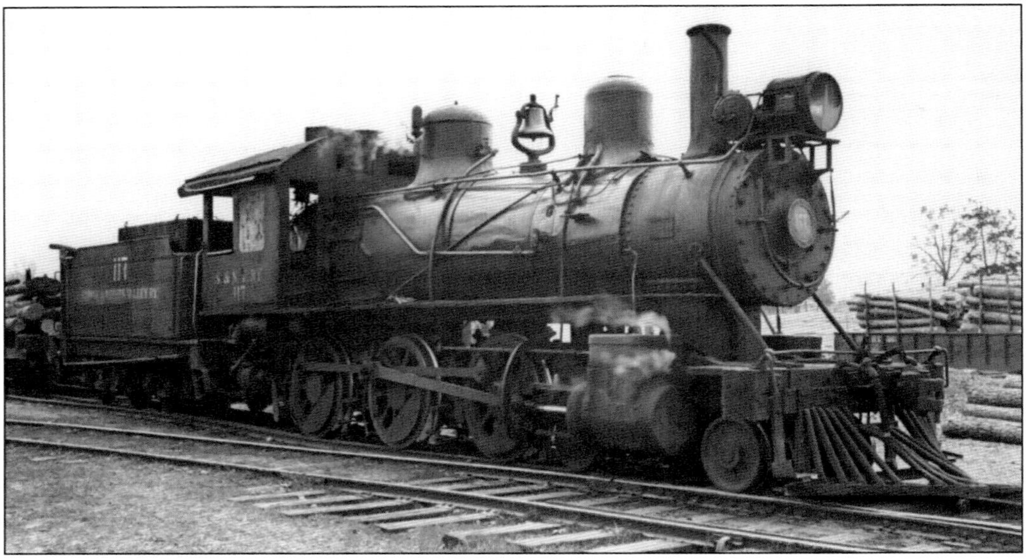

In 1919, Peavy-Moore Lumber Company purchased the mill and railroad properties of the Sabine Tram Company at Deweyville in Newton County. The tram was refurbished and extended to a new connection with the Orange & Northwestern at Gist. It was then chartered as the Sabine & Neches Valley Railway (S&NV) on November 21, 1921. On December 31, the new lumber company officially purchased the railroad, and log train movements were from then on made over the Sabine & Neches Valley. The above photograph taken in March 1941 shows one of the workhorses of the new S&NV, the No. 117, which was purchased second-hand in March 1923. Below, a sea of logs and forest destruction is found on the S&NV around 1940. (Both, courtesy Texas Transportation Archive.)

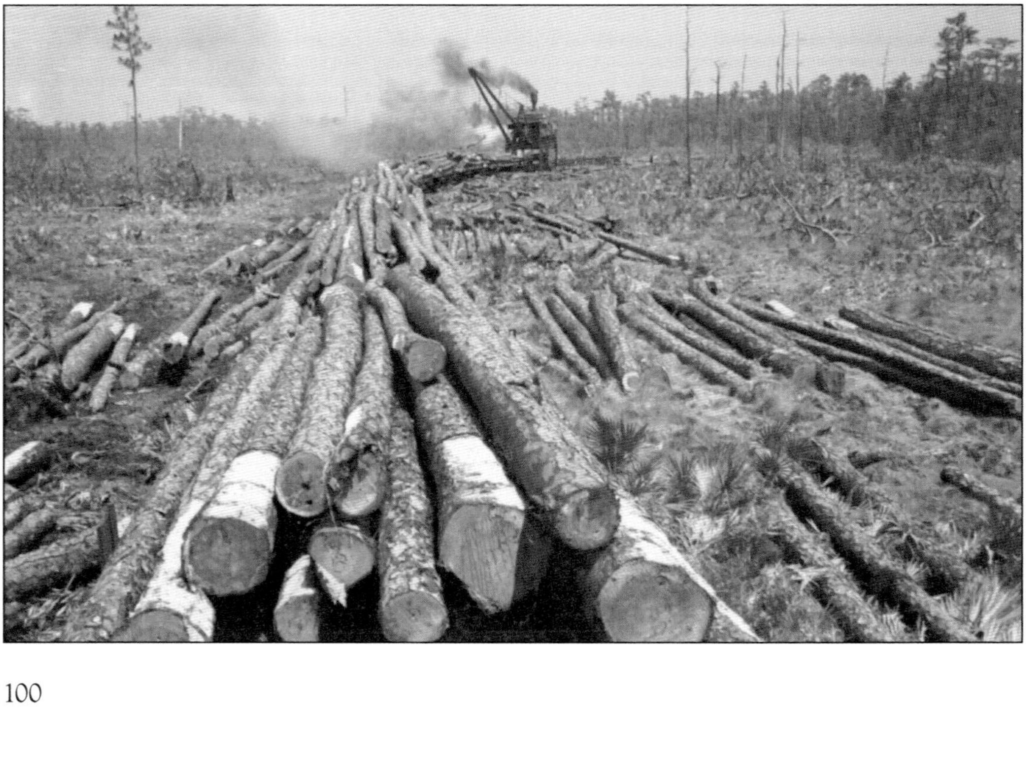

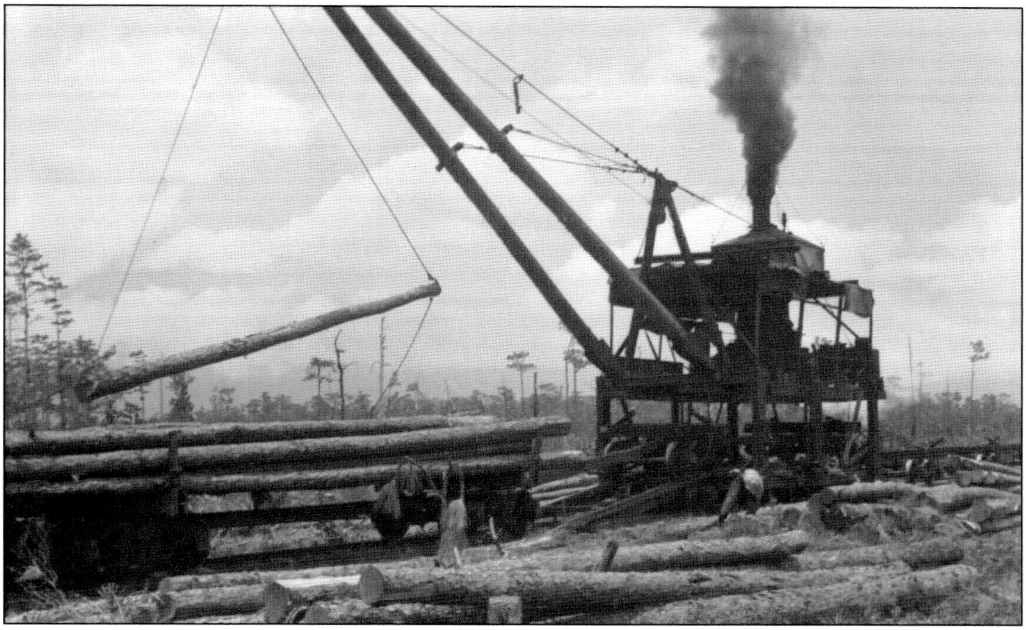

The Peavy-Moore log loader works at a front somewhere in Newton County around 1940. Peavy-Moore operated a logging camp at Camptown, about four miles west of Deweyville, and this may be a photograph of logging in that area. (Courtesy Richard W. Keeling Collection.)

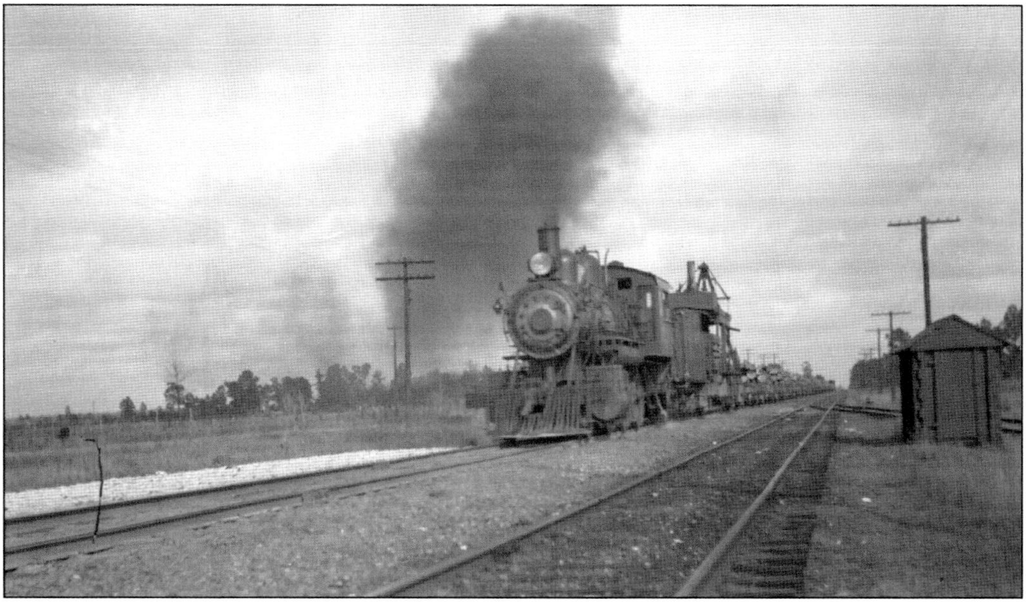

Sabine & Neches Valley No. 122 moves a Peavy-Moore train over the Kansas City Southern Railway (KCS) near Ruliff around 1940. Peavey-Moore built trams off the KCS mainline east of Ruliff and arranged for the trackage rights that enabled the movement of trains directly from the cutting areas to the mill. The only stipulation was that all trains be equipped with automatic couplers and air brakes. (Courtesy Richard W. Keeling Collection.)

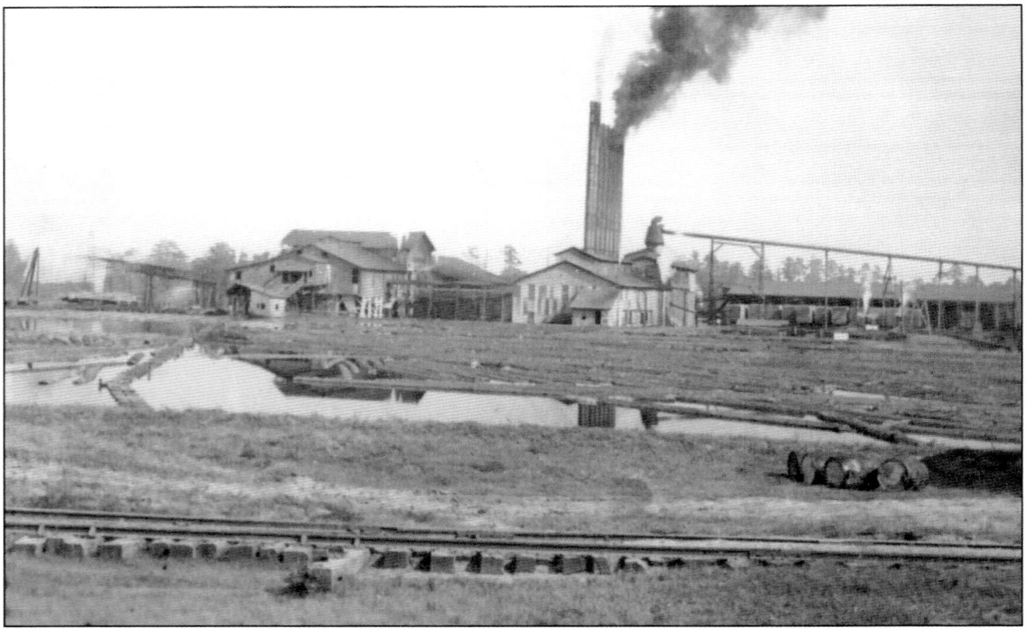

In 1917, Lutcher-Moore granted brothers R.W. and T.P. Wier the rights to harvest timber from 90,000 acres that the company held in Newton County. The Wier Long Leaf Lumber Company was formed and, throughout 1917, erected mill buildings, established the new mill town of Wiergate, and constructed the 15-mile short-line Gulf & Northern to connect Wiergate with the Orange & Northwestern Railway at Newton. By the time logging operations commenced at the end of 1918, the Wiers operated the largest mill west of the Mississippi River, above. Wier's railroads penetrated a park-like environment, below, which was a visual reminder of the industry's early days in the old-growth forests. (Above, courtesy Texas Transportation Archive; below, courtesy Richard W. Keeling Collection.)

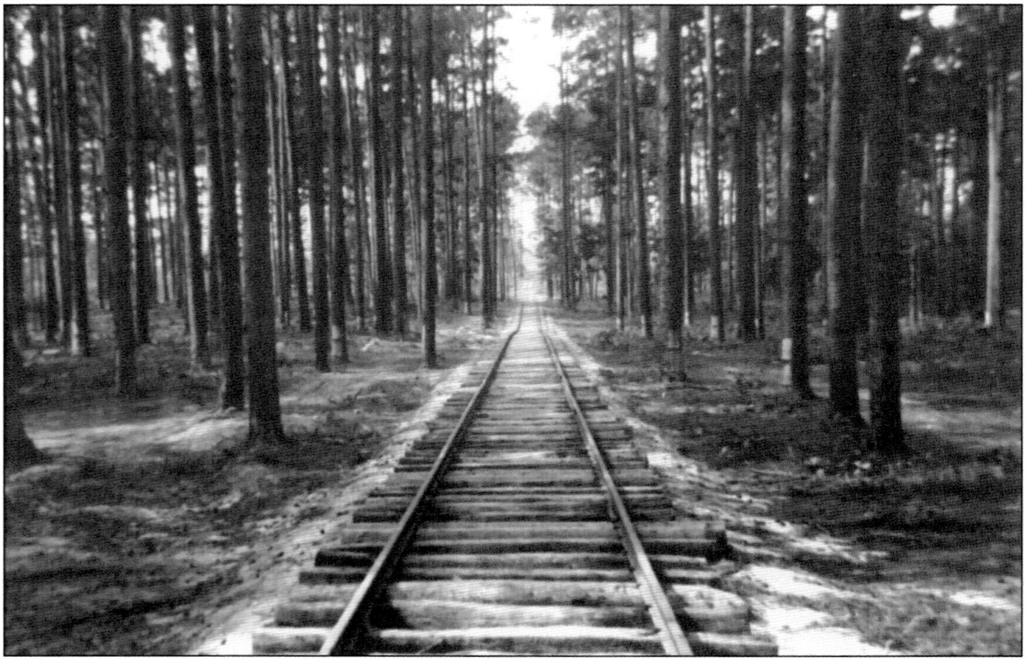

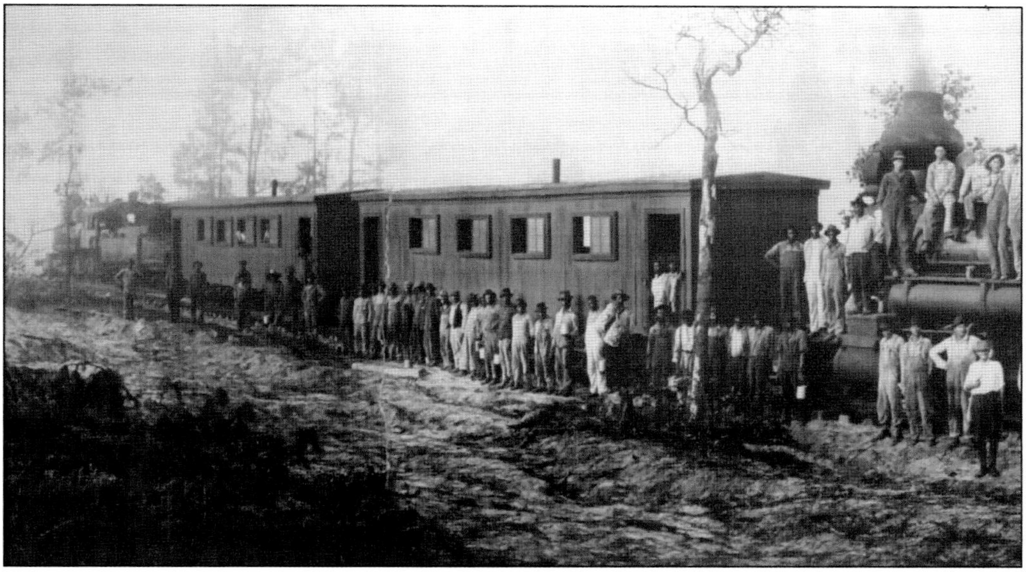

The Wier Long Leaf woods crew pose alongside two camp cars used for transporting workers to and from the cutting and loading areas. Many Wier loggers lived at Wiergate and were transported to and from the work areas each day. Engine No. 6 is on duty at the head end. (Courtesy Newton County Museum.)

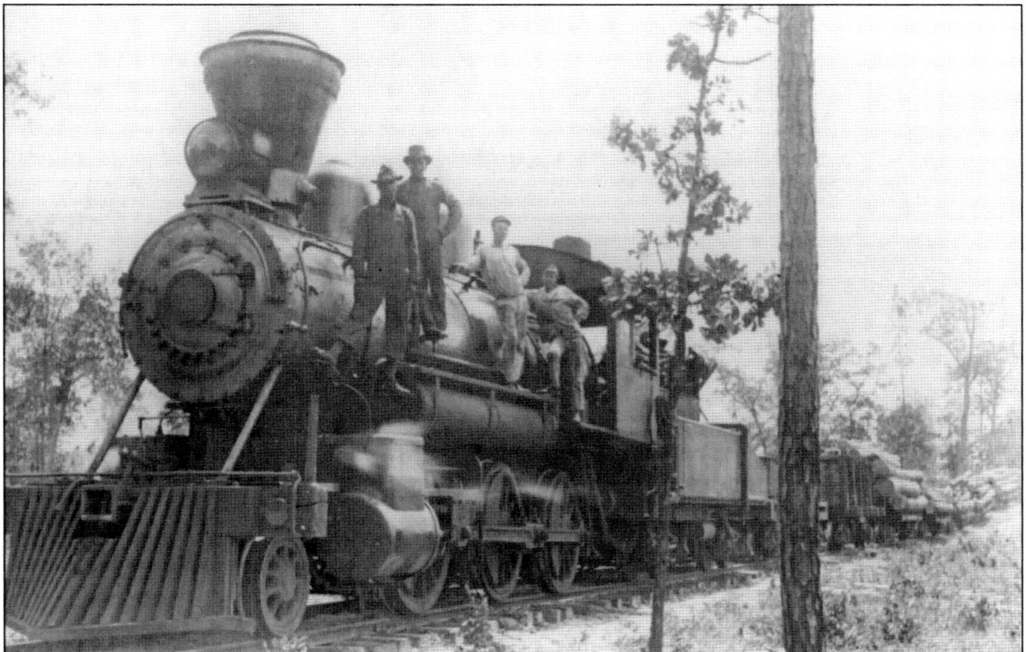

Engine No. 6 heads up a full log train along either the Wier tram or Wier's Gulf & Northern Railroad. The No. 6 was used extensively in logging work throughout the life of the company. (Courtesy Newton County Museum.)

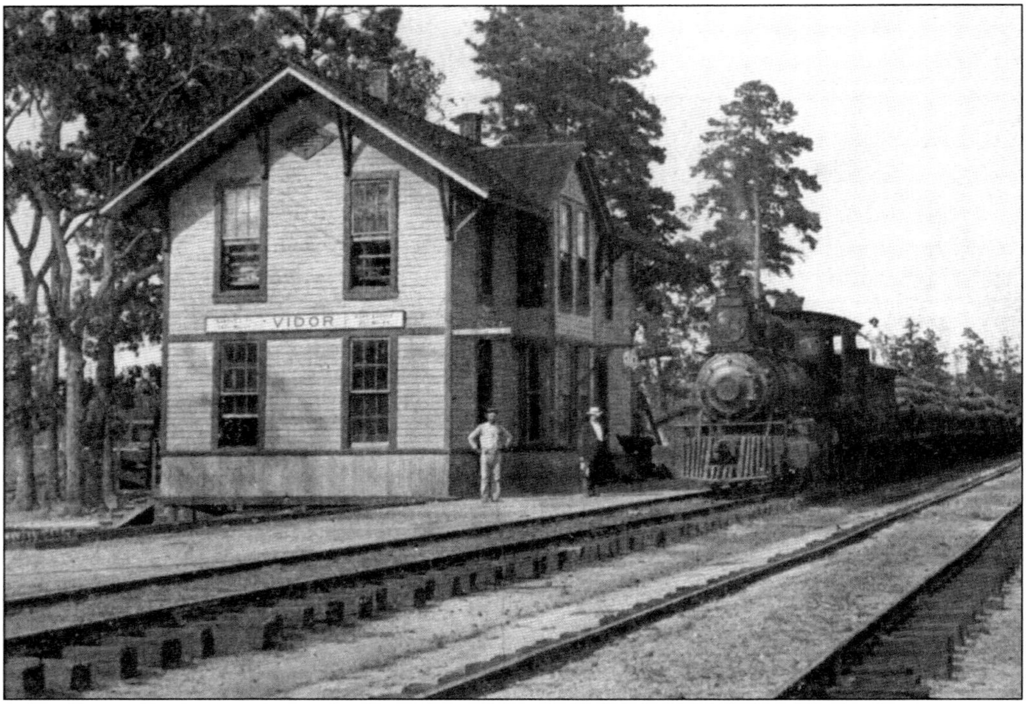

In 1902, the Miller-Vidor Lumber Company purchased the Beaumont Sawmill Company at the port city of Beaumont. Logs were generated by camps in the vicinity of Vidor in Orange County. A 17-mile tram known as the Galveston Beaumont & Northeastern moved logs to both the Neches River and directly to the mill by trackage rights over the Kansas City Southern Railway. In the photograph above, one of Miller-Vidor's log trains passes the KCS depot at Vidor on its way to Beaumont in the summer of 1910. Tiny Porter-built No. 102 of the Galveston Beaumont & Northeastern is pictured below in 1910, taking on water at Vidor.

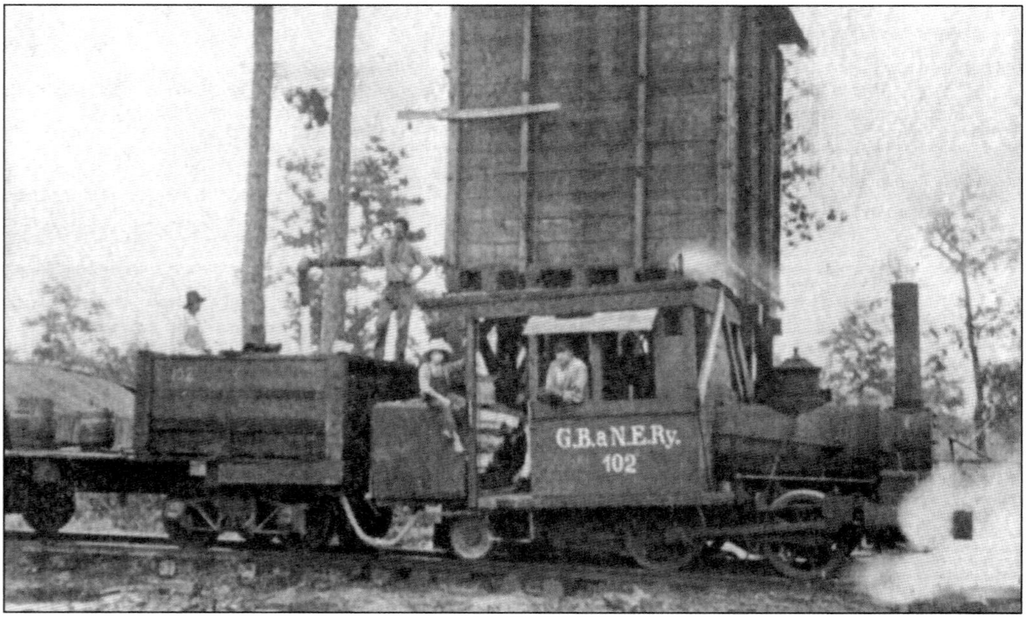

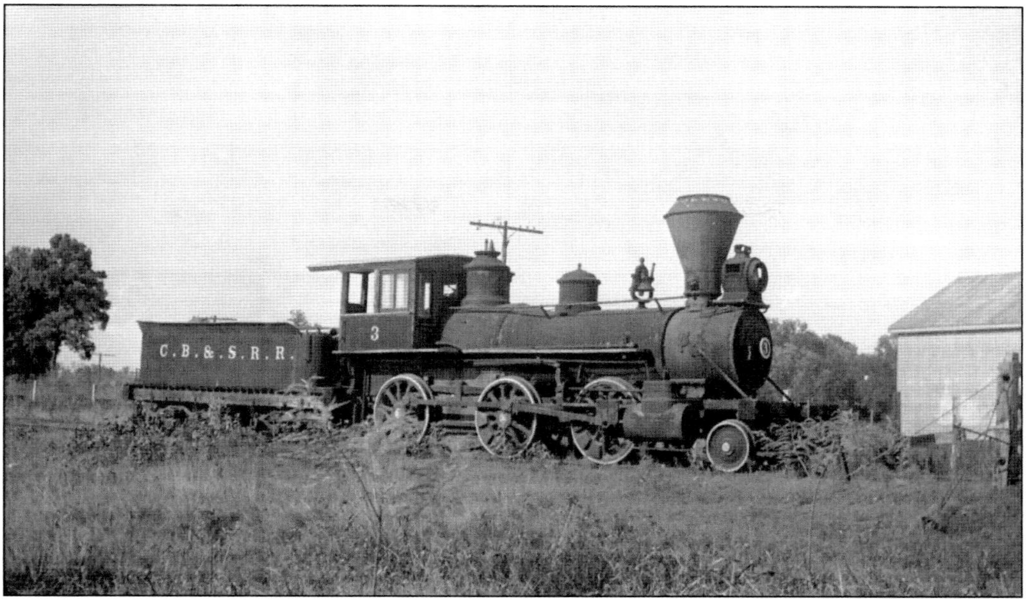

In 1889, Charles A. Bender purchased a mill at Humble on the Houston East & West Texas Railway and began harvesting about 26 square miles worth of timber purchased the year before. A 15-mile tram was laid in a northwesterly direction from Humble, powered by several locomotives. In this view, Engine No. 3 is in storage at Humble in 1933, after operations had ceased. (Courtesy Texas Transportation Archive.)

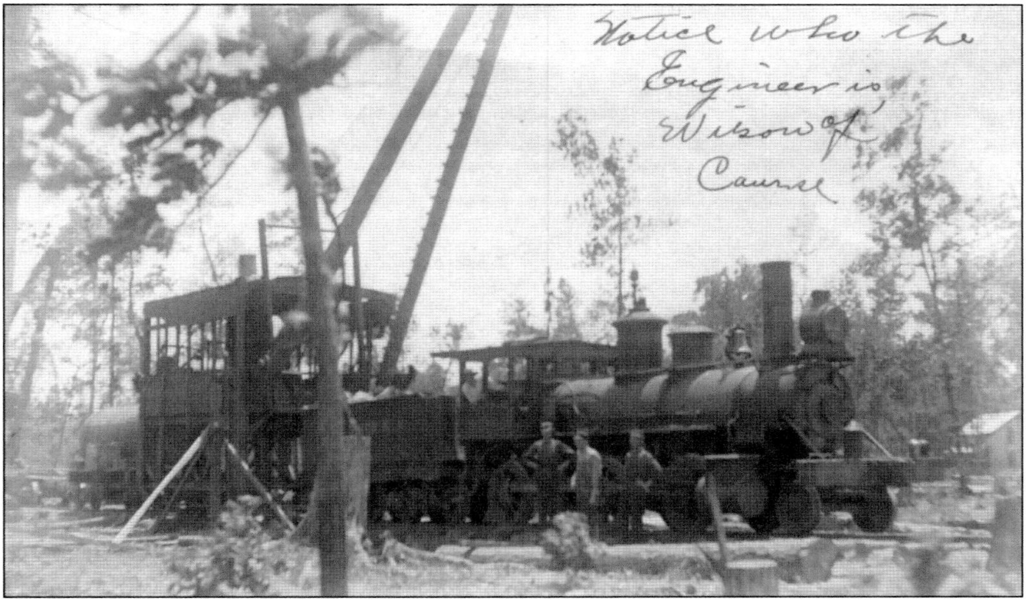

In 1902, Miller-Vidor erected a 75,000-board-foot mill at Timber on the Santa Fe in Montgomery County. A tram built in 1902 was incorporated in 1904 as the Peach River & Gulf Railway (PR&G). The PR&G operated the Miller-Vidor log trains and provided free passenger transportation on its single coach. Here, PR&G Engine No. 1 is pictured with a log loader in May 1908. (Courtesy Texas Transportation Archive.)

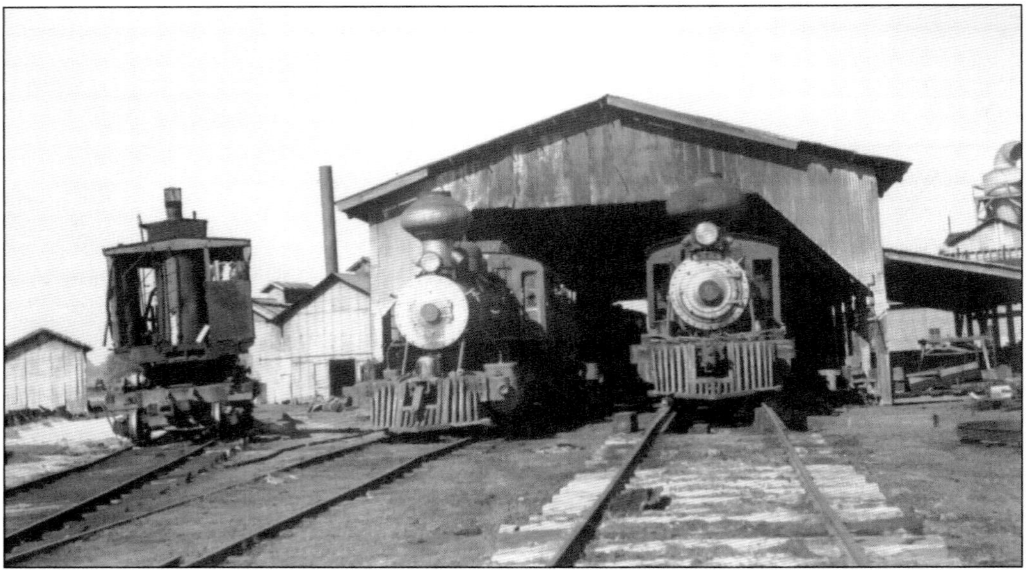

In 1901, Foster Lumber Company established a mill at Clinesburg on the Santa Fe, 17 miles east of Conroe in Montgomery County. Foster renamed the town "Fostoria," and until operations ceased in 1957, the company operated a large mill logged by a well-built tram that extended up to 25 miles in length. This view shows Engines Nos. 6 and 8 at the machine shop in 1938. (Courtesy Texas Transportation Archive.)

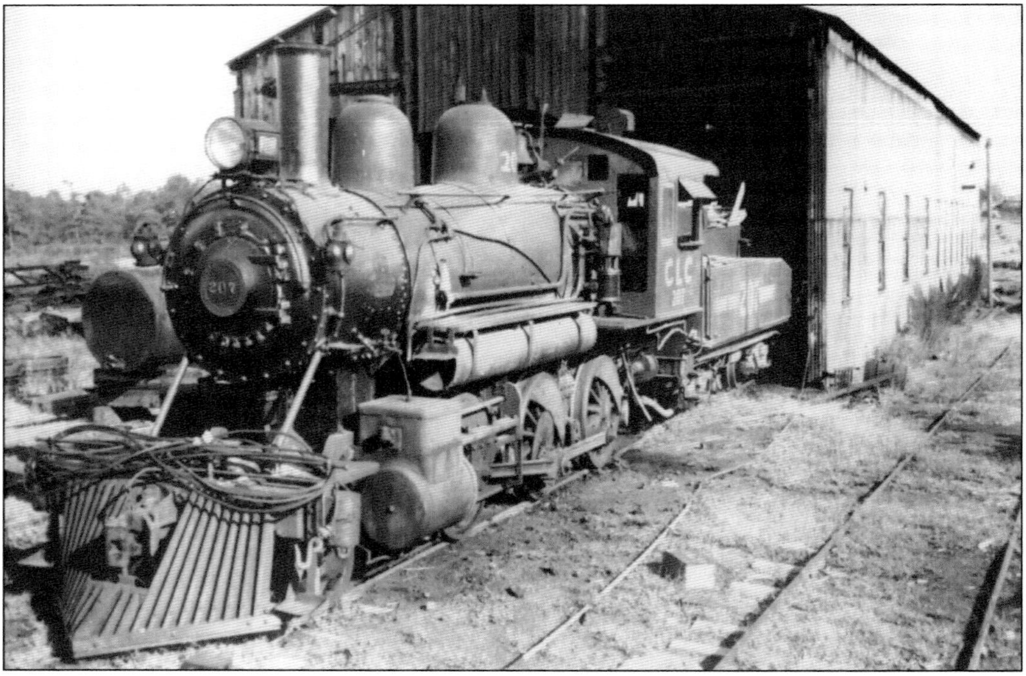

In 1933, Conroe Lumber Company began operating the former Delta Land & Timber at Conroe in Montgomery County. Included in the deal was Delta's 20-mile tram and four locomotives. Logging was also conducted off the Santa Fe east of the mill and at Crockett on the International–Great Northern. In this view, Engine No. 207 rests outside the machine shop in 1939 shortly before the end of operations. (Courtesy Texas Transportation Archive.)

Six

Twilight of Railroad Logging in Texas

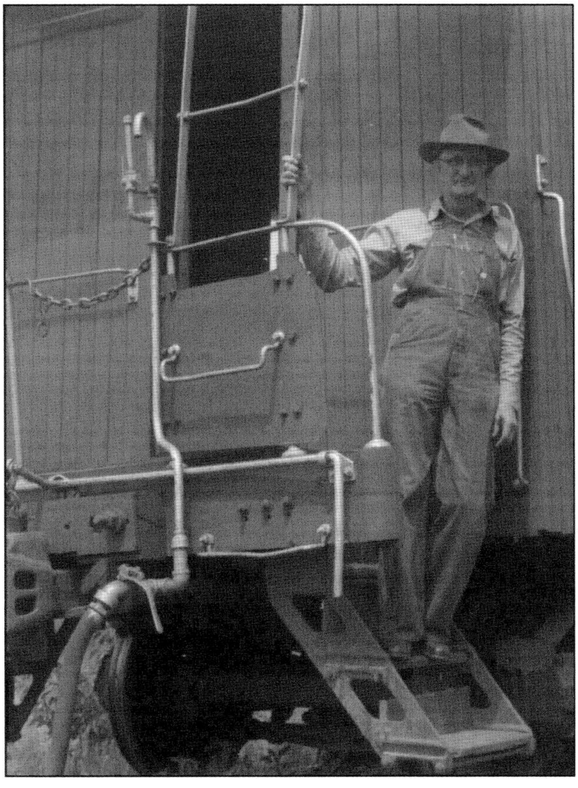

In the spring of 1957, conductor June Terry looks out from the back of a caboose attached to a short Angelina County Lumber log train that has completed its work at New Camp and is about to begin the trip home at the Keltys mill in Lufkin. The period after the 1920s saw industry-wide changes in the methods of moving logs from the woods to the mills. Automobile transportation in the woods, which had been an experiment for lumber companies in the 1910s, was common by World War II and dominant by 1950. The cost of maintaining a private industrial railroad had simply become unsustainable, and thus trucks and tractors were in and railways were out. The 1950s and early 1960s saw the last log trains of Frost, Kirby, Kurth, Angelina County, Temple and Southern Pine, and Carter Companies. The last log train in Texas finished its run at Diboll on the Southern Pine Lumber Company in 1963. (Courtesy Richard W. Keeling Collection.)

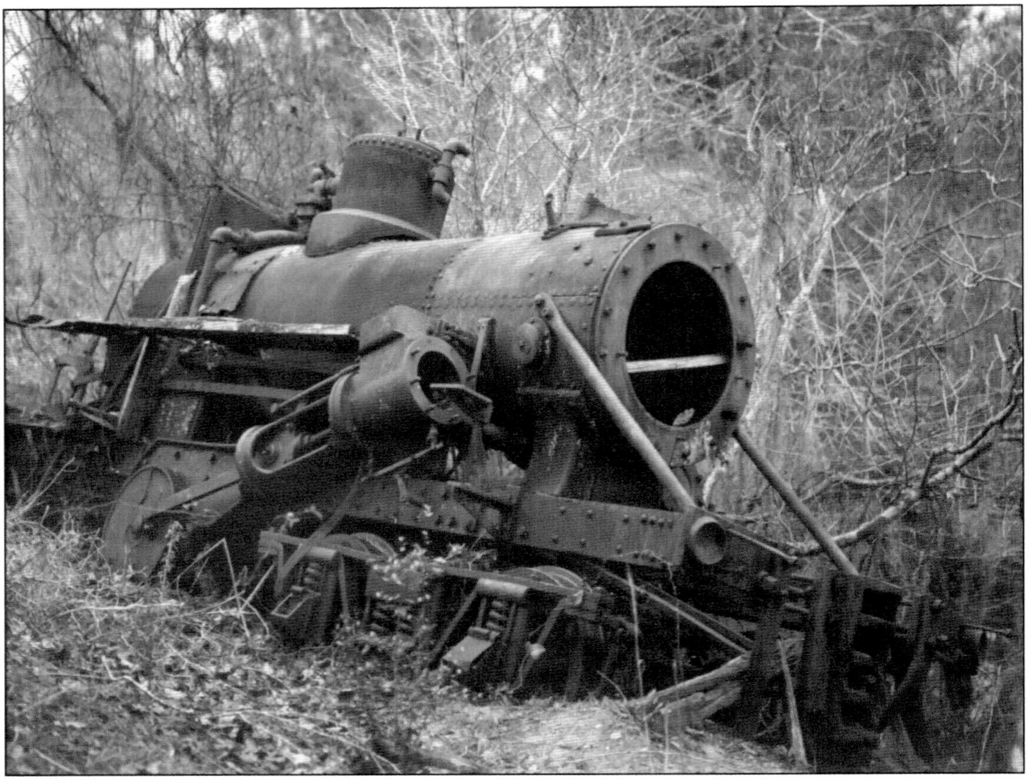

For years, a story circulated about a locomotive abandoned in the woods near Romayor in Liberty County. In 1964, rail historian Joe R. Thompson hiked to the location and used his camera to turn legend into fact. The engine turned out to be a Climax Machine Works "Class B" model, built in 1893 for a Michigan railroad. In 1913, it headed south to work for various lumber companies and gravel pits in Texas and Louisiana. Its last employer was Texas Construction Materials at Romayor, where it had an accident significant enough that it was abandoned in place. It remained there until 2014, when it was moved for display at a resort at Romayor. Below is the engine as it looked in 1919, when it was being refurbished by Southern Iron & Equipment. (Courtesy Richard W. Keeling Collection.)

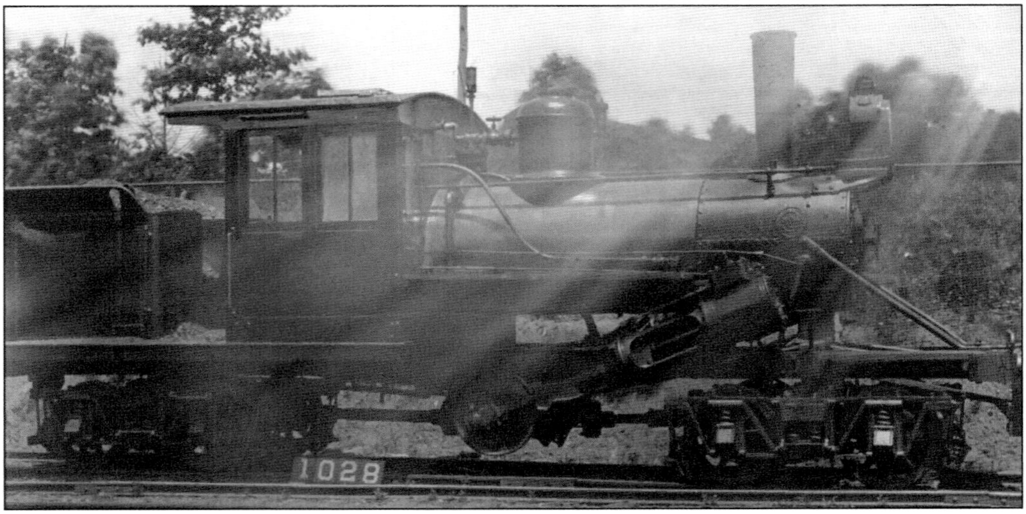

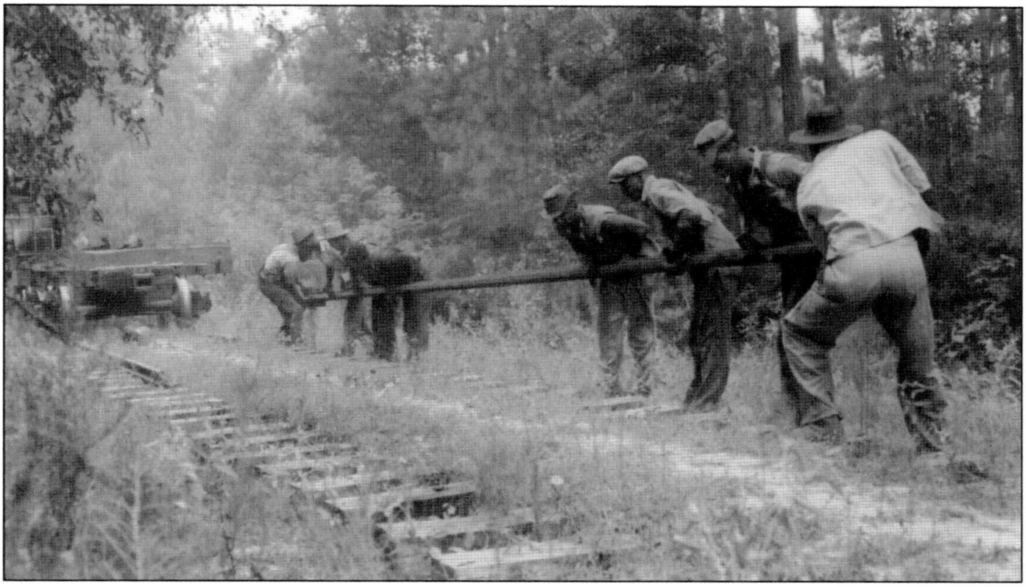

In the 1950s, W.T. Carter & Brother Lumber Company made the decision to scrap all existing tram lines and use highway trucks to move logs to its Camden mill. At 9:30 a.m. on August 19, 1955, historian Richard Keeling recorded the steel gang pulling up the last tram north of Camden. This track once extended as far north as Manning in Angelina County. (Courtesy Richard W. Keeling Collection.)

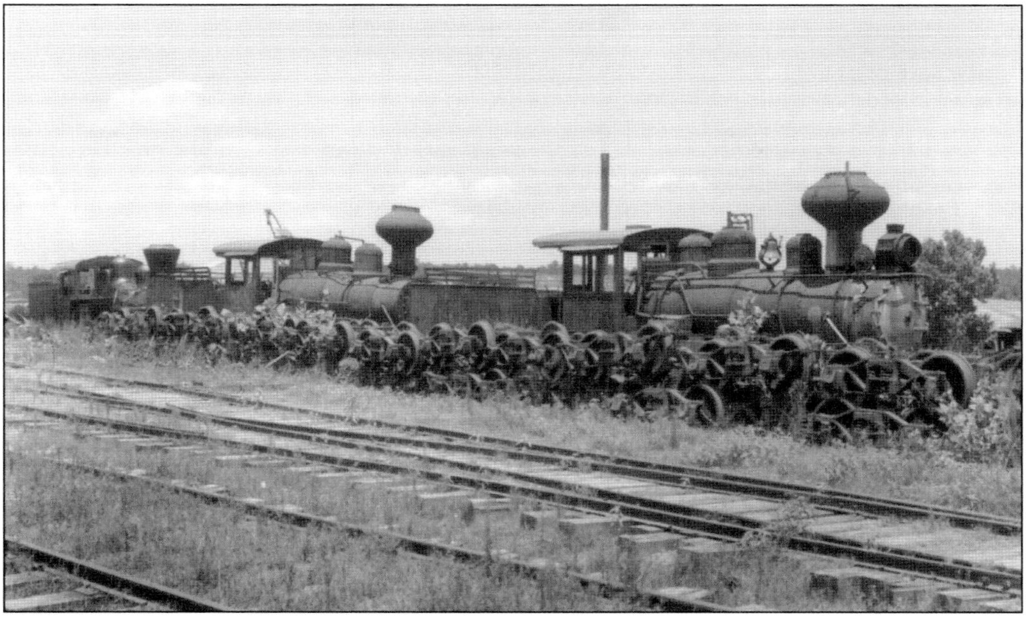

Because W.T. Carter tended to store its old engines rather than scrap them, the Camden mill yard became littered with historic locomotives and wonderfully old-timey and home-brewed rolling stock, making Camden a favorite destination of rail photographers. (Courtesy Richard W. Keeling Collection.)

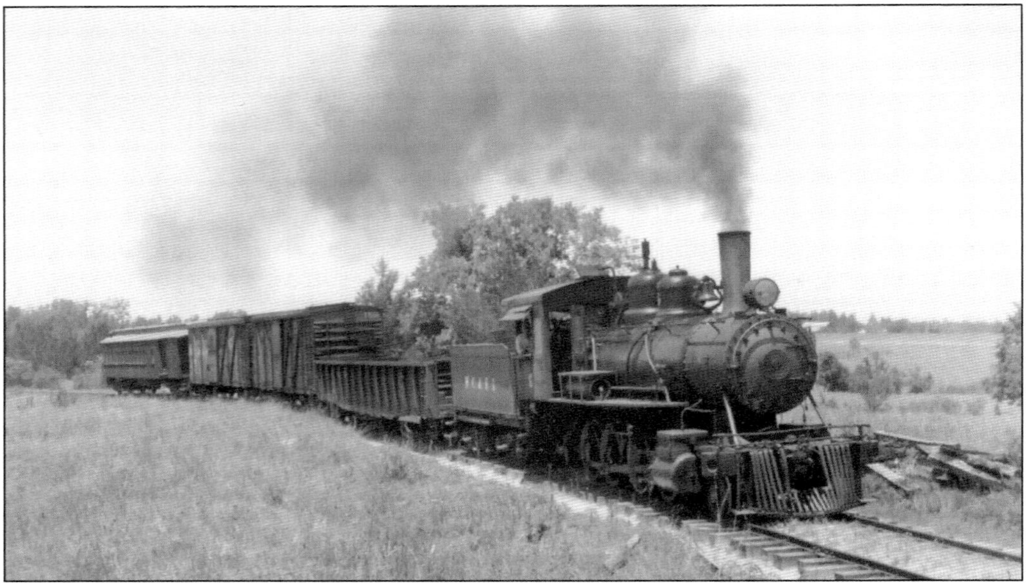

From the late 1950s until the last run in 1973, Carter's 1898 short-line Moscow, Camden & San Augustine Railroad added a coach to the regular freight train for the benefit of tourists. The 50¢ fare was collected informally by popular conductor Carl Vinson, and the round trip took about 90 minutes. The photograph above shows the train near Moscow behind No. 6. Pictured below, the train has made it to Moscow, and No. 6 is being turned on the Moscow turntable to enable the engine to run forward on the return trip. (Courtesy Richard W. Keeling Collection.)

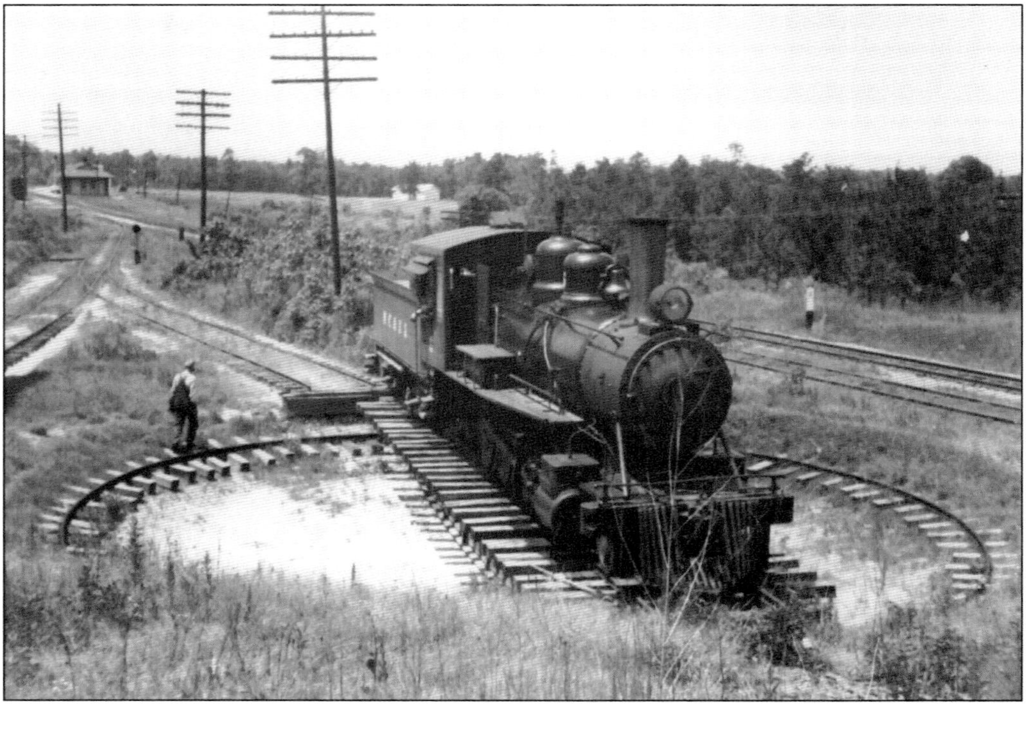

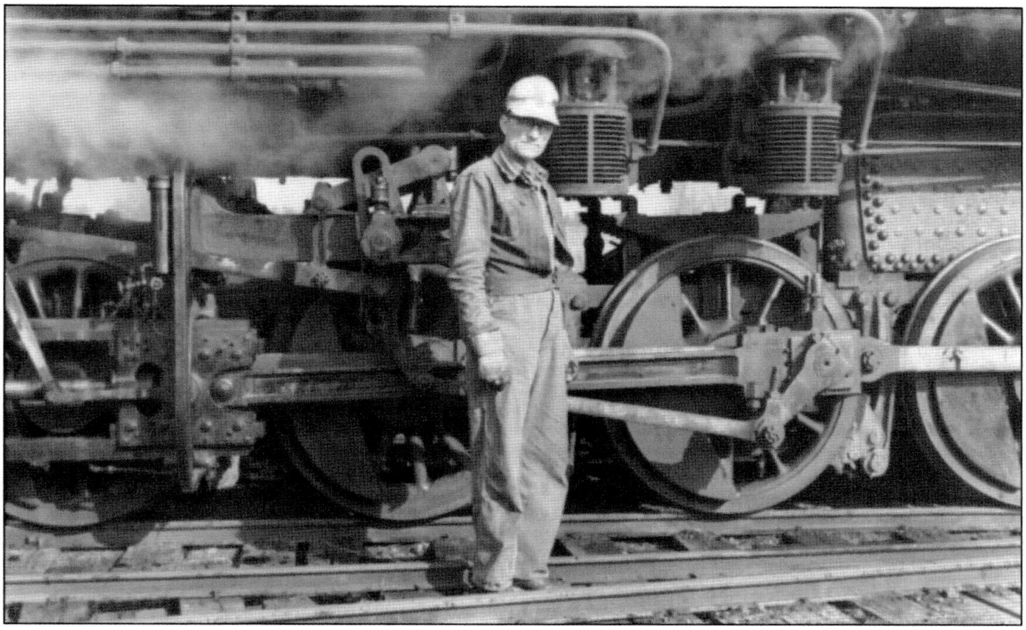

Earl Amerine was a veteran crewman for W.T. Carter and a popular engineer with those visiting the Moscow, Camden & San Augustine Railroad tourist train. Here, Amerine obliges photographer Richard Keeling for a personal portrait on December 21, 1964. (Courtesy Richard W. Keeling Collection.)

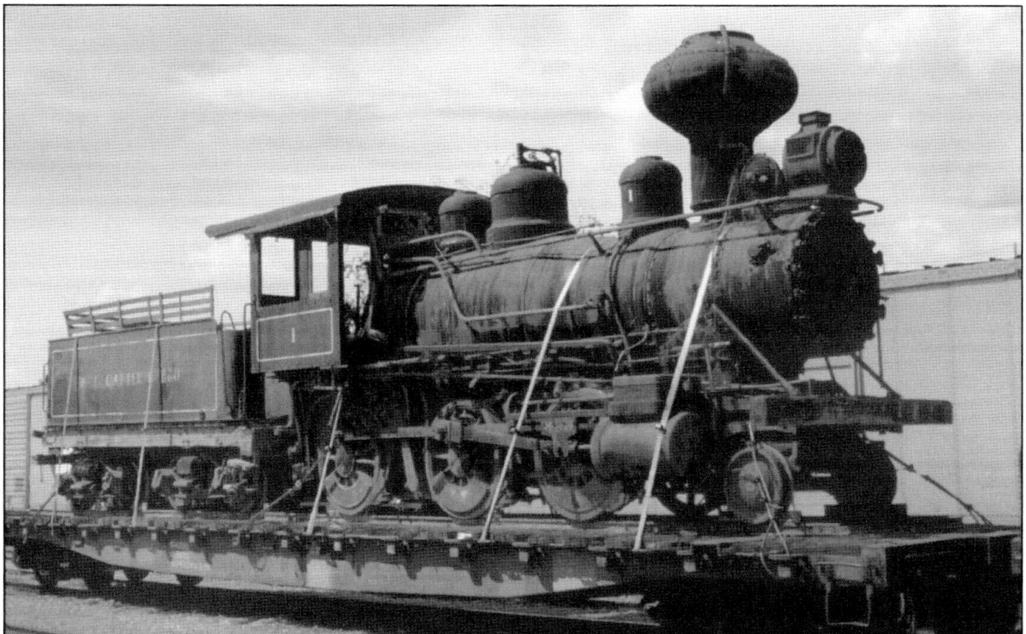

Another W.T. Carter veteran, Carter's third No. 1 locomotive leaves the property for good. The engine is headed for full restoration and return to train service at the Eureka Springs & Northern Arkansas Railroad at Malvern, Arkansas. (Courtesy Texas Transportation Archive.)

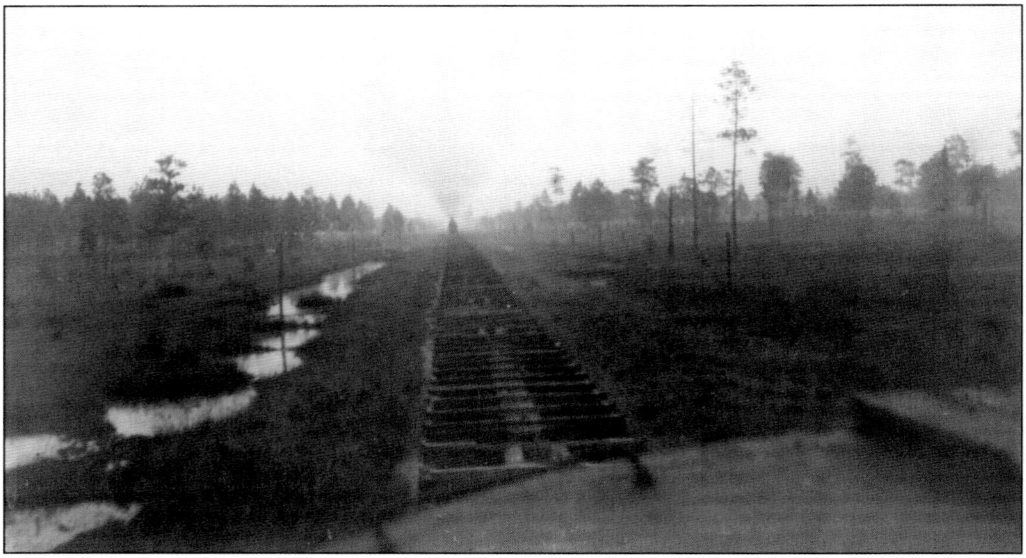

This series of images shows one of Kirby Lumber Company's movements to and from a log front near Silsbee late in the company's history. In the first view, the No. 90 has entered the Santa Fe mainline in a light rain with a string of empty log cars. Kirby was allowed trackage rights over the Santa Fe as long as trains were equipped with automatic couplers and air brakes. The Santa Fe also required the presence of a "pilot conductor," a Santa Fe crewman paid by Kirby to advise the engineer in maneuvering over that portion of the Santa Fe mainline. Once at the tram switch, the train moved off the Santa Fe and back onto Kirby tracks. At the Kirby loading site, below, No. 66 is making progress loading the train up with logs. (Courtesy Richard W. Keeling Collection.)

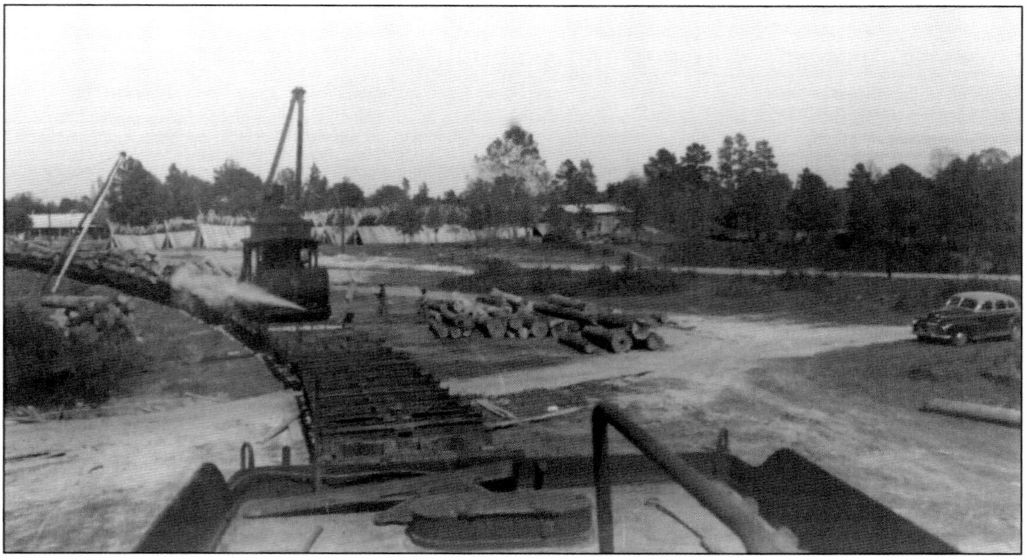

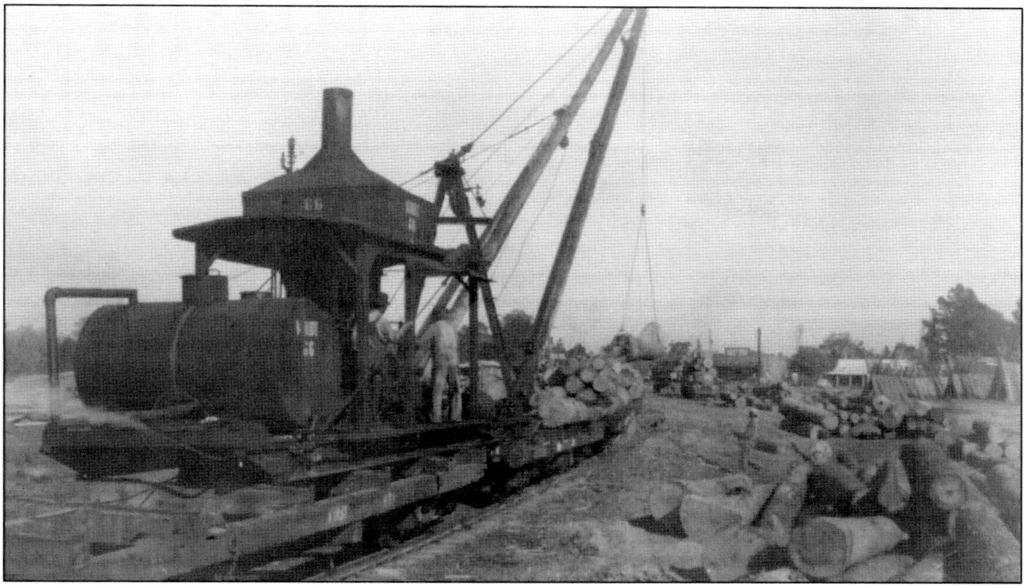

Above, Kirby Loader No. 66 positions a log over a partially loaded car, aided by hand signals from a worker on the ground. In the distance, a log truck can be seen unloading its contents, likely for the next day's train. In the last decades of railroad logging, gasoline trucks, bulldozers, tractors, and even passenger vehicles are a common sight in photographs—in stark contrast to those 19th and early 20th century images that show a world of remote wilderness, inaccessible to all but those riding in via animals or log trains. Below, the train is loaded, the loader's boom has been lowered and chained, and the engineer readies to move toward the Santa Fe mainline for the return trip to Silsbee. (Courtesy Richard W. Keeling Collection.)

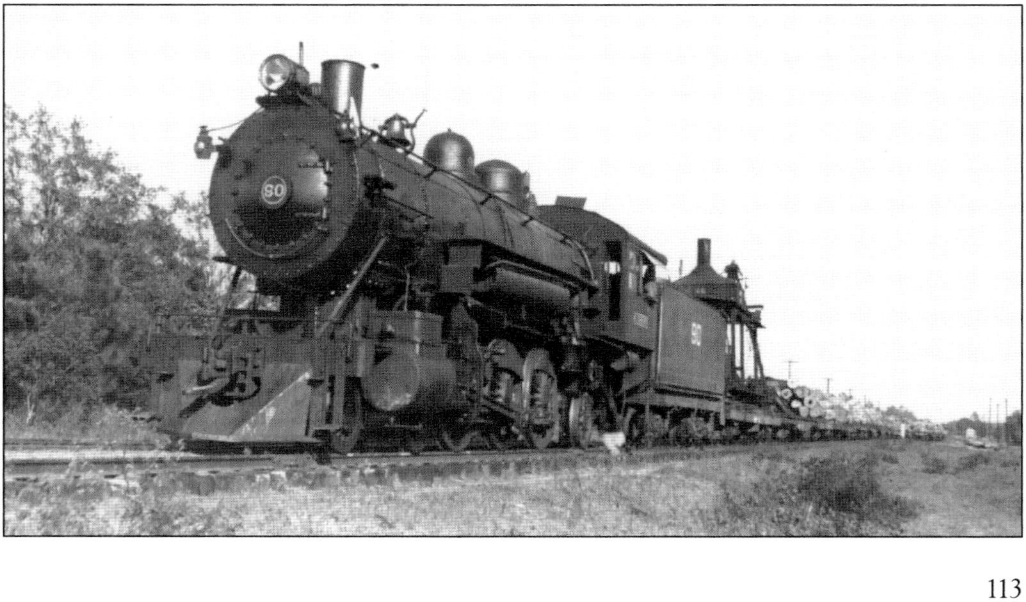

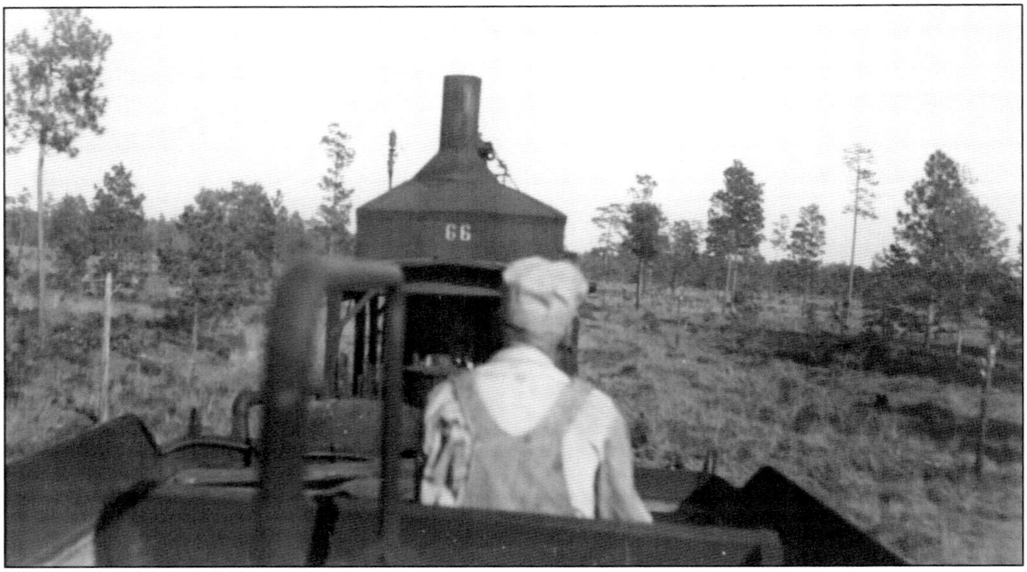

Above, a member of the train crew looks out over the back of No. 90's tender as the train moves outbound over the tram toward the connection with the Santa Fe. Below, the train arrives at the tram switch that will allow it to reenter the Santa Fe mainline. The Kirby train is bound by the Santa Fe schedule. All train movements are conducted under specific instructions called track warrants, and the Santa Fe pilot conductor onboard will make sure that all instructions are followed. (Courtesy Richard W. Keeling Collection.)

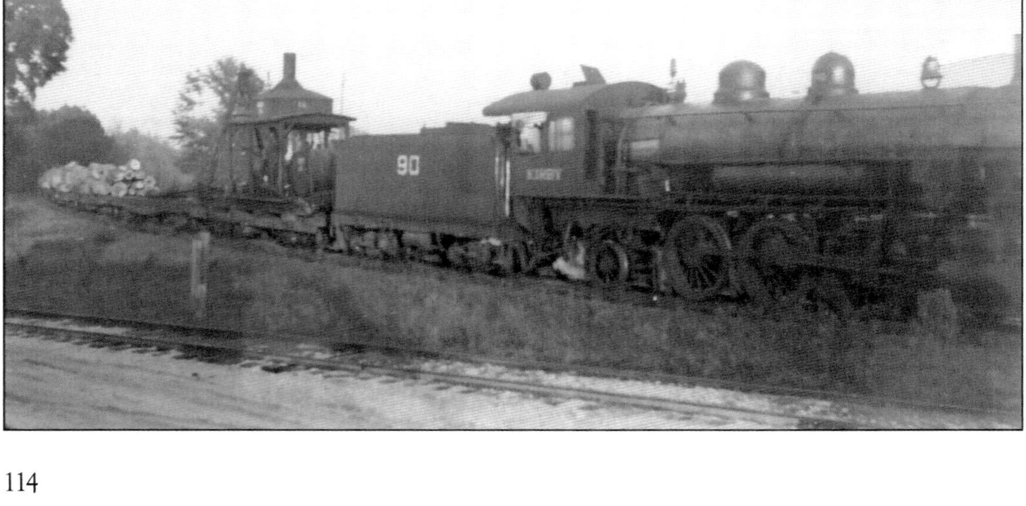

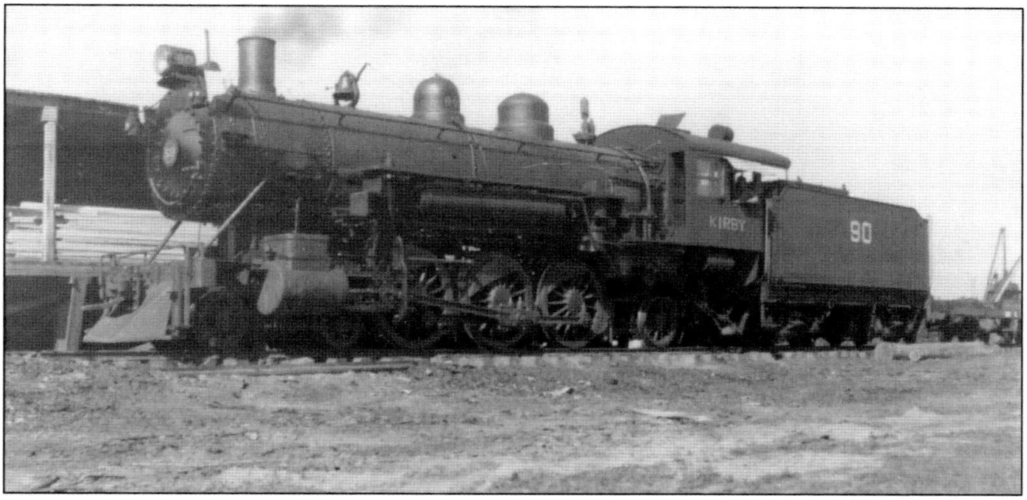

Back at Silsbee, the No. 90 ties up at the engine house to be readied for the next day's log movement. The No. 90 worked on the Santa Fe log run until 1950, when it was finally retired from service and scrapped. After 1952, Kirby ceased running trains over the Santa Fe altogether, and logs thereafter were hauled as regular freight on the Santa Fe trains. (Courtesy Richard W. Keeling Collection.)

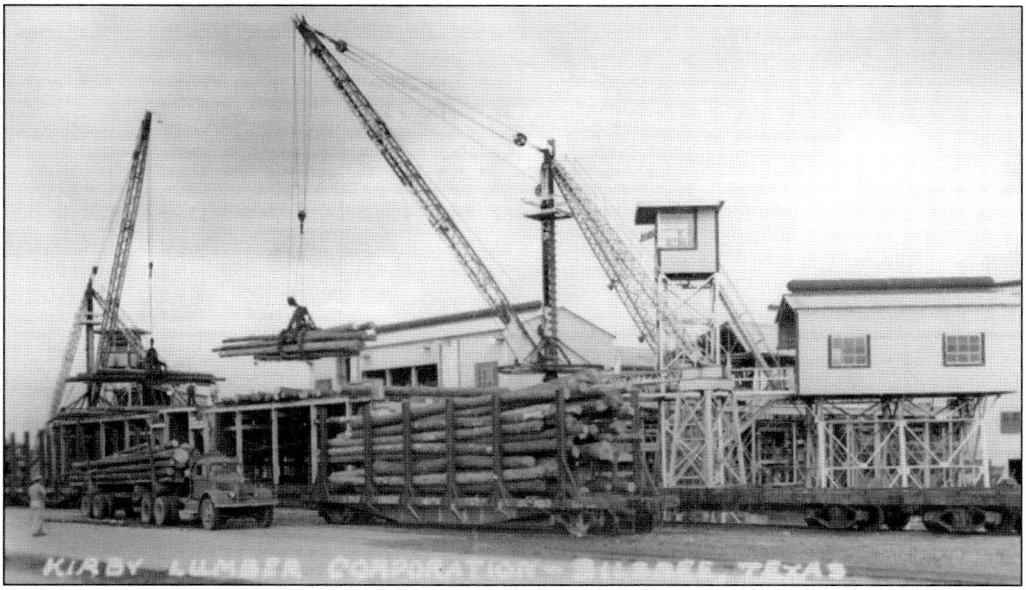

By the early 1950s, Kirby no longer used trams to log any of its mills. Logs were loaded onto mainline roads like the Santa Fe and treated as regular freight. Silsbee's new mill was a modern all-electric facility, and Kirby opted to concentrate its energies there, leading to the closure of its former mill giants at Call, Honey Island, and Bessmay. Trucks replaced trains in the woods, and Kirby railroad logging now belonged to history. (Courtesy Texas Transportation Archive.)

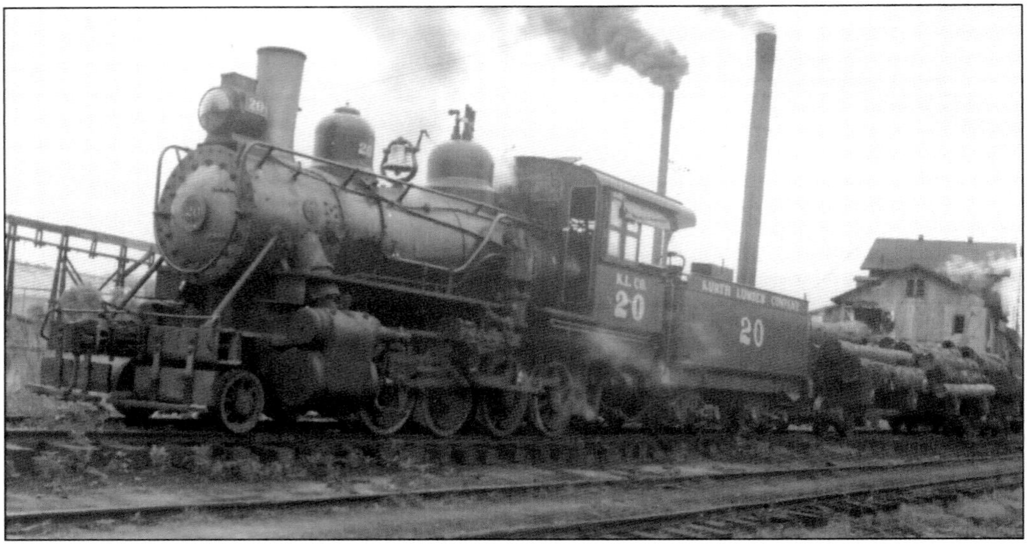

The Jasper County Lumber Company was purchased by J.H. Kurth in 1946, becoming the Kurth Lumber Company. Kurth operated its own tram at Jasper, powered by Locomotive No. 20, pictured above in the mid-1950s. The No. 20 was a 1916 ex–Sierra Railroad engine that Kurth purchased from the US Army. It was scrapped along with the mill and its railroad in the early months of 1962. Below, Kurth No. 20 heads out for the Santa Fe connection in Jasper on August 17, 1955, with cars of finished lumber from the Kurth mill. (Both, courtesy Richard W. Keeling Collection.)

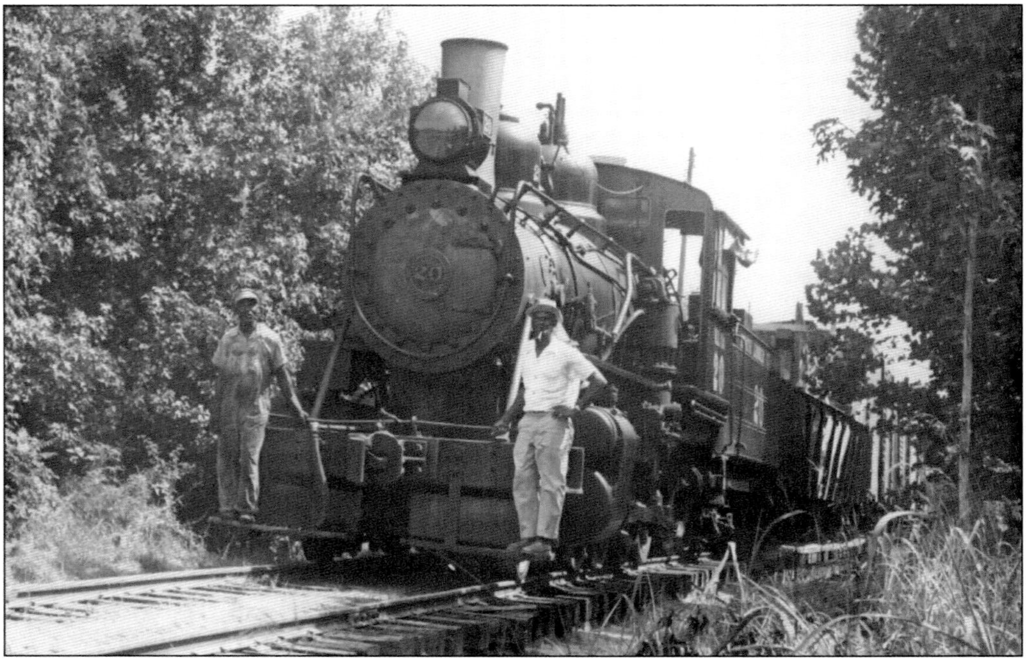

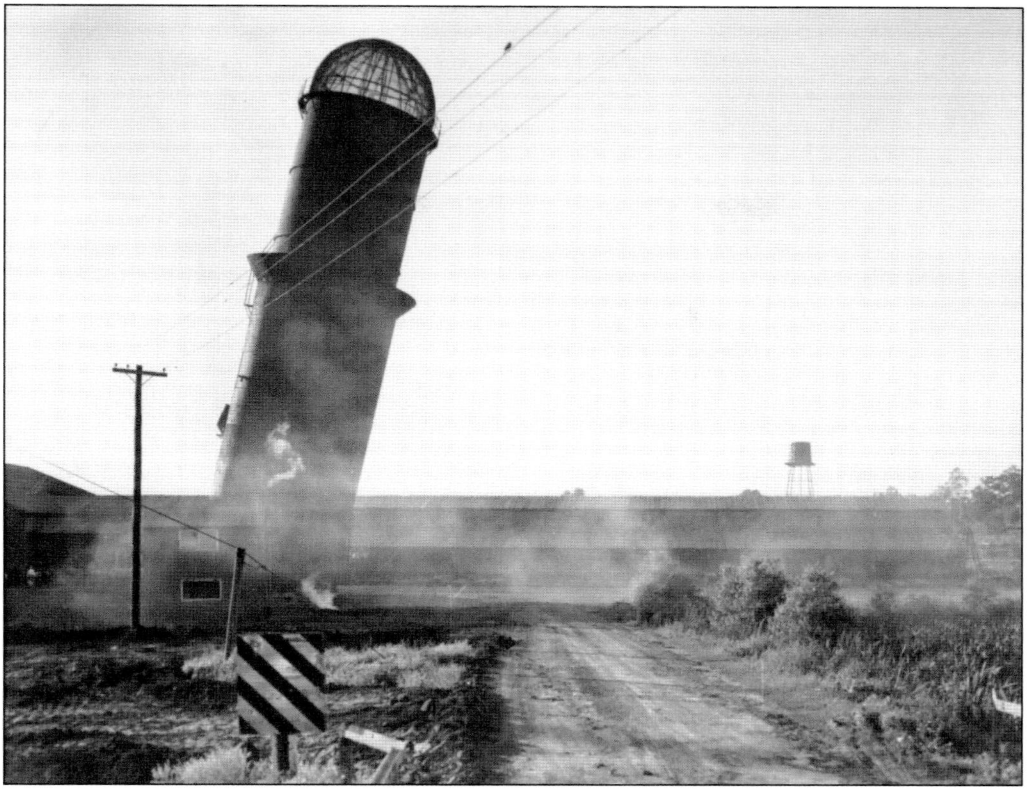

The 1954 wrecking of the sawdust burner of the former Frost-Johnson Lumber Company at Nacogdoches marked the end of over 50 years of nonstop operation by Frost and its predecessor, Hayward Lumber Company. Scenes like the one above became common in East Texas by the World War II years. Frost-Johnson and its associated lines operated three dozen steam locomotives throughout its history, yet it was the little gasoline Plymouth engine below that was the sole motive power at the end. (Above, courtesy Pyrtle Tuetsch; below, courtesy Richard W. Keeling Collection.)

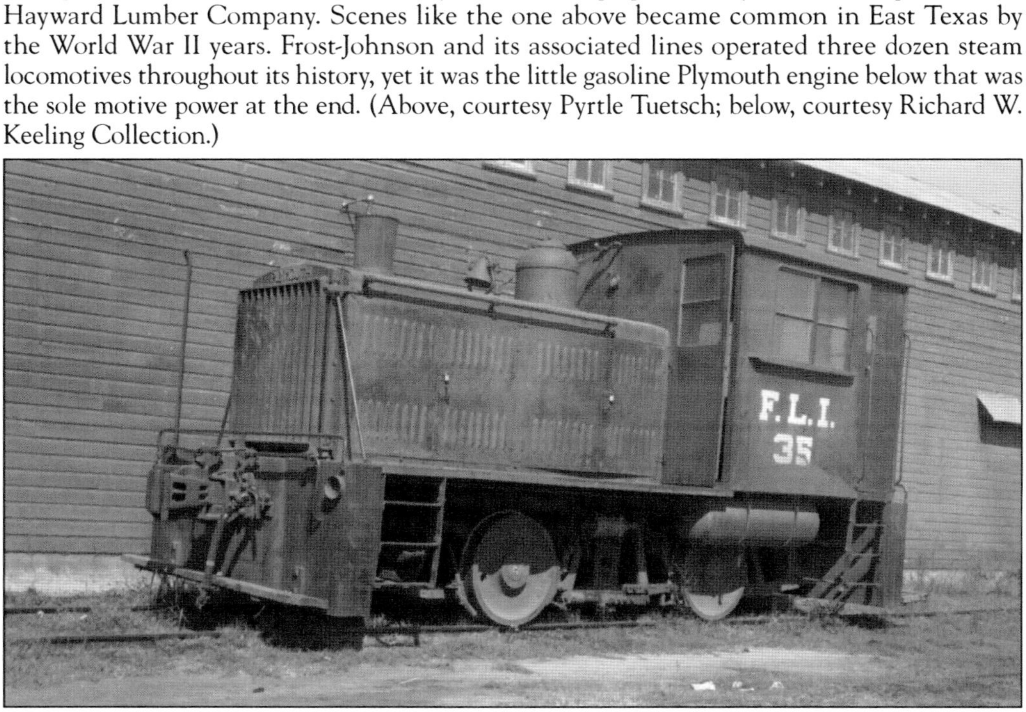

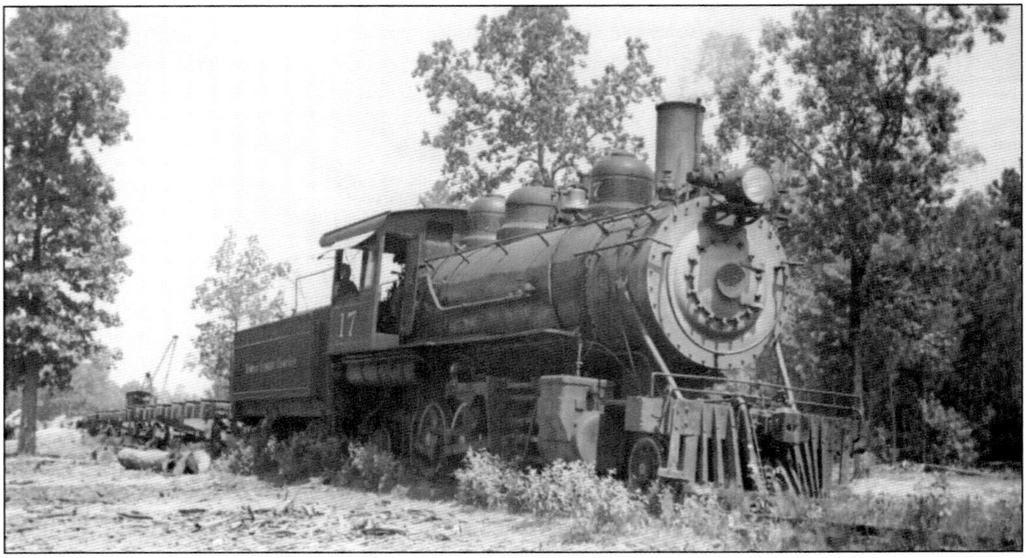

Photographed on August 17, 1955, No. 17 works at the Temco camp north of Evadale in Jasper County, a point accessed only by a trip over the Santa Fe. The name "Temco" was a contraction of "Temple" and "Company," shorthand for its Jasper County camp but not in reference to any community in particular. At the business end of the train, the loader pictured below moves at a good pace. After cutting at Temco concluded in the late 1950s, the No. 17 was left in the weeds there until it was finally scrapped in late 1963. (Courtesy Richard W. Keeling Collection.)

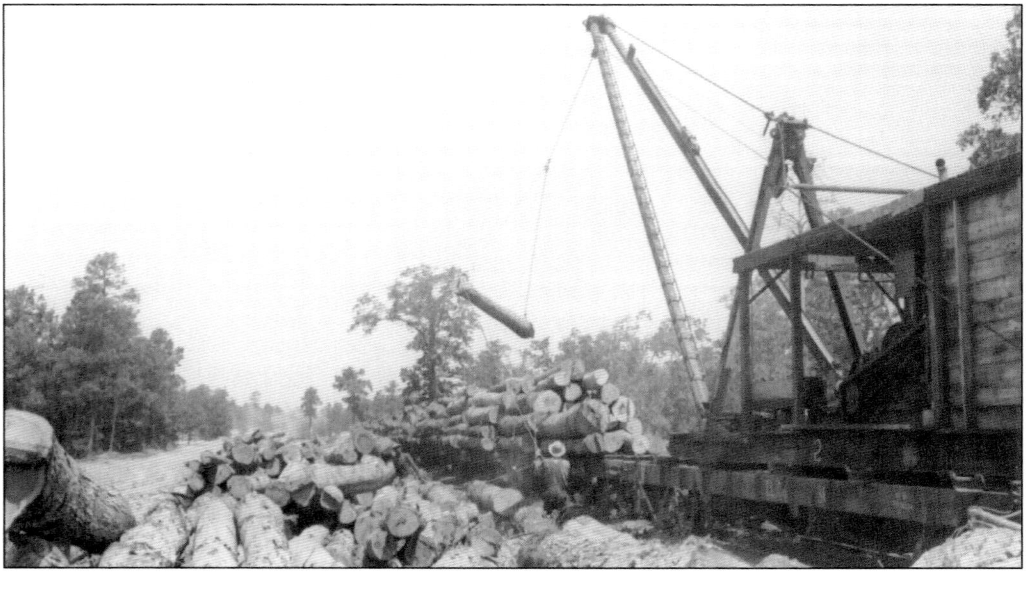

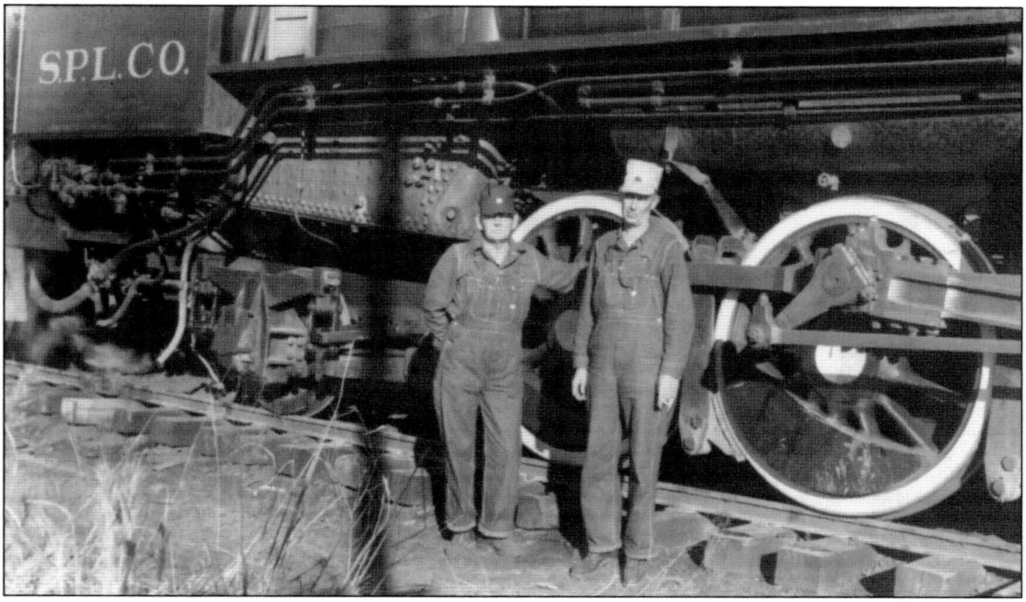

Engineer C.A. McDaniel (above at left) and his fireman (at right) pose in front of Southern Pine Lumber's big Engine No. 20 on October 8, 1957. McDaniel began his career as a fireman on Temple Lumber's Shay No. 16. He was promoted to engineer and piloted trains for both Temple and Southern Pine. In the mid-1950s, the company kept him busy with the regular log train run that originated at Temco in Jasper County, but by the early 1960s, the steam engines were retired and McDaniel took that opportunity to retire himself. Below, the No. 20 embarks from Pineland at speed with McDaniel at the throttle. (Courtesy Richard W. Keeling Collection.)

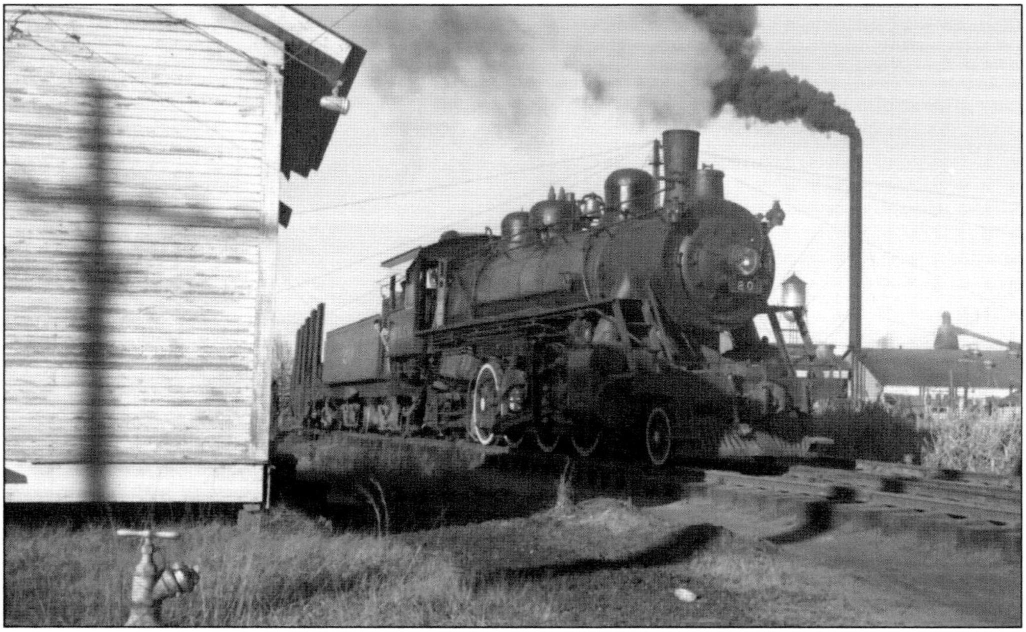

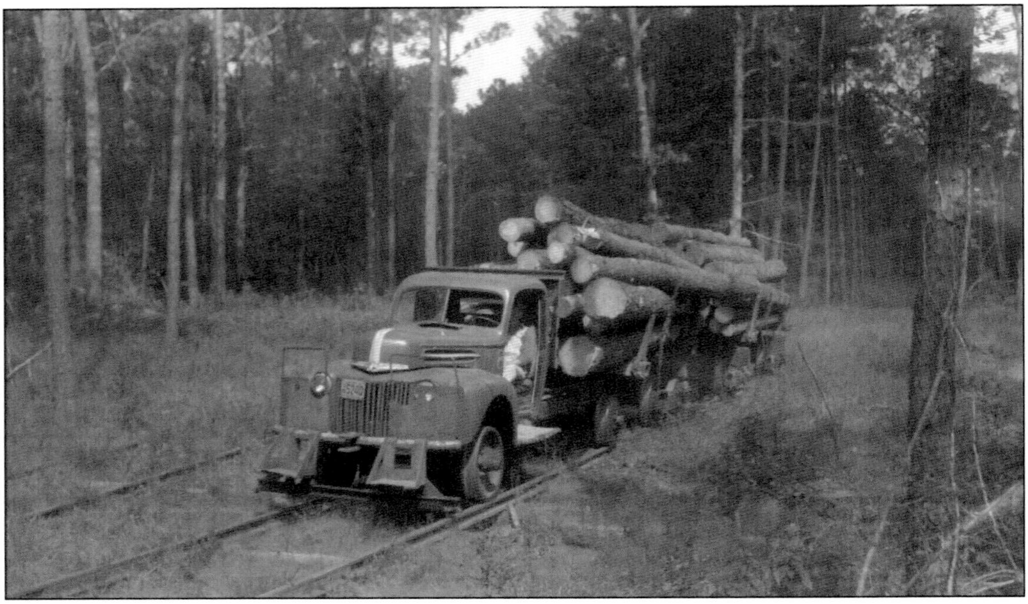

From the late 1940s into the 1950s, Southern Pine Lumber came up with a creative solution to the problem of logging a tract of Hardin County timber that was under swamp water most of the year. The company laid a six-mile-long tram and powered it with a Ford V-8 highway truck modified to run on rails. Log cars were similarly modified trailers, using wheel sets salvaged from ancient railroad logging cars. The first "train" made the connection with the Missouri Pacific at Strain on August 23, 1948. Crews referred to the tram variously as the "Hull Tram," the "Strain & Keep Straining Railroad," or simply, the "Swamp Buggy." Below, a Swamp Buggy trailer is loaded at the skidway at the end of the tram. (Courtesy Richard W. Keeling Collection.)

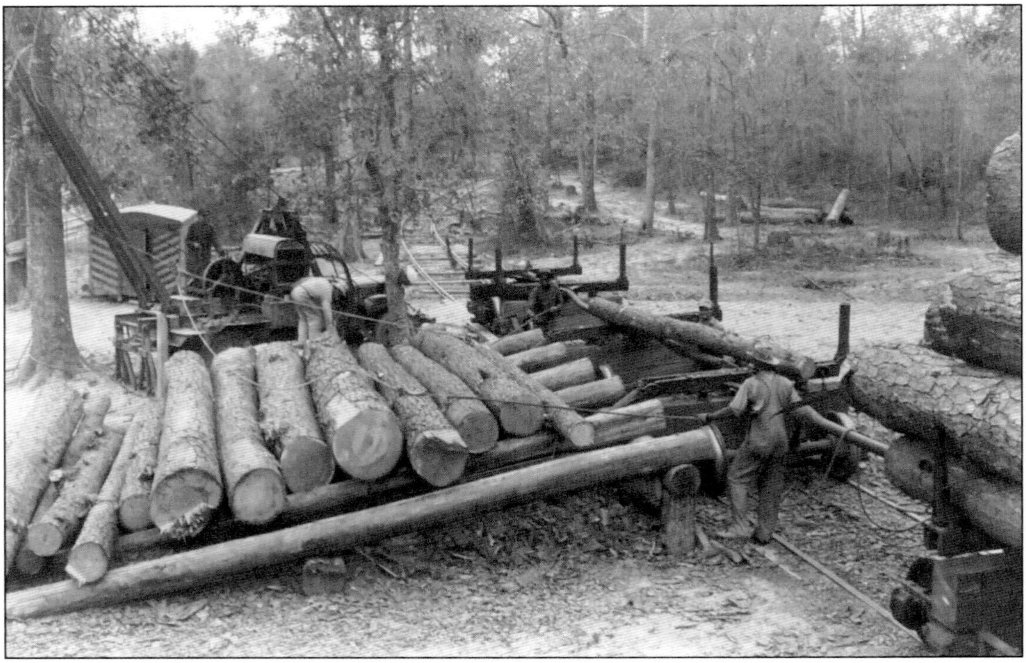

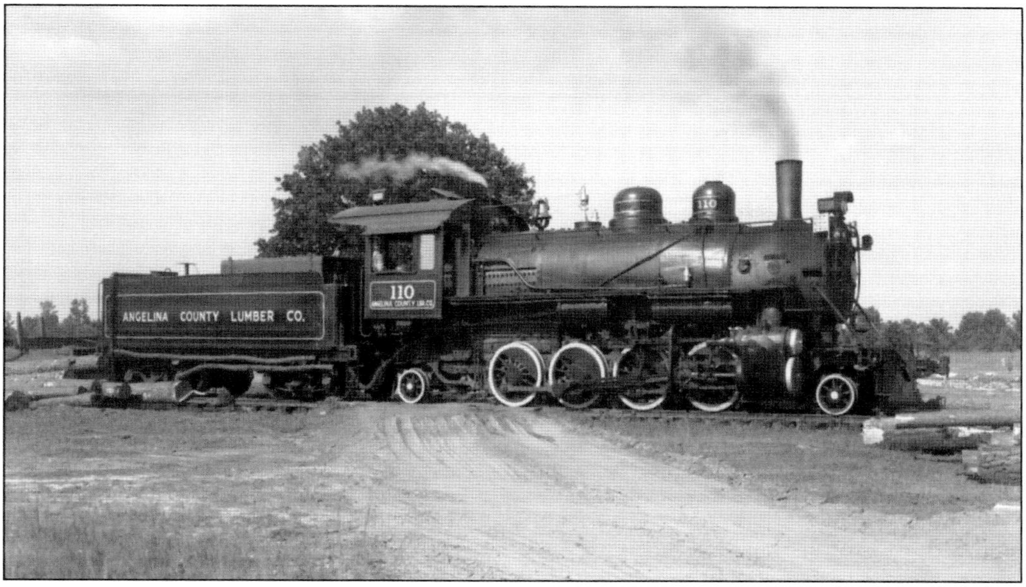

New Camp, located about three miles southwest of Chireno on the Angelina & Neches River Railroad, was a loading point for the Angelina County Lumber Company. In the spring of 1957, historian Richard Keeling took a series of photographs documenting logging at New Camp and the log train's return to Keltys that evening. In the above photograph, Engine No. 110 is attached to empty log cars for loading and is uncoupled in order to make a quick run south of New Camp for a water refill. By noontime, the steam loader crew has made good progress loading the train. This work, pictured below, will continue throughout the afternoon. (Courtesy Richard W. Keeling Collection.)

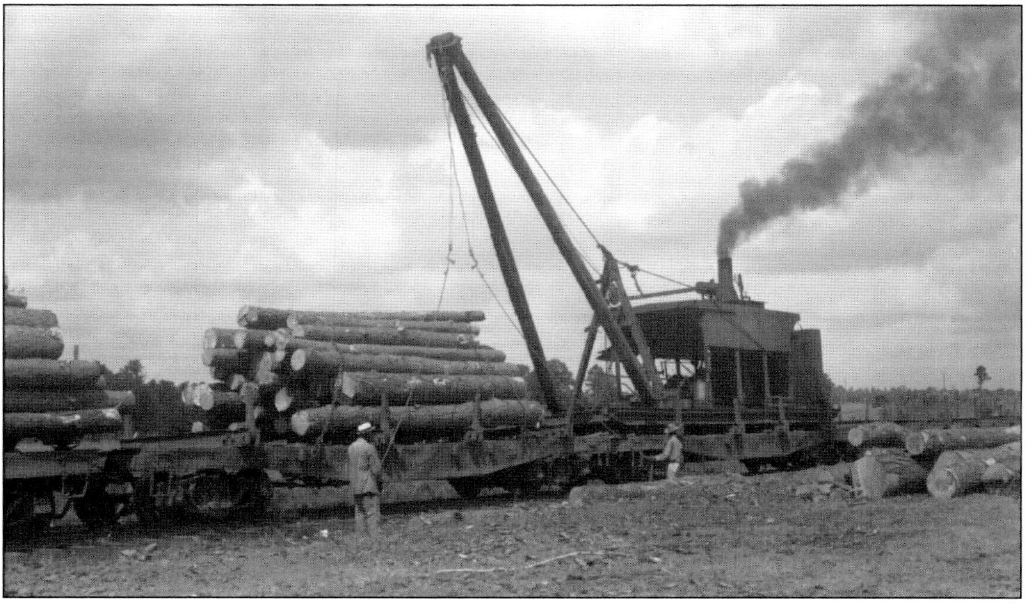

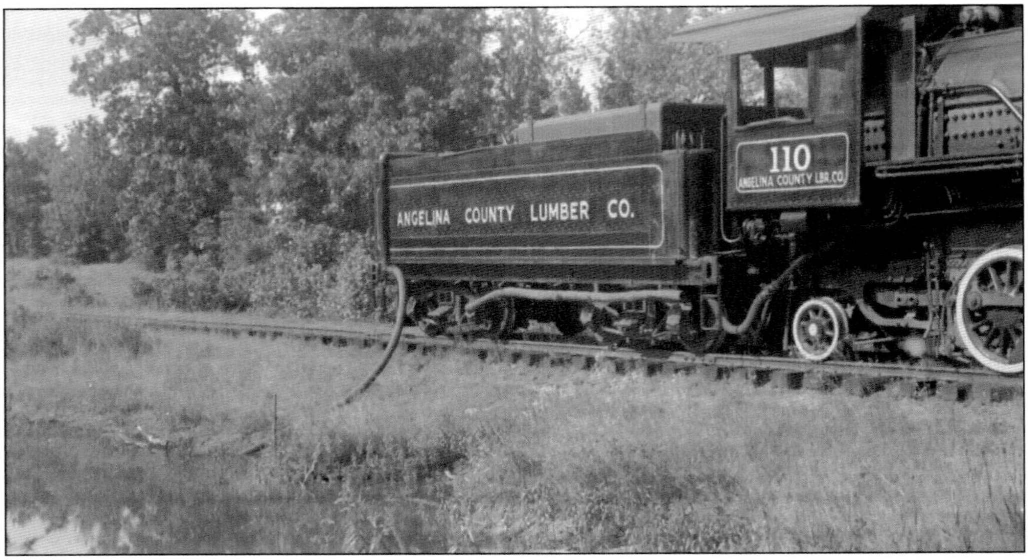

While loading continues, the No. 110 makes a quick run down the line toward Etoile to refill its tank with water pumped from the adjacent pond (above). The water is not ideal but, with a filter, is good enough for the boiler. A hose attached to the tender is extended to the edge of the pond, and then a pump is activated, drawing water into the tender's tank. This system for watering locomotives was vastly less expensive than maintaining a proper railroad water tank and thus was adopted by countless lumber companies during the heyday of railroad logging. Below, the log cars are loaded to capacity, the loader's boom is tied down, and the train prepares to begin its 27-mile, two-hour return trip to the mill at Keltys. (Courtesy Richard W. Keeling Collection.)

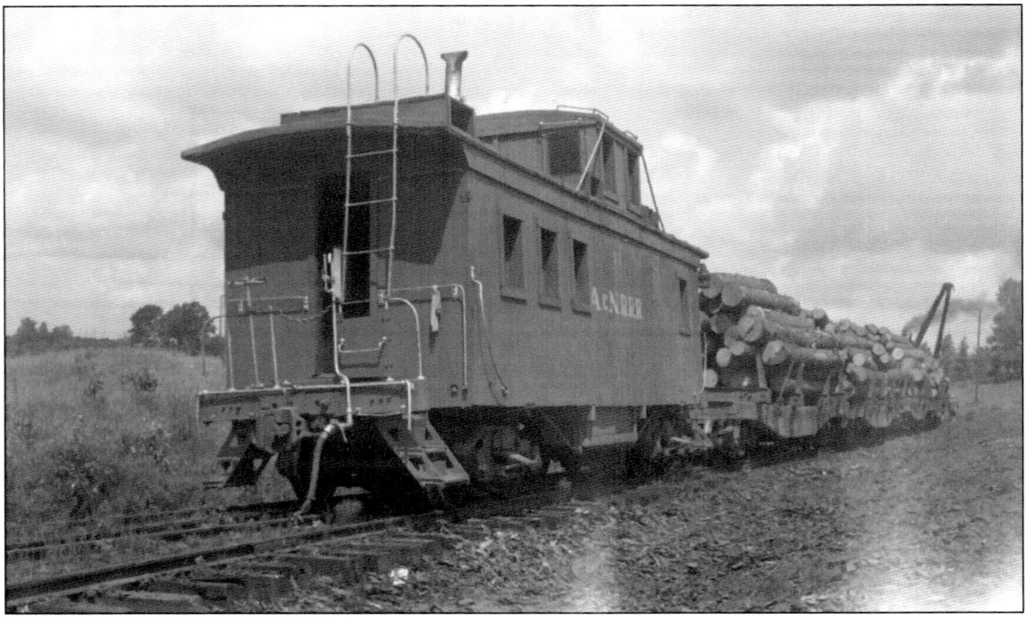

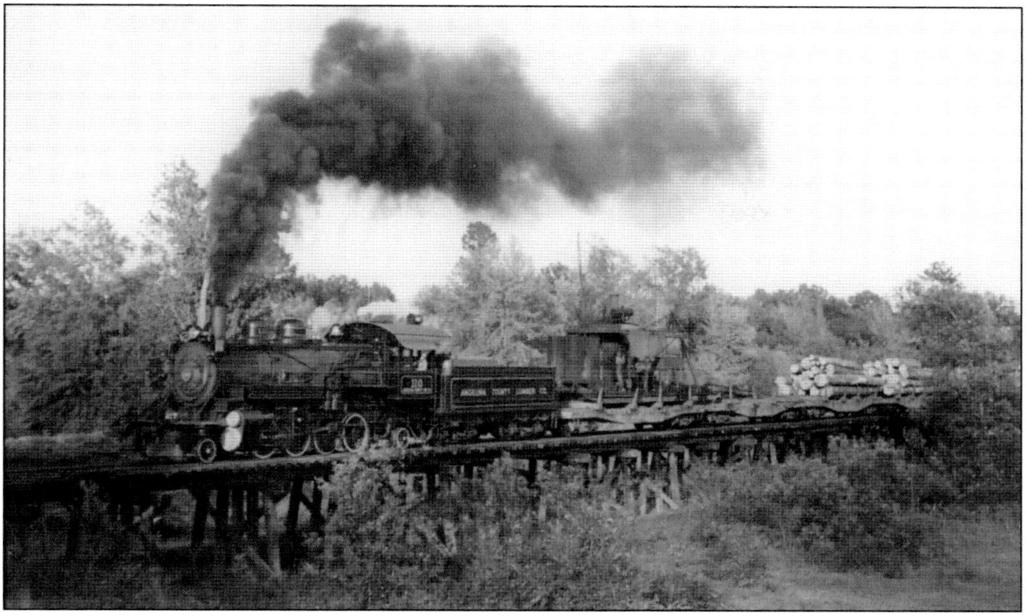

The shadows are getting long as Angelina County Lumber No. 110 moves through the rural countryside between Ewing and Lufkin. In 30 minutes, the train will pull into Keltys and deposit its logs into the millpond. By 1962, the No. 110 was retired from log train service and assigned to work one day per month, switching the Southland Paper mill at Herty on the eastern edge of Lufkin. The below September 1963 photograph shows the No. 110 switching the mill. In 1966, ICC inspectors determined that the No. 110 had a damaged firebox, so the engine was retired for good. In 1970, it was donated and placed on display at Lufkin's Ellen Trout Zoo. (Courtesy Richard W. Keeling Collection.)

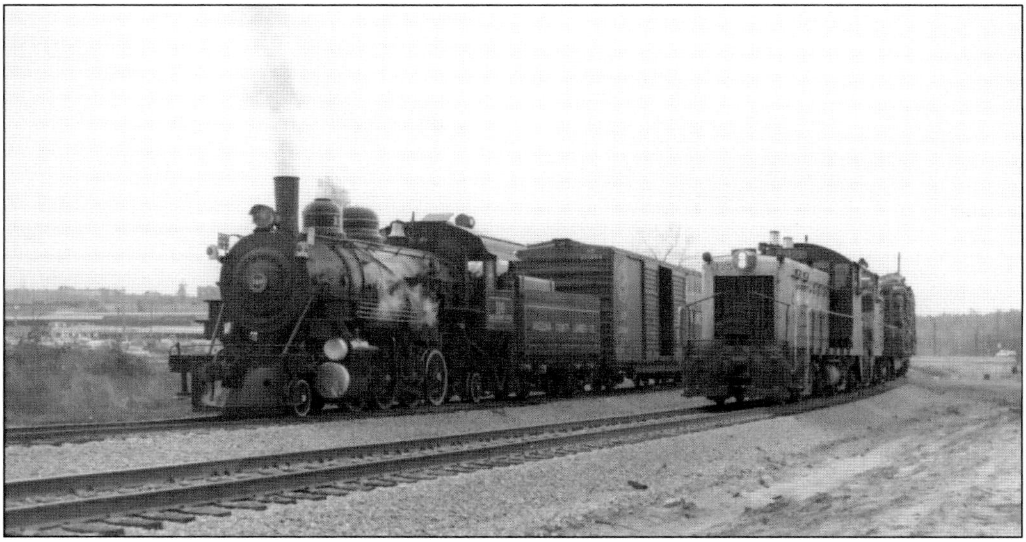

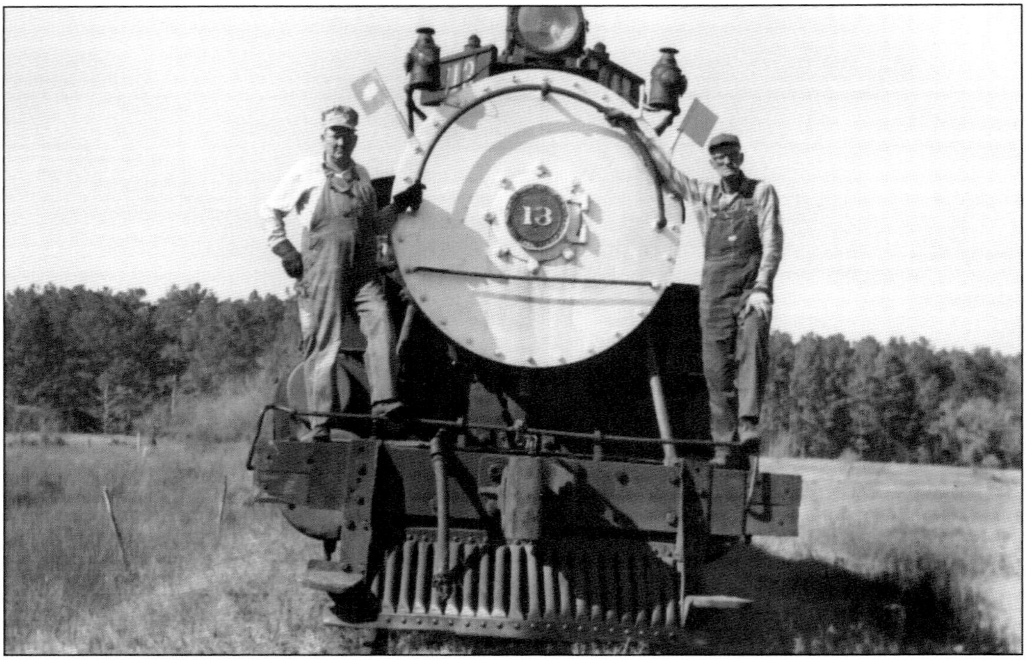

Log trains operated on Southern Pine Lumber rails until the spring of 1963. The next few images, taken on January 10, 1963, capture a day of logging at a site northwest of Diboll near Vair. In just a matter of weeks, Engine No. 13 was retired, and the trams were scheduled for removal. In the photograph above, engineer Louis Minton (left) and fireman and loaderman Bill Powers (right) pose for a personal portrait with No. 13 as they head back to Diboll at the end of the workday. The workday began with No. 13 leaving Diboll, pulling a string of empty log cars, reaching the long Neches River bridge at 7:45 a.m., and heading for the loading site just east of Highway 103. (Courtesy Richard W. Keeling Collection.)

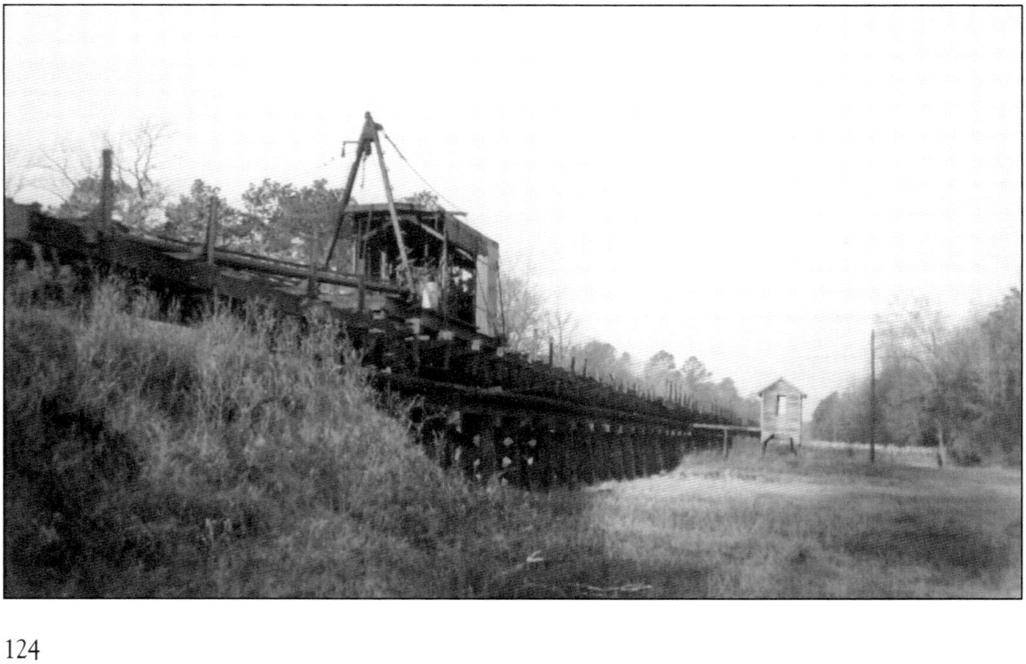

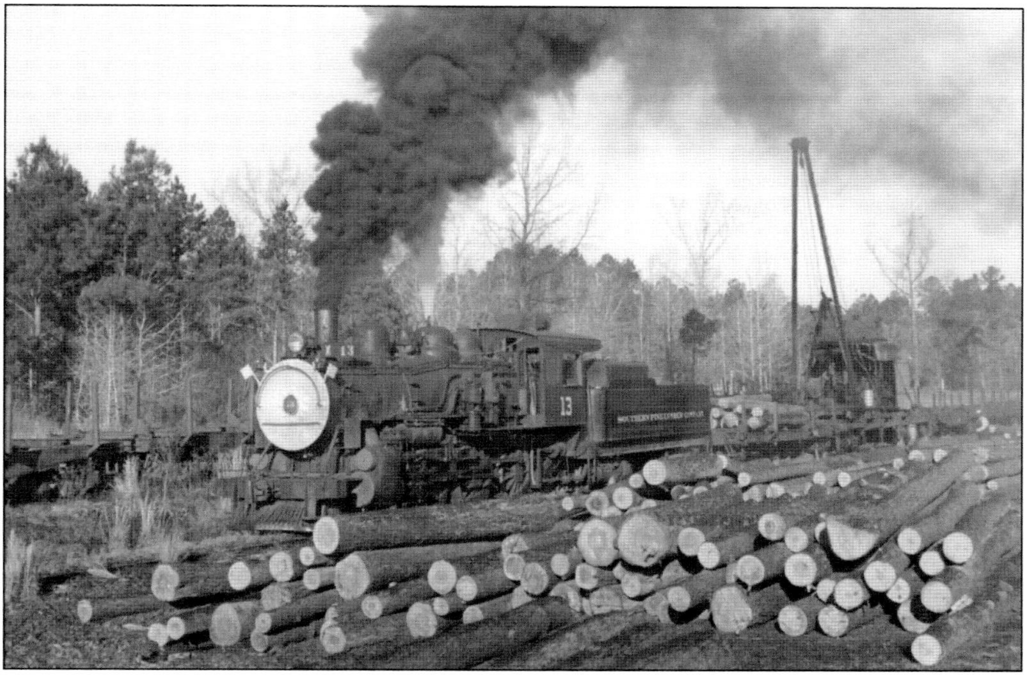

Above, at the loading site, the No. 13 puts up a great deal of smoke and steam as it moves the loader along the many stacks of logs waiting to be loaded. Despite the January weather, the work is hard enough that some workers wear short sleeves under their overalls. The work of loading the train, pictured below, will continue throughout the day. Another full train load will await the next day's run. (Courtesy Richard W. Keeling Collection.)

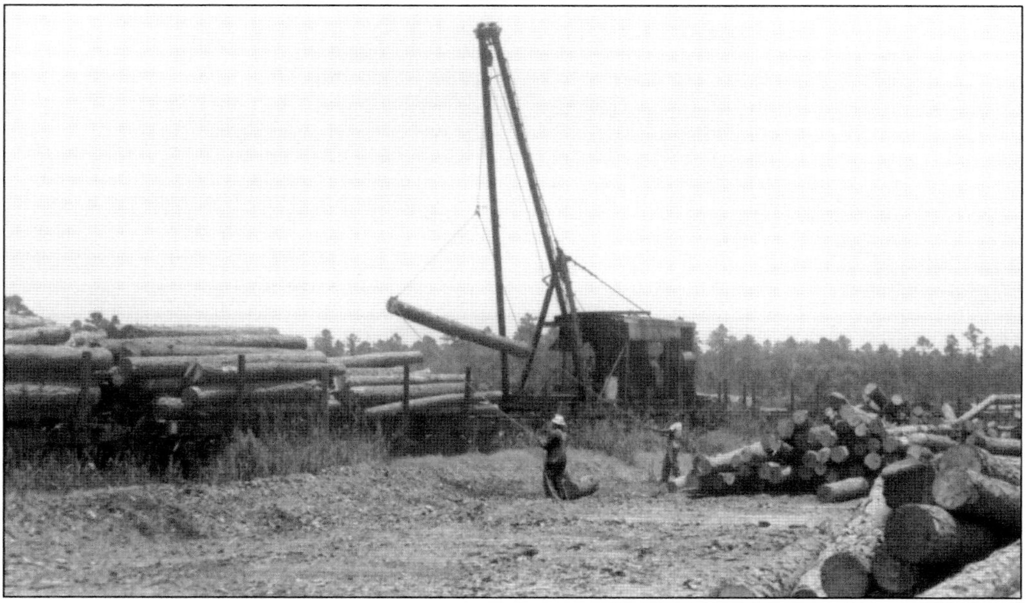

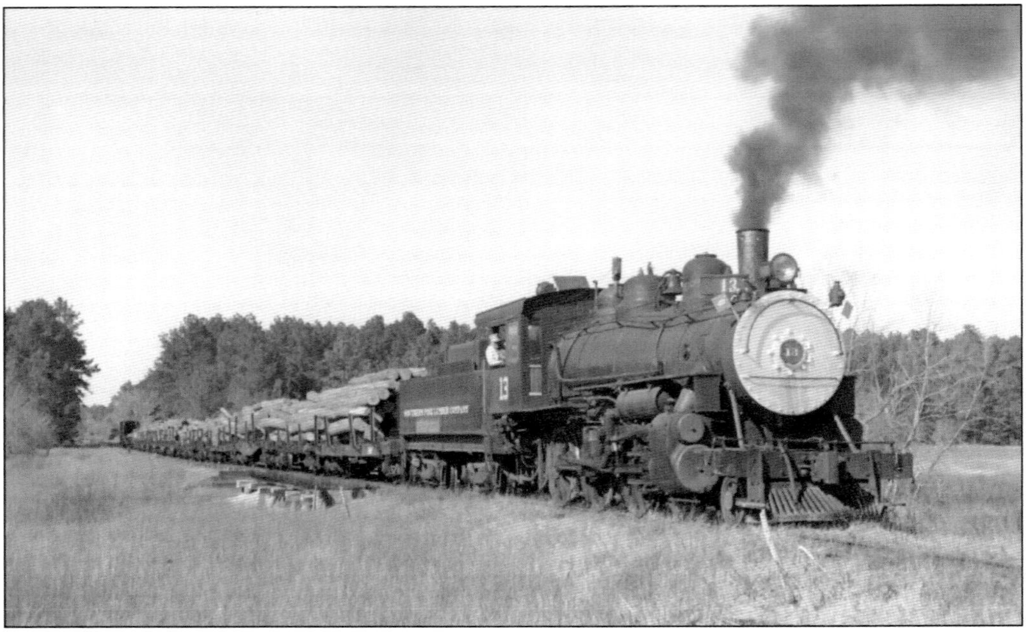

After all cars are loaded to capacity, the loader is placed at the tail end, and the train moves back toward Diboll. Engineer Lewis Minton pauses the train briefly so that Richard Keeling can capture the scene for posterity. Below, a brakeman looks out from the back of Southern Pine's Caboose No. 1 as the train picks up speed and clears the Highway 94 crossing. This view is looking east toward Vair. (Courtesy Richard W. Keeling Collection.)

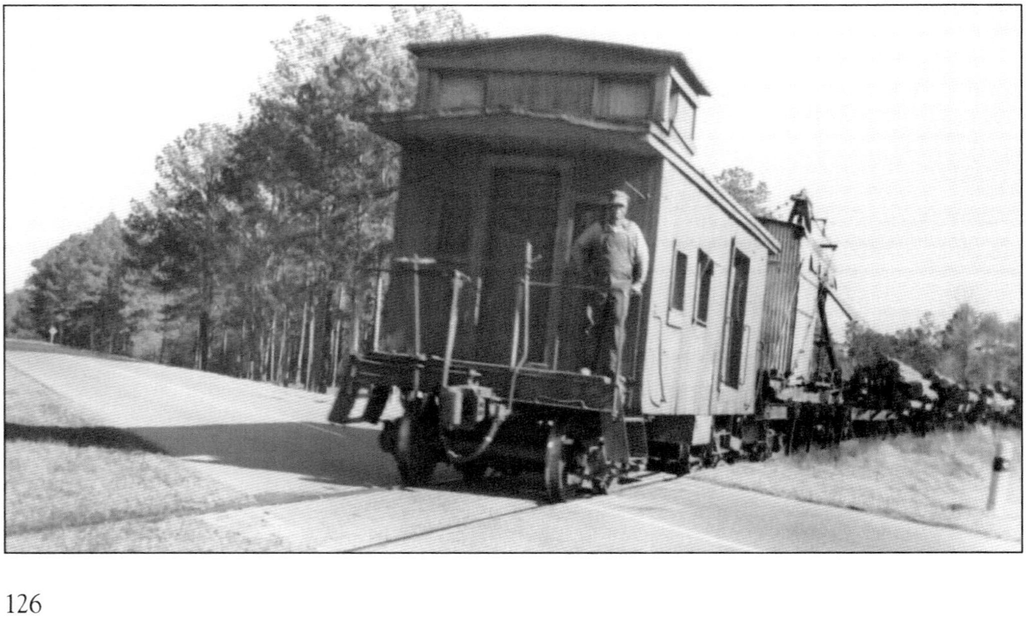

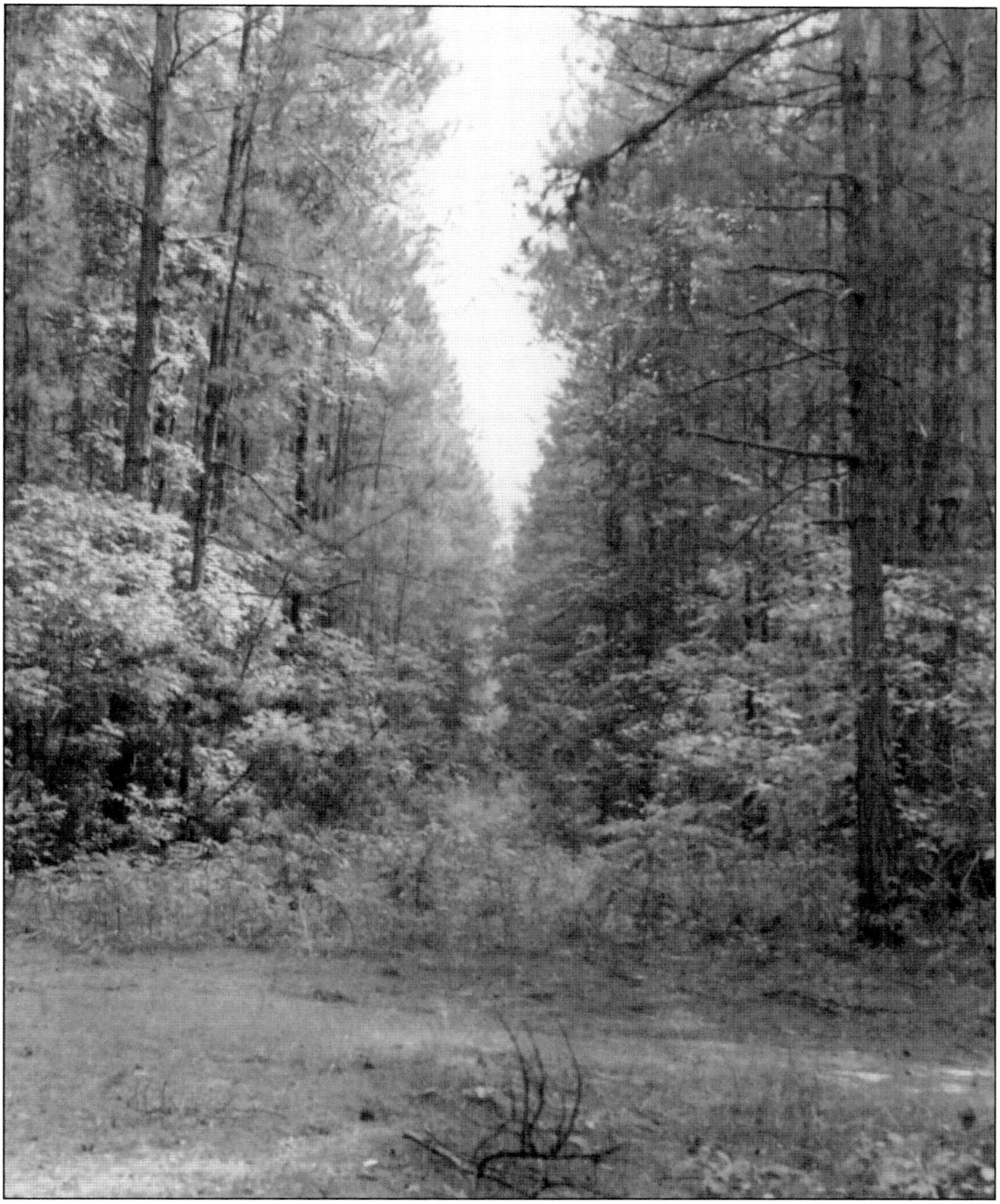

In the 1950s, on a visit to their old mill community of Wiergate in Newton County, members of the Wier family recorded this view of what remained of the old Wier Long Leaf Lumber Company tram. The last Wier train moved through here in 1943, when there were almost 20 lumber trams still operating in Texas. A decade later, that number was down to five. One by one, surviving Texas lumber giants left the railroad business. W.T. Carter ran its last log train in 1955, Kurth Lumber in 1961, and Temple Lumber and Angelina County Lumber in 1962. Finally, in the spring of 1963, Southern Pine Lumber's No. 13 returned to Diboll with what historian Richard W. Keeling considers the last steam log train to run in Texas. It was finished. What had once been vital to the world of the 1880s no longer had a place of importance in the world of the 1960s. But like all unique chapters of history, while it would not be relived, it would certainly be retold. (Courtesy Joan Weatherly.)